THE RAGE AGAINST
THE LIGHT

THE RAGE AGAINST THE LIGHT

WHY CHRISTOPHER HITCHENS WAS WRONG

Peter Harris

RESOURCE *Publications* • Eugene, Oregon

THE RAGE AGAINST THE LIGHT
Why Christopher Hitchens was Wrong

Resource Publications
An Imprint of Wipf and Stock Publishers
199 W. 8th Ave., Suite 3
Eugene, OR 97401

www.wipfandstock.com

PAPERBACK ISBN: 978-1-5326-5197-7
HARDCOVER ISBN: 978-1-5326-5198-4
EBOOK ISBN: 978-1-5326-5199-1

APRIL 23, 2019

For Andrew Hall who led me to faith in Christ when I was only twelve years old and for my greatest teacher, Roger Cooke, who inspires me more than any other to keep the faith. Above all, I dedicate this book to my wife Hasina and children Joel and Chloe who in their unique ways have encouraged me to complete my book. That means a great deal.

Contents

Preface

WHEN THE JOURNALIST CHRISTOPHER Hitchens died on 15 December 2011, the most eloquent of New Atheism's spokespersons fell silent, but because of his ubiquitous presence in the Media and online, and because of the continuing popularity of his magnum opus, *God is Not Great: How Religion Poisons Everything*, Hitchens' brand of anti-theism and anti-religionism continues to attract attention and reinforce or change people's beliefs about religion. The response of Christian apologists has been comprehensive and vigorous. Yet the Christian argument with Hitchens is far from complete, and Hitchens, who enjoyed debating religious people, would probably have welcomed this fact and perhaps even this book. It is the purpose of this book to do three things: To define more precisely than has been done hitherto Hitchens' worldview with regards to religion, in particular, identifying differences between his opinions and those of other leading New Atheists such as Richard Dawkins; to develop and refine existing Christian counterarguments; and to present new lines of argument. This book is therefore a Christian apology because the author is a Christian who does not accept Hitchens' description of God and Christianity.

This book will argue that Hitchens' most fundamental beliefs are that personal and political freedom are vital to human flourishing, that there are objective moral values, and that reason and evidence are the best ways of understanding the world. These axioms are the basis of his anti-theism and anti-religionism. As there is no good evidence for the existence of God, Hitchens is an atheist, but he is a specific kind of atheist: He is an anti-theist. This means that Hitchens does not want God to exist and is glad He does not because if God did exist, He would be a superlative totalitarian who would nullify human freedom. Hitchens is also an anti-religionist because he dismisses religion as irrational and egregious on the grounds that it requires people to believe the most preposterous beliefs and commit the most immoral acts.

Christian responses to Hitchens have been very successful; atheist criticisms have been very effective also. This book will contribute to the debate by demonstrating that God cannot be a totalitarian and by proposing that the great totalitarian is the law of sin. It will argue that Christianity ought to be and has been an effective opponent of totalitarianism, whereas militant atheism devoid of theological trappings has been responsible for the persecution of believers. The argument then takes us to a third point: There is no basis for Hitchens' moral objectivism and that his anti-theodicy fails. Demonstrating the rationality of the Christian faith against the view that Christianity demands unproven and illogical beliefs will be the final focus.

Though my primary aim is an academic one in that I seek to understand the truth with regards to Hitchens' anti-theism, my purpose is also an evangelistic purpose. It seeks not only to persuade the unbelieving audience to consider the desirability of God's existence, but also by its respectful manner, invite the unbelieving audience to consider a relationship with God. through Christ.

Acknowledgments

MANY THANKS GO TO Dr Braxton Hunter at Trinity College of the Bible and Theological Seminary for helping me to write my book and to Justin Brierley for the opportunity to discuss Christopher Hitchens on Premier Radio.

1

Introduction

HITCHENS DEFINES HIS VIEW of religion by two propositions which are neither necessarily connected nor incompatible, but which he holds simultaneously:

1. All religious beliefs are untrue.

2. All religious beliefs are harmful.

As shall be argued in chapter two which defines in more detail what Hitchens' anti-theism is, there are other beliefs that constitute his world view. At the core of Hitchens' worldview is his anti-theism which consists of three propositions:

3. There is no good evidence that God exists.

4. Therefore probably God does not exist.

5. It is a good thing that God does not exist, for if He did, His rule would be the most powerful dictatorship one could imagine.[1]

Propositions 1 and 2 are anti-religionist whereas propositions 3 and 4 are atheist. Proposition 5 is anti-theist.

Hitchens' anti-theism and anti-religionism are nothing new. Bertrand Russell, for example, in his famous lecture to the South London Sceptical Society in 1927 entitled *Why I am Not a Christian*,[2] encapsulates the essence

---

1. Christopher Hitchens, *Letters to a Young Contrarian*, p. 57.

2. Bertrand Russell, *Why I am Not a Christian*, at https://www.andrew.cmu.edu/user/jksadegh/A%20Good%20Atheist%20Secularist%20Skeptical%20Book%20Collection/Why%20I%20am%20Not%20a%20Christian%20-%20Bertrand%20Russell.pdf (accessed 29 September 2015).

of Hitchens' case when he presents the moral problem of hell, interprets religious belief as the immature wish for a caring big brother and indicts the Church with retarding civilization's progress. But even if ideas are not new, they can still have great influence when they are recycled and repackaged for a culture that is not familiar with them. It seems as if each generation must grapple with the same philosophical problems, often coming to different conclusions. New Atheism is doing exactly that: It is thinking through the age-old questions of God's existence and the effect of religious belief on society and presenting standard atheist conclusions in ways and by means that are attractive to contemporary audiences.

For those who have an academic knowledge of atheism, New Atheism might appear superficial,[3] but it has had and continues to have real influence within popular culture where the easy, sensational formulas of disbelief rather than the painstaking objectivity of scholarship are often preferred.[4] New Atheism has influence because there is a huge audience for their publications. The leading sacred text of New Atheism, Richard Dawkins' *The God Delusion*, reached number four on the *New York Times* hardcover non-fiction best-seller list within two months of publication.[5] Hitchens' contribution to the mass marketing of New Atheism has been to write a best-selling book *God is Not Great: How Religion Poisons Everything* and then to continue to preach that message through major media outlets and in high-circulation publications such as *Vanity Fair* and *Slate*. The text which arguably kick-started the New Atheist 'movement' was Sam Harris' *The End of Faith: Religion, Terror and the Future of Reason*. Published in 2004 in response to the 9/11 terrorist massacre, the paperback edition entered the *New York Times* best seller list at number four.[6] Harris' *Letter to a Christian Nation* was reported by the *Washington Post* to have attracted large audiences of supporters and opponents.[7] Daniel Dennett's scholarly tome, *Breaking the Spell: Religion as a Natural Phenomenon*, has not sold as widely as the more provocative texts of his New Atheist colleagues, but it certainly attracted the critical attention of well-known publications such

3. David Bentley Hart, 'Believe it or Not', at http://www.firstthings.com/article/2010/05/believe-it-or-not (accessed 11 September 2015 at 16:02 pm).

4. 'David Bentley Hart interview on New Atheism', You Tube, 19 April 2013, at https://www.youtube.com/watch?v=99onNksSYA0 (accessed Saturday 26 September 2015).

5. 'Hardcover Notification-New York Times', *The New York Times*, 3 December 2006.

6. 'Sunday Book Review', *New York Times*, July 2005.

7. David Segal, 'Atheist Evangelist in His Bully Pulpit, Sam Harris Devoutly Believes That Religion is the Root of All Evil,' *The Washington Post*, 26 October 2006.

as Britain's *The Guardian* newspaper[8] and the US' *The New York Times*.[9] In the aftermath of the 9/11 atrocity, other terrorist outrages carried out in the name of Allah and the increasingly multi-religious nature of Western societies, the question of religion is very much on many people's minds.

New Atheism does not want only to be a form of entertainment: It wants to create a successful intellectual and cultural revolution. New Atheism is a determined effort to transform the *zeitgeist* through an aggressive skeptical secularism. It is an attempt at a new Enlightenment achieved not over decades as was the case with the 18th century Enlightenment, but with the speed thought possible through the contemporary Media. It is a project to jolt societies away from religious insanity and back to their rational roots.

This grand secular dream, however, has not come to pass. It is now just over a decade since Dawkins' *The God Delusion* was published and there has been no turning away from religion wherever the New Atheist Gospel has been preached. But New Atheism has retained some of the momentum of the heady days of 2006. Despite the death of Hitchens in 2011[10] and Richard Dawkins' stroke in 2016[11] (which happily he survived), New Atheism continues to seek to dominate the discourse around religious belief. Despite the possibility that New Atheism is being superseded by atheists with a respect for religious belief and a stronger social justice agenda,[12] there still exists a mass market for New Atheist writings. Hitchens' *God is Not Great* remains a popular text to buy. At the present time of writing, the online bookseller, Amazon, reports that *God is Not Great* is ranked 1,826 among its bestsellers.[13] The tenth anniversary edition of Dawkins' *The God Delusion* was published in May 2016 with an afterword by Daniel Dennett. People are still buying into the New Atheists' message.

Though Hitchens' anti-theism is unoriginal within the history of philosophy and Western culture, his contribution has been to present anti-theism attractively to contemporary Occidental culture which is perhaps more attracted to anti-theism than it has ever been in its history. Among New Atheism's leadership,[14] Hitchens is the writer who gives the movement

8. Andrew Brown, 'Beyond Belief', *The Guardian*, 25 February 2006.

9. Leon Wieseltier, 'The God Genome', *The New York Times*, 19 February 2006.

10. Peter Wilby, 'Christopher Hitchens obituary', *The Guardian*, 16 December 2011.

11. Calla Wahlquist, 'Richard Dawkins stroke forces delay of Australia and New Zealand tour', *The Guardian*, 12 February 2016.

12. Chris Hall, 'Forget Christopher Hitchens: Atheism in America is undergoing a radical change', *Salon*, 5 June 2014.

13. https://www.amazon.co.uk/God-Not-Great-Religion-Everything/dp/1843545748 (accessed 22 February 2017 at 09:29).

14. The Four Horsemen of the Non-Apocalypse as the New Atheist leadership have

its rhetorical polish both in writing and in speech. Hitchens too brings to New Atheism a substantial though tendentiously deployed *corpus* of historical knowledge and contemporary events. Though under scrutiny the inaccuracies and fallacies in his work become apparent, it is true that Hitchens packages old ideas in new and challenging ways. Among Hitchens' most striking contributions are pithy principles such as the Hitchens' Challenge and Hitchens' Razor, his vivid descriptions of the universe in chaos as a challenge to teleological arguments, and parables such as what might be called 'the God with folded arms' who is indifferent to human suffering. He writes too with intense moral conviction. Hitchens therefore may well deter people from becoming religious believers, or at least from considering religious belief seriously. He may well weaken or extinguish the faith of some who believe. As importantly, his anti-theism and anti-religionism are untrue and refutation is necessary. Anti-theists for the sake of their salvation need to hear the Christian message. Hitchens, therefore, for the sake of these people, needs to be refuted in the strongest terms possible. This book, however, is certainly not that last word *contra* Hitchens, but an invitation to others to continue the debate with a man who so loved to debate.

Contributing to the Debate

How specifically will my book contribute to the debate with Hitchens? There is no specialized, comprehensive, evaluative study of Hitchens' anti-theist and anti-religionist *weltanschauung* within the critical literature. Though my aim is to critique Hitchens' work from a Christian point of view, my first purpose is to present objectively a systematic exposition of his ideas which draws on a very wide range of primary sources. Unless Hitchens' worldview is properly understood, no accurate criticism of it is possible. The initial focus of this exposition will be upon how he defined his anti-theism and his anti-religionism and the axioms upon which these two views rest. Part of this exposition also will be the exploration of what Hitchens uniquely contributes to New Atheism and how some of his ideas challenge New Atheist orthodoxy, a theme that has had little or no recognition within the literature. Second, I will provide a systematic description and evaluation of the counter-arguments of both Christian and atheist opponents. My aim is to identify what is effective and poor about their arguments. My most important aim is that of the Christian apologist: Using new lines of argument,

---

been called are Richard Dawkins, Daniel Dennett, Sam Harris and Christopher Hitchens. The leadership would have been a quintet if Ayaan Hirsi Ali had been able to attend the meeting in Hitchens' Washington apartment in 2007.

I will demonstrate that the God of Christianity is not a totalitarian, that Hitchens' moral philosophy and anti-theodicy fail, and that Christianity is a rational religion. My task is not only academic, but apologetic too in that it seeks to help those Christians whose faith has been shaken or even lost because of Hitchens, to draw people to Christ and appeal to those who are agnostics, atheists and anti-theists.

Specifically, my text will make its contribution by asking four fundamental questions. First, why was Hitchens an anti-theist and anti-religionist and what did he mean when he said he was this? Second, what responses have already been provided by Christian apologists and to what extent do they meet the Hitchensian challenge? Third, what existing counter-arguments within the apologetic literature can be developed further? Finally, what new arguments against Hitchens are possible?

An Outline of the Chapters

Chapter two will identify what Hitchens means when he says he is an anti-theist and why he defines himself as such. It will argue that Hitchens is not only an anti-theist, but also what might be called an anti-religionist in that not only does he hate the idea of God's existence, but he opposes all religions. Chapter two will reveal that though Hitchens seeks the destruction of extremist religion, there are limits to Hitchens' anti-religionism with regards to moderate religion, a fact that the critical literature does not recognize sufficiently. In this chapter, Hitchens' worldview will be shown to be foundationalist and opposed to postmodernism, an observation that also is absent from the critical literature. Chapter three is a critical review of the major lines of criticism made by Christian and non-Christian critics to Hitchens and the New Atheists. Chapter four critically assesses Hitchens' view that God's existence is undesirable because if He did exist He would be the total totalitarian. The chapter responds by demonstrating that the Christian God does not possess totalitarian traits, but instead, possesses traits that disqualify Him as one, including His creation and guarantee of human free-will in the midst of a deterministic universe. The chapter will demonstrate that sin is the great totalitarian, not God who on the contrary is humanity's liberator from its deadly effects. It will present hell as evidence of how humans are free though God exists. Hitchens fails to note that the Son of God Himself suffered at the hands of autocracies for challenging their authority and therefore this chapter will contend that God ought not to be viewed as the friend of tyrants. The chapter will conclude with the evidence from the *Song of Solomon* that God loves His people and therefore cannot be viewed as a totalitarian. Chapter five takes on Hitchens' argument that Christianity is theocratic and that all totalitarian regimes, though seeming secular, are theocratic after all as they demand worship of the leader and his state. This chapter's argument is that Christianity is and ought to be the friend of political freedom because the principle of the separation of church and state is a Christian one. Christianity is also the cultural soil in which democracy took root. The American Revolution, Hitchens' favorite revolution, was stimulated by the preaching of American ministers and Christians were at the forefront of the resistance to the East German Communist dictatorship. As for the argument that secular dictatorships are theocratic, the unused counter-example of Khrushchev's Soviet regime is a clear example of an atheist dictatorship devoid of theological trappings that murdered and persecuted Christians. These arguments need application to the debate with Hitchens. Finally, the chapter will explore in a more developed way than before Hitchens' admiration for the totalitarian revolutionary, Leon Trotsky, and how this seems inconsistent with Hitchens' anti-totalitarian attitude. Chapter six is a scrutiny of Hitchens' moral philosophy and anti-theodicy. It will argue that Hitchens' moral objectivism and his belief that morality is a product of natural selection are a contradiction because natural selection leads only to moral relativism. God will be seen to be the best foundation for moral objectivity and for the intrinsic value of humans to which Hitchens subscribes. These are established arguments, but they need to be stated within the context of the debate with Hitchens. If there is no moral objectivity in an atheist universe, the chapter will challenge Hitchens to explain why one ought not to choose Nietzsche's anti-democratic philosophy instead. This is a wholly new line of argument within the debate and a very powerful one. In the last part of the chapter reasons will be given for why God might allow appalling moral and natural evil without attempting to create a full-blown theodicy. Chapter six will also present the observation that Hitchens' abuse of his body through alcohol and cigarettes and his justification for doing so undermines his anti-theodicy based on natural evil. As Hitchens accuses religion of being irrational and wish-thinking, chapter seven will develop the argument that the Bible values rationality and that a focus on the truth is a necessary element of Christian daily living. I describe Paul as a strong compatibilist in terms of faith and rationality and argue that the work of the Holy Spirit within the act of salvation is a rational one, something that within the debate with Hitchens is missing. Chapter eight is the conclusion which summarizes my case.

The Sources

` My approach is a holistic, comprehensive one, for it seeks to select from all the relevant primary material of Hitchens' *oeuvre* information that will enable me to form an accurate view of his anti-theism to criticize it more effectively. The primary sources available for Hitchens are his polemical writing and speaking and the autobiographical data of *Hitch 22: A Memoir*. Hitchens' polemics consist of books, journals, and newspaper articles; his oral communication consists of public speeches, lectures, and debates. It will also make use of the secondary sources of the writings of critics and commentators. The secondary sources come in book, article, and oral form also and are the subject of chapter three.

Hitchens' anti-theist *magnum opus* is *God is Not Great: How Religion Poisons Everything*. This is the main source of information, but there are other useful written sources. There is the large collection of extracts from atheist and anti-theist writings called *the Portable Atheist: Essential Readings for the Nonbeliever*, the published transcripts of Hitchens' debate with two Christian opponents, the debate with Pastor Douglas Wilson and the former British Prime Minister, Tony Blair, Hitchens' disquisition on mortality published posthumously and named *Mortality*, and Hitchens' first book length foray onto the battleground of belief and anti-belief, the diatribe against Mother Theresa called *The Missionary Position: Mother Theresa in Theory and Practice*. The primary sources that do not have Hitchens' anti-theism as their focus but which contain useful summations of and comments on his anti-theism are *Letters to a Young Contrarian* and *Thomas Paine's Rights of Man*.

All sources have their advantages and disadvantages. *God is Not Great* is a frustrating book for its chapters' names can be misleading as to their content. For example, chapter five, though promising to show that religion's metaphysics is false, contains no critical discussion of metaphysical arguments used by theists such as the cosmological and ontological arguments. The book, though providing some footnotes, fails at times to reference important texts. For example, on pages 66 and 67, Hitchens summarizes some of the opinions of Paul, Laplace, and Nietzsche, yet no footnotes are provided. Checking Hitchens' facts is therefore not always easy. The chapters also do not have a logical sequence. The discussion of religions' origins, for example, does not occur in chapter one, but is chapter eleven's topic. The book is repetitive. For example, chapter thirteen asks the question which most of the chapters are answering, namely, does religion make people behave better? Chapter fifteen repeats the question by attacking the immorality of religion's precepts.

Though to some extent unsystematic, *God is Not Great* is the most detailed and developed presentation Hitchens ever made of his anti-theism, and therefore it is fundamental to this dissertation's aims. It reveals most forcefully Hitchens' moral outrage at religion's irrationality and immorality that is situated at the heart of his anti-theism. Most importantly, it provides an ample target for those who wish to criticize Hitchens' anti-theism, which of course, is one of the aims of this dissertation.

The Portable Atheist is a valuable primary source for though it is a book that Hitchens edited from other atheists and anti-theists' writings, its introduction is a highly organized summary of Hitchens' anti-theism and demonstrates Hitchens' skills as an essayist at their finest. In fourteen pages, Hitchens presents his most important ideas about God and religion. It is therefore an easily accessed guide to his thought.[15] the *Portable Atheist* is important for another reason. It shows Hitchens was aware of the anti-theist tradition into which he fits because he includes the anti-theist essay, 'The Philosophy of Atheism' by Emma Goldman, the late 19th century Russian anarchist.[16]

The two transcripts *Is Christianity Good for the World* and *Hitchens vs. Blair: Is Religion a Force for Good in the World?* are useful primary sources, for though they repeat arguments and variations of those arguments from *God is Not Great*, they provide arguments Hitchens has not used before. They also reveal Hitchens' polemical strategies when debating Christian apologists. Additionally, they are an important part of the critical response to Hitchens for they reveal counter-arguments used by two seasoned debaters, Pastor Douglas Wilson and the former British Prime Minister, Tony Blair.

The fifth book-length text, *Mortality*, is useful to my study of Hitchens' anti-theism for though most of the book cogitates on the experience of terminal illness, section two returns to the theme of religion. It reveals that Hitchens did not condemn those who prayed for him, but he was bemused by it. *Mortality* also introduces the reader to Hitchens' most developed discussion of Nietzsche which in the light of Nietzsche's anti-theism and anti-religionism is surprisingly short. It is this discussion of Nietzsche that plays an important part in chapter six's comparison of the two men's anti-theism and the argument that on Hitchens' moral philosophy, there is no reason to accept Hitchens' moral code over Nietzsche's.

The next primary book source is *The Missionary Position: Mother Teresa in Theory and Practice*. This is Hitchens' earliest full text denunciation of religion and it features the arguments that his audience and critics have

---

15. Christopher Hitchens, ed. *the Portable Atheist*, pp. xiii-xxvi.

16. Ibid., pp. 129-133.

become accustomed to in his later work: religion is a friend of dictatorships, causes suffering whilst creating the impression that it alleviates it, and is marked by a naive belief in miracles. It is an important book for it reveals how consistent the axioms of Hitchens' anti-theism remained and that Hitchens' anti-theist methodology not only censures ideas and institutions, but also individuals.

Chapters nine and ten of *Letters to a Young Contrarian*, published six years before *God is Not Great*, concern Hitchens' anti-theism. Similarly, to the introductory essay of *the Portable Atheist*, these chapters in *Letters* are an example of Hitchens at one of his most succinct, lucid, and organized on the topic. The lines of argument found in this chapter are all to be found in *God is Not Great* which demonstrates again the consistency of Hitchens' position. These chapters provide easily accessible quotations for chapter two's exposition.

Hitchens' *Thomas Paine's The Rights of Man* explores Paine's central belief that all hereditary monarchy was doomed and that it should and would be replaced by a democracy based on universal suffrage.[17] The importance of this text is that it provides evidence of Hitchens' belief in objective moral values that transcend time and space in the form of human rights. From his twenty-first century standpoint, Hitchens praises *Rights of Man* as providing the moral ideas for a sane society.[18] Paine's moral values, adumbrated in the 18th century, are adopted by Hitchens as a guiding light for his society.

Hitchens' articles can be accessed in the online archives of the newspapers and journals in which they were published. Most of the articles that are relevant to this dissertation were published in the following publications: *Slate*, *Vanity Fair* and *The Nation*, *Newsweek* and *The Atlantic Monthly*. The advantage of using Hitchens' articles is that they provide information on how his anti-theist and secularist principles determined how he wrote about contemporary religious matters, such as the allegations against and prosecutions of Catholic priests for the sexual abuse of children.

The Internet provides access to a vast amount of Hitchens' debates and speeches. You Tube is an excellent source.[19] Sometimes the recordings are excerpts of speeches and debate, but often the recordings are complete and therefore Hitchens' argument can be discerned in full. Other websites such as fora.tv provide access to Hitchens' speeches.[20] There is an online

---

17. Christopher Hitchens, *Tom Paine*, p. 83.

18. Ibid., p. 11.

19. https://www.uk.youtube.com (accessed 25 February 2017 at 17:27).

20. The website can be accessed through the simple online address, fora.tv. Within its catalogue, Hitchens' speeches and presentations can be found at library.fora.tv/search?q=Christopher+Hitchens+ (accessed 25 February 2017 at 17:29).

repository of transcripts of Hitchens' debates at hitchensdebates.blogspot. com. Another website, dailyhitch.com, is a compendium of videos, articles and excerpts from Hitchens anti-theist writings presented in an approving fashion. The debates and speeches are useful for they provide information about the additional lines of argument to those he deploys in his written work, formulated in response to the arguments of his opponents. Hitchens' spoken polemics also repeat arguments found in his writings which provide an indication as to which of his arguments he considered the best.

Interviews that Hitchens gave also provide important material on his views.[21] Again, much of what Hitchens says in interviews is a repetition of his written opinions already published. The interviews, nevertheless, provide the opportunity to see Hitchens challenged and asked for further clarification and justification for his opinions, and the developments and qualifications he makes to his arguments in response.

What is the usefulness of *Hitch 22* to this present study? Hitchens makes it clear that his text is not an autobiography which tells his story comprehensively, but a selective account.[22] The degree to which Hitchens' memory is reliable is not an important question. What is significant is how Hitchens' memories, whether true or not, galvanize and sustain his anti-theism.[23] *Hitch 22* is useful in that it provides Hitchens' definition of what totalitarianism is. It reveals how consistent his hatred for totalitarianism has been and through the inclusion of his responses to the famous Proust Questionnaire, information about his normative ethics. *Hitch 22* also reveals information that suggests that Hitchens' personal experiences of the Church might have been one of the reasons for his hardened attitude against it, though he himself never makes this assertion.

21. One of the most revealing and interesting interviews Hitchens gave was his response to the 'Proust Questionnaire'. See Christopher Hitchens, *Hitch 22*, pp. 333-335.

22. Deborah Solomon, 'The Contrarian: Questions for Christopher Hitchens', *The New York Times*, 2 June 2010.

23. Sources that ratify some of what Hitchens remembers and which were published before Hitchens wrote his memoir, do exist. Ian Parker's profile of Hitchens, written four years before Hitchens wrote his memoir and one year before the publication of *God is Not Great*, provides biographical material that corroborates some of Hitchens' account. See Ian Parker, 'He Knew He Was Right: How a former socialist became the Iraq war's fiercest defender', *The New Yorker*, 16 October 2006.

My World View

Before I continue, I acknowledge the need to lay my intellectual cards upon the table. With what sort of worldview am I coming against Hitchens? Clearly, I am a Christian, but what sort as there are many who go by this name? The most succinct way in which I can identify my Christianity is through the fact that I affirm the truth of the Apostle' Creed which reads as follows:

> 'I believe in God the Father Almighty, Maker of heaven and earth. And in Jesus Christ his only Son our Lord; who was conceived by the Holy Spirit,[24] born of the virgin Mary; suffered under Pontius Pilate, was crucified, dead and buried; the third day he rose from the dead; he ascended into heaven; and sitteth at the right hand of God the Father Almighty; from thence he shall to come judge the quick and the dead. I believe in the Holy Spirit; the holy catholic Church; the communion of saints; the forgiveness of sins; the resurrection of the body; and the life everlasting. Amen.'[25]

I am therefore a Bible believing Trinitarian for reasons which will become apparent to the reader as s/he proceeds through the text. If anyone wishes to read a book which provides excellent reasons for why the Bible is a sure foundation for belief, I would recommend *Why Trust the Bible: Answers to 10 Tough Questions* by Amy Orr-Ewing. As for the Trinitarian perspective, I would recommend that the reader consults an easily accessible and very thorough treatment of the subject by the Christian philosopher, Peter S. Williams in his article, 'Understanding the Trinity' at the bethinking.org website.[26]

I accept that there is such a thing as logical truth and empirical evidence. I am not a postmodernist which is meant to be the defining view of our age.[27] Postmodernism fundamentally rejects the idea that there is such a thing as absolute truth. It will be part of my description of Hitchens' antitheism that he was under no circumstances a postmodernist. For Hitchens, there were such things as universal truths and universal untruths, of which religion was one. That Hitchens was not a postmodernist does not prevent a postmodernist critique of his work, but as I am not a postmodernist either, it is necessary to justify why I do not adopt that approach.

24. Holy Ghost is the original translation of the name of the Trinity's Third Person. Wayne Grudem, whose version of the Creed I am using, uses the modern translation. See Wayne Grudem, *Systematic Theology*, p. 1169.

25. Taken from *Systematic Theology: An Introduction to Biblical Doctrine* by Wayne Grudem Copyright 1994. Used by permission of Zondervan. www.zondervan.com

26. Peter S. Williams, 'Understanding The Trinity' at https://www.bethinking.org/god/understanding-the-trinity (accessed 3 March 2018 at 11:44).

27. J. P. Moreland and William Lane Craig, *Philosophical Foundations for a Christian Worldview*, p. 145.

Of all the things postmodernists believe, the most significant to the present discussion is their rejection of absolutes. Absolute truth does not exist. The correspondence theory of truth which leads to the view that truth is absolute is the theory that truth is 'a matter of propositions . . . corresponding to reality.' In other words, 'truth obtains when reality is the way a proposition represents it to be.'[28] To put it more succinctly: What we say must match what is the case. If there are no absolute truths, there can be no metanarratives which provide all-encompassing explanations for the universe. There are therefore a range of competing worldviews among which no one worldview can be said to be exclusively the truth.

The idea of competing worldviews extends to morality. It is no surprise that postmodernists reject the idea that there are morals that are binding absolutely on all people. No moral facts in fact exist according to postmodernism. Rather, there are moral codes that reflect the conditions of different cultures and no one code is superior to another.

The fundamental problem with postmodernism is that its assertion that there is no such thing as absolute truth is a self-refuting proposition. To assert there is no absolute truth is to assert an absolute truth, therefore there is such a thing as absolute truth. The same incoherence is seen in postmodernism's assertion that the correspondence theory of truth is untrue. To state that the correspondence theory is untrue is to assert a proposition that is true according to the correspondence theory. In other words, this statement asserts that there is a state of affairs where there is no truth that is a verbal expression that matches what is the case; but to assert this proposition is to assert there is a correspondence between the words of this proposition and a state of affairs, thus claiming a truth that is in correspondence with the world. Postmodernism denies the absolute truth of metanarratives, but to deny that there are metanarratives is to write a metanarrative itself, albeit a negative one which seeks to dissolve all metanarratives into a *mélange* of worldviews that are chosen purely subjectively. The metanarrative is therefore there are no metanarratives. Postmodernists deny that there is universal moral truth, but one may ask legitimately how postmodern writers would react to the plagiarism of their written work. The copyright symbol that occupies and legally guards their writings is the consequence of the universal moral principle that theft is wrong, and intellectual theft is something that universities and academics take very seriously. Surely on postmodern terms, if I chose to plagiarize Derrida's work, I am merely and excusably operating to a different moral code that reflects my local, culture and subjective preferences?

28. Ibid., p. 130.

My third presupposition is that apologetics is a God-given method of appealing to the unbeliever. Some Christians do not agree: They are fideists who argue that a rational defense of the Christian faith is unnecessary and even impossible and that it is a case of taking Christian beliefs on ungrounded faith. Fideism's denial of Christianity's rational nature is unscriptural. Peter the Apostle speaks of the Gospel's truth as founded on 'eyewitnesses' of Christ's majesty rather than 'cunningly devised fables' (2 Pet. 1:16). Peter is therefore appealing to evidence for the Gospel. Peter also exhorts Christians to 'always be ready to give a defense to everyone who asks you a reason for the hope that is in you' (1 Pet. 3:15). Christian testimony therefore ought to provide reasons for faith. Faith too is a matter of evidence, for it is defined as 'the substance of things hoped for, the evidence of thing not seen' (Heb. 11:1). Faith is formed based on evidence for the hope we have in God. A further discussion of the rational nature of faith can be found in chapter three where I examine the response of Christian apologists to Hitchens' anti-theism.

Methodology

Evidence is indispensable to Hitchens and so my approach is to present the evidence that his anti-theism and anti-religionism with regards to Christianity is untrue. Much of my evidence is historical, for many of Hitchens' arguments against Christianity are historical. I therefore play the part of the historian who draws upon primary and secondary sources to provide causal analysis and narratives to upset at points Hitchens' version of religious history. Specifically, I seek to provide historical facts that demonstrate that secular totalitarianisms have existed and have been destructive towards religions and their devotees. I seek also to show that Hitchens' reverence for Trotsky is paradoxical by the same historical method.

My second method is philosophical because Hitchens' moral philosophy and his anti-theodicy demand philosophical responses. Hitchens is not a sophisticated philosopher, but his philosophy raises robust questions that if Christianity is true, it must answer.

Third, my method can be described as hermeneutical. It is through the correct interpretation of Scripture that it is possible to demonstrate that Christians ought to be epistemically virtuous, that God is absolute but not a totalitarian and a guarantor of human freedom, and that sin is the greatest enemy of human freedom. It is also through the correct interpretation of the New Atheist 'sacred texts' of Hitchens and others such as Dawkins which will enable me to identify their beliefs and demonstrate their weaknesses.

In Summary so Far

My aim is therefore not to disprove Hitchens' atheism by proving that there is a God, but to disprove his anti-theism by demonstrating that God is not how he describes Him to be, that there are good reasons to desire God's existence and that Hitchens' anti-religionism, moral philosophy and anti-theodicy are untenable. It is not only an academic treatise, but also a pastoral instrument and an evangelistic appeal through its desire to strengthen the beliefs of Christians and to call the atheist and anti-theist to repentance based on evidence and the promptings of the Holy Spirit.

2

The Anti-Theism and Anti-Religionism of Christopher Hitchens

Introduction

THE TITLE AND SUBTITLE of Hitchens' book *God is Not Great: How Religion Poisons Everything* reveals the two sides of his attitude to religious belief: He is an anti-theist and an anti-religionist. Hitchens' anti-theism and anti-religionism in turn rest on three axioms. These principles do not necessarily lead to anti-theism and anti-religionism, but in Hitchens' case, they have. First, Hitchens believes that humans possess free-will and values personal and political freedom as the organizing principle of individual, social and political life. Second, Hitchens possesses a belief in universal, objective moral values. Third, for Hitchens, reason and evidence are the best ways of understanding the world.

It is the task of this chapter first to trace the connection between Hitchens' first principles and his anti-theism and anti-religionism. It will argue that as a libertarian, Hitchens' principal objection to God's existence and belief in God is that God, if He existed, would be a totalitarian because of his omniscience, omnipresence and omnipotence and therefore would nullify human freedom. As he accepts that there are such things as universal moral values, Hitchens' moral objection to religion is that it poisons, or ruins, our enjoyment of life and is responsible for egregious crimes. Hitchens argues that there are universal moral values because these have been encoded inside humanity by the process of natural selection. Morality is objective, not relativistic. It is Hitchens' rationalism and demand for evidence that leads him to reject religion in another way: That it is irrational because it expects people to believe propositions that are not supported by evidence.

15

The chapter's second purpose is to demonstrate that there are limits to Hitchens' anti-religionism. Hitchens neither believes that religion will wither away nor is it desirable to abolish it. Religion will not disappear because it was established in our species by natural selection and its abolition would be undesirable because that would be a totalitarian act. Hitchens' response to religion is two-fold: armed struggle against the extremists which unfortunately will be unending and the taming and accommodation of moderate religion within secular society. In this Hitchens maintains both a secular Manicheanism and a neo-conservatism in his outlook. Against extremists, there is the unending struggle of good against evil, but for moderate religionists, there is a private space within a democratic secular society, the epitome of which is the U.S constitution. Though essentially distrustful of all religion, Hitchens recognizes some merit in religious belief and sees the argument with moderate religionists as a way of defining what is civilized, which puts into question the assertion that religions poisons everything. This chapter will also contend that Hitchens' anti-theism and anti-religionism is a form of anti-postmodernism. Hitchens does not present his views as one among a competing range of views within the marketplace of ideas. Rather, he is a foundationalist who believes that his arguments are true because they are backed up by evidence.

Definitions: Hitchens the Anti-theist

The most fundamental questions that underlie intellectual and academic endeavor concern what there is and what is not, why there is what there is and what our reactions to what there is and is not ought to be. Atheism is the view that there is no God, or gods, or that there is no evidence for these beings' existence. According to Jonathan Miller the distinguished British physician and theatre director, the term 'atheism' is unnecessary. Miller does not see why there has to be a term for unbelief in God when there is no term for not believing in such things as fairies.[1] Though Hitchens prefers to call himself an anti-theist rather than an atheist, Hitchens regards the word atheism as necessary, for it expresses a legitimate position which distinguishes those who have no religious beliefs from those who do.[2] I agree. As a distinct position *contra* belief, atheism can be the logical outcome of having adopted a substantive worldview. Hitchens is an atheist because he accepts the tenets of scientific materialism. According to scientific materialism, all that exists is matter and the best people to ask about the nature

---

1. Hitchens, ed., *the Portable Atheist*, p. xx.
2. Ibid., pp. xx-xxi.

of matter are scientists. On this view, there is no reality to religion which believes in non-material substances such as spirits and souls.[3] Atheism is also a cause for accepting other beliefs such as it is wrong to teach children about creationism and hell. It does not necessarily follow that an atheist will oppose these teachings, but opposition to them does follow on from many people's atheism. Of course, there are probably atheists who do not think about what their atheism might entail, but for thoughtful atheists, atheism is a process of working out why one does not believe in God and what one does believe now that one no longer believes in God. Thinking about one's atheism therefore means one cannot remain in a negative position denying God, but rather one must work out the implications as far as one can see of one's atheism.

But Hitchens seeks a better word than atheism for there are types of atheists with which he would disagree. He recognizes that there are atheists who cannot believe in God, but who have reluctantly rejected faith as they would like there to be a God for all the benefits that His existence is perceived to bring.[4] McGrath adds another category: Those atheists who neither hate God nor actively oppose religious belief, but who are apathetic or indifferent atheists.[5] Hitchens is neither of these types of atheist, for although he does not accept that there is any evidence for the existence of God, he prefers to define himself as an anti-theist.[6]

What sort of anti-theist is Hitchens? Kahane understands anti-theism to be the belief not that God ought not to exist because He is bad, but that it would be bad, or worse, if God did exist. Anti-theism is therefore by Kahane's lights not a denial of God's goodness, but a denial of the goodness of God's existence.[7] Alternatively, an anti-theist might conceivably hate God as He is presented by the world's religions but might somehow wish that God did and could exist in a way that has only benefits and no disadvantages. It is conceivable too that one might oppose the existence of God without any particularly strong aversion to God. Hitchens' anti-theism is none of these for he is 'delighted that there is absolutely no persuasive evidence for the existence of any of mankind's many thousands of past and present deities.'[8]

3. David Cook, *Blind Alley Beliefs*, p.130.

4. Hitchens, ed., *the Portable Atheist*, p. xxii. See also https://fora.tv/2007/05/10/ Christopher _Hitchens (accessed 6 November 2015 at 05:49).

5. Alister McGrath, *Why God Won't Go Away*, pp. 23-24.

6. Christopher Hitchens, 'On God and North Korea', You Tube, 16 June 2009 at https://www.youtube.com/watch?v=f4oTRJl5vvI (accessed 6 November 2015 at 14:27).

7. Guy Kahane, 'Should We Want God to Exist?' in *Philosophy and Phenomenological Research*, May 2011, Volume 82, Issue 3, p. 674.

8. Christopher Hitchens and Douglas Wilson, *Is Christianity Good for the World?*, p. 12.

Unlike Kahane's definition of anti-theism, Hitchens denies the desirability of God's existence because of His superlative badness. To understand why Hitchens views God in this way, one must understand the most fundamental value that Hitchens hold: that of personal freedom.

In the last interview he gave before he died, Hitchens said to his interlocutor, Richard Dawkins:

> 'I have one consistency, which is [being] against the totalitarian—on the left and on the right. The totalitarian, to me, is the enemy—the one that's absolute, the one that wants control over the inside of your head, not just your actions and your taxes.'[9]

Hitchens was speaking not only of God here, but of human totalitarians too. Hitchens' life and work demonstrate how right he is to say of himself that he has been an unstinting enemy of arbitrary government. We have said and will have much to say about the anti-totalitarianism of Hitchens' work, but it is appropriate to say a little about his anti-totalitarian personal life. Whilst at Oxford University, Hitchens joined the International Socialists who opposed the left-wing totalitarianism of Maoist China and the Soviet Union.[10] When visiting Castro's Cuba, Hitchens was appalled by Castro's support for the Soviet Union's repression of Czechoslovakia.[11] Hitchens' break with the International Socialists came when they failed to see, or refused to see, that the communist regime that seized power in Portugal was a Stalinist one.[12] Hitchens has been a consistent opponent of right-wing dictatorships also. He has written against the American-backed right-wing regimes of South America[13] and approved of the military action to liberate the Falklands from the Argentinean overlord General Galtieri.[14] Before he was officially known as a New Atheist, Hitchens was defying theocracy. He wrote in defense of the right to free speech of the novelist Salman Rushdie who had been marked out for death by the Ayatollah Khomeini for blasphemy and took the risk of hosting Rushdie at his Washington apartment when Rushdie came to the U.S. to meet unofficially President Clinton.[15] Hitchens' vigorous

---

9. 'Preview: Richard Dawkins Interviews Christopher Hitchens' at https://www.newstatesman.com/blogs/the-staggers/2011/12/dawkins-hitchens-catholic (accessed 5 December 2015, 12:00).

10. Hitchens, *Hitch 22*, pp. 85-87.

11. Ibid., p. 119.

12. Ibid., pp. 183-185.

13. Ibid., p. 200.

14. Ibid., p. 201.

15. Ibid., pp. 268-280.

and unrepentant support of the overthrow of Saddam Hussein is his most well-known act of anti-totalitarianism.[16]

There is possibly a deeply personal note to Hitchens' war of words with theocracy. He reveals in his memoir that after his mother, Yvonne Hitchens, had committed suicide in a hotel in Athens, the Anglican minister of the city's Protestant cemetery was reluctant to bury his mother in consecrated ground. Hitchens describes that he had to bribe the stubborn cleric to conduct his mother's funeral.[17] Though Hitchens' opposition to theocracy and religion generally is motivated by intellectual and moral reasons, one cannot help speculating to what extent the priest's callous officiousness hardened Hitchens' anti-clericalism.

It is Hitchens' opinion that if God existed, He would be akin to a human totalitarian, but immeasurably worse. God would be, and this is my expression, not Hitchens', the total totalitarian. This is the cause of Hitchens preferring to call himself an anti-theist rather than an atheist, although atheism forms part of the anti-theist worldview.[18] If God existed according to Hitchens, His authority would be an everlasting regime established without human consent, capable of reading people's minds and enslaving them.[19] Hitchens has also described God as 'a supreme and absolute and unalterable ruler whose reign [is] eternal and unchallengeable' and who requires 'incessant propitiation' and who keeps everyone under 'continual surveillance' which intensifies after death.[20] Such a form of government would render the idea of freedom meaningless.[21] God would be the last stage totalitarianism for He would be able to do what the regime in Orwell's *1984* could not do: He could detect thought crime as soon as it occurred. Those held guiltless will go heaven whereas thought criminals will be dispatched hell.[22] What makes eternity with God a hellish idea is that those living in it will be required to worship God incessantly.[23] What makes God's reign unbearable is that one cannot escape or overthrow it, whereas at least with human dictatorships there is the possibility of defecting from or rebelling against them. For those

16. Ibid., pp. 307-326.

17. Ibid., p. 26.

18. Hitchens and Wilson, *Is Christianity Good for the World?*, p. 12.

19. 'Christopher Hitchens On God and North Korea', You Tube.

20. Hitchens and Wilson, *Is Christianity Good for the World?* p. 12.

21. Ibid.

22. Christopher Hitchens, 'An Atheist Responds', *Washington Post*, 14 July 2007.

23. 'Christopher Hitchens On God and North Korea', YouTube.

who can do neither, death is at least some form of release! Thus, to seek to live under God's rule is the wish to be a slave.[24]

Alongside the loss of freedom that God's government entails, there are rules which are too demanding to be kept,[25] the absence of personal value[26] and the loss of critical thought.[27] At the heart of this government is a designer or creator whose method of creation results in the deaths of millions of creatures.[28] God's sky-based regime[29] has made humans immoral and yet orders them to be good.[30] God demands worship from His subjects whilst they are alive on earth and whilst they are in heaven. What is worse is that God also demands not only obedience from his terrified devotees, but also their love[31] which in the light of God's cruelty is masochism.[32] Those who live in a dictatorship are not permitted to think critically or independently, and this is the same with those subjected to God's authority. Salvation is offered at the price of the surrender of one's critical faculties because religion requires belief in baseless propositions.[33] It is no surprise that Hitchens celebrates what he purports to be the absence of evidence for God's existence.[34]

Hitchens anticipates the following objection to his anti-theism: what if God were a benevolent Deity? Would His existence on balance be better than His non-existence, and if so, would his existence not be desirable? According to Hitchens, if God were benevolent, He would be a benevolent dictator whose existence is undesirable because of His patronizing approach. Such a God would be like a father who keeps his growing children in a state of dependency by permanently supervising them.[35] He would be the shepherd who treats His followers like a flock of sheep, which for Hitchens is supremely cruel.[36] His knowledge of what is good for you and His determination that you have it whether you like it or not is more debasing than the demands

---

24. Christopher Hitchens, 'Axis of Evil' at https://fora.tv/2007/05/10/Christopher_Hitchens (accessed 16 November 2015 at 09:25).

25. Christopher Hitchens, *God is Not Great*, p. 212.

26. Hitchens, ed., *the Portable Atheist*, p. xvi.

27. Ibid.

28. Ibid., p. xviii.

29. Ibid., pp. xxii.

30. Rudyard Griffiths, ed., *Hitchens vs. Blair*, p. 8.

31. Ibid., p. 13.

32. Hitchens and Wilson, *Is Christianity Good for the World?* p. 13.

33. Ibid.

34. 'Christopher Hitchens On God and North Korea', You Tube.

35. Benjamin Hawkins, 'Dembski, Hitchens debate God's existence', *Baptist Press*, 23 November 2010).

36. Christopher Hitchens, *Mortality*, p. 25.

of the evil totalitarian. More preferable than the benevolent dictator is the evil one who cannot care less for his subjects.[37] For Hitchens, therefore, what makes both the benevolent and the evil God superlatively evil is that they are both dictators, and dictatorship is by definition evil, with the benevolent God's patronage less tolerable than His evil counterpart's oppression.

Moral and natural evils give Hitchens further reason to believe that if God exists, He is evil. To demonstrate this, Hitchens tells a parable. He begins by asking his audience to accept for the sake of argument that humanity has existed for 150,000 years and asserts that it is impossible to believe in an omnibenevolent Creator when humans have been created and placed in a world of enormous and overwhelming suffering.[38]

Hitchens therefore turns to the problems of moral evil and pain to deny logically the existence of a benevolent God, and to argue that the only God who could conceivably exist in the light of human suffering is an evil one or an incompetent one whose rescue attempts are too late and insufficient. It is therefore best that such a God does not exist.

Anti-theism and Anti-religionism

In the introduction, Hitchens was defined as an anti-religionist with limitations to his anti-religionism. The anti-religionism he feels, though it has limits, is very powerful for he is prepared to resist moderate religious influence through polemics and legislation, and extreme religion through armed force.[39] It might seem unnecessary to define Hitchens as both an anti-theist and an anti-religionist because the latter seems to follow on from the former and *vice versa*. If a person is an anti-theist, it is surely the case that s/he would also oppose the religions that celebrate the God or gods s/he does not believe in and to whom s/he is opposed. If someone hates religion, they would also end up hating the deities who are at the heart of religion. But though anti-religionism may follow on from or lead to anti-theism, it does not necessarily follow. A person may be opposed to the forms that religion takes, and yet believe in and love God; and a person might not believe there is a God and be glad that is the case, and yet still see the social benefit of

37. 'Christopher Hitchens: The Moral Necessity of Atheism (2/8), YouTube, 8 September 2007 at https://www.youtube.com/watch?v=JiBvgAS7vKQ (accessed 21 February 2016, 16:23).

38. Hitchens, ed., *the Portable Atheist*, p. xix.

39. 'Christopher Hitchens responds to a Jihad sympathizer', You Tube, 20 August 2009 at https://www.m.youtube.com/watch?v=axHR8AOXXKC (accessed 10 September 2016 at 21:19).

religion such as creating a sense of community and encouraging voluntary work. An anti-theist might, for example, recognize the comfort that religion brings to those at the end of their lives. Another permutation might be a person who chooses to adopt a religion that does not worship a personal deity such as Buddhism. Hitchens combines anti-theism with anti-religionism by condemning God as the arch dictator, seeking the destruction of malevolent forms of religion, and keeping tame through a secular separation of state from religion the moderate forms of religion so they do not mutate into something harmful. As the two positions can be logically separate, it is important to identify Hitchens as both.

Immoral and Irrational: Why Hitchens is Anti-religion

Hitchens asserts the universal proposition that all religions poison all things. This is the statement that subtitles *God is Not Great*. Logically, Hitchens' proposition takes the form of a universal: all religions are poisonous, or all x is y. To avoid the defeater of universal propositions, which is to find just one single exception to the rule being proposed, Hitchens presents the following justification: Religion ruins the context and foundation of human lives. In other words, though religion has done good things for humanity, it ultimately spoils everything because of the servile attitude it requires of its devotees. Hitchens writes that once we have accepted that we are worthless sinners, everything we do is lived in the darkness of this belief and life is spoiled.[40]

Religion therefore poisons by abolishing certain pleasures through prohibition, but when pleasures can remain, they can only be partially and tentatively enjoyed. There are two ways by which religion poisons according to Hitchens: through its immorality and its irrationality.[41]

Hitchens expresses the twin faults of immorality and irrationality through four basic assertions: Religion misrepresents the truth about human origins and the beginning of the universe, makes people narcissistic, promotes wishful thinking, and represses sexuality.[42] Sexual repression and servility are immoral in Hitchens' view for they rob humanity of two essential freedoms: the freedom to enjoy sexual relations and the freedom to exercise political liberty. The solipsism Hitchens refers to is the view that the universe was created for the benefit of humanity, which is superlative

---

40. https//:hitchensdebates.blogspot.co.uk/2010/08/hitchens-vs-kresta-ave-maria-radio.html (accessed 10 December 2015 at 08:17).

41. Christopher Hitchens: 'Talks at Google', YouTube, 16 August 2007 at https//:www.youtube.com/watch?v=D0B-X9LJjs (accessed 20 February 2016 at 15:00 pm).

42. Hitchens, *God is Not Great*, p. 4.

egotism and therefore a form of immorality too. The irrationality of religion is seen in its mythical explanations for human and material origins and its preference for believing what it hopes to be true rather than what is true determined by evidence.

Religion is Immoral

Just as God is a totalitarian, or would be if He existed, in Hitchens' opinion so too are the religions created in His name. As Hitchens' most fundamental value is that of freedom, his anti-religionism is visceral. Turning once more to the last interview he gave, Hitchens theorized that the origins of totalitarianism were theocratic:

> 'The beginning of that [totalitarianism] is the idea that there is a supreme leader, or infallible pope, or a chief rabbi, or whatever, who can ventriloquise the divine and tell us what to do.'[43]

In this statement, Hitchens discerns that the authority of the tyrant originally came from his capacity to hear God and speak on His behalf. No one would dare contradict one who had such an intimate connection with God. Secular authority denies the existence of God but claims to have the same infallible wisdom as to how to create utopia. What enables the theocrat and the secular ruler to govern is the desire to worship and be servile on the part of the masses and the illusory promise made by theocrats that either by following their commands the faithful will enjoy eternal bliss, or in the case of secular tyrants, heaven on earth.

Hitchens' fullest analysis of totalitarianism is found in God is Not Great.[44] Hitchens makes the distinction between ordinary dictatorship, or authoritarianism, which seek people's outward obedience and totalitarianism's desire to control people at the level of their thoughts and which considers people its property. Dictatorships are kept in place by the sadomasochistic desire to be subjected and the desire to see others subjected.[45] Totalitarianism is normally regarded as systematic, but Hitchens identifies arbitrariness as dictatorship's quintessential attribute. Those within its grip are never allowed to relax and are never sure if they have followed the rules

---

43. George Eaton, 'Preview: Richard Dawkins Interviews Christopher Hitchens', at https//:www.newstatesman.com/the-staggers/2011/12/dawkins-hitchens-catholic (accessed 5 December 2015, 12:00).

44. Hitchens, God is Not Great, pp. 229-235.

45. Ibid., p. 230-231.

correctly or not[46] as the rules might be altered at any point with rulers' subjects not certain if they are obeying the latest version of the law.[47]

Hitchens provides historical evidence for absolutism's theocratic origins: Oriental monarchs, South American emperors and medieval kings were either seen as gods or combined the office of the high priest with their regal position. Hitchens asserts that totalitarianism remained a problem even in modernity when the concept of the divine right of kings had died out. We hear that the ideal of a utopian state on earth has led people to commit terrible crimes in its name. By way of an example, Hitchens refers us to the Jesuit dictatorship in Paraguay which won egalitarianism at the cost of freedom. He concludes that section of his text with the statement that behind dictatorships lies the religious instinct.[48]

Though Hitchens denounces Calvinist prototypical totalitarianism,[49] Hitchens more frequently denounces Catholicism's alliance with Fascism. According to Hitchens, Fascism has been for the Church a welcome barrier to atheist Communism. Fascism's anti-Semitism is also attractive to the Catholic Church for the Church teaches that the ancient Jews murdered Christ. Collaboration between Fascism and Catholicism began when Pope Pius XI signed the Lateran Treaty with Mussolini in 1929 which recognized Mussolini as Italy's legitimate ruler in return for his recognition of Catholicism as Italy's official religion. On July 8th, 1933, a diplomatic accord was signed between Hitler and the Pope in which the Pope retained control over the education of German Catholic children in return for the abolition of the Catholic Centre Party. Hitchens concedes that Pius XI distrusted Hitler and that from the early days the German Catholic clergy denounced the Nazi policy of eliminating the physically and mentally handicapped, but argues that his successor, Pius XII, was an admirer of the *Fuehrer* who believed that God had entrusted the German people to Hitler's care. The Vatican continued its support for Nazism after its defeat by helping Nazi fugitives to flee to South America by providing an escape network.[50] A contemporary example of the natural alliance between Catholicism and Fascism is provided by Mother Theresa who according to Hitchens took donations from the Duvaliers.[51]

46. Hitchens, *Hitch 22*, p. 51.

47. Hitchens, *God is Not Great*, p. 231.

48. Ibid., pp. 231-232.

49. Ibid., p. 233.

50. Ibid., p. 240.

51. Christopher Hitchens, 'Mommie Dearest: The pope beatifies Mother Teresa, a fanatic, a fundamentalist, and a fraud', *Slate*, 20 October 2003.

According to Hitchens, the most common objection his atheist allies meet is the double assertion that the worst crimes against humanity have been perpetrated by atheist, secularist tyrannies and that without the moral bridling of religion, humanity descends into the worse crimes imaginable. The most common examples given of such regimes are those of Hitler and Stalin.[52] As this chapter has already just devoted space to Hitchens' argument that Catholicism colluded with Nazism and Fascism, I will focus on how Hitchens meets the accusation that Stalin the atheist was more murderous than religion has ever been.

Hitchens argues that neither Stalin nor his regime were secular and atheist, but theocratic. Stalin always kept the Church on his side by maintaining and even appointing bishops. He acted in a religious way by hunting down heretics.[53] Stalin acted like the Pope when he submitted science to dogma by endorsing Lysenko's pseudo-scientific claims.[54] During the Second World War the Russian Orthodox Church, in return for Stalin's protection, reinforced Stalinism by preaching loyalty to it.[55]

Hitchens turns to Trotsky as an example of how a left-wing atheist leader can adhere to enlightened political policies without becoming the object of a personality cult. In an edition of Radio 4's 'Great Lives', Hitchens explains why he admires Trotsky.[56] Trotsky is admirable because of his opposition to Stalinist totalitarianism and his prophetic understanding of the dangers posed by Nazism. He was also a man of action and ideas, an intellectual, a talented journalist and a military genius. If Trotsky had seized power in 1905, the First World War would have been avoided and Nazism would never have emerged. Trotsky was responsible for mass executions of Red Army deserters and cowards during the Civil War, but his severity was a military necessity rather than the result of personal sadism. By winning the Civil War, Trotsky prevented a far-right government from being created in Russia. In a later debate over Trotsky with the historian and biographer Robert Service,[57] Hitchens added more reasons for his Trotskyism. Trotsky

52. Hitchens, *God is Not Great*, p. 230.

53. http://hitchensdebates.blogspot.co.uk/2010/08/hitchens-vs-kresta-ave-maria-radio.html (accessed 25 February 2017 at 15:29).

54. Hitchens, *God is Not Great*, p. 244.

55. Ibid., p. 245.

56. 'Christopher Hitchens-On BBC Radio 4 "Great Lives" Discussing Leon Trotsky [2006]', You Tube, 16 September 2012 at https://www.youtube.com/watch?v=98uw-qzFq88 (accessed Monday 28 August 2016 at 02:30).

57. 'Trotsky with Hitchens and Service', YouTube, 3 August 2009 at https://www.youtube.com/watch?v=cuzXR-5w4Qu (accessed 29 August 2016 at 12:03).

was a man of great courage[58] and if Trotsky had become the leader of the Soviet Union rather than Stalin, there would have been no purges, Russian and Georgian chauvinism, and less anti-Semitism.

Religion as Original Sin

Religion is a form of original sin because its founding precepts are evil. Hitchens lists the following as religion's sinful axioms: It presents to the credulous untruths about the nature of the world,[59] holds to the doctrines of blood sacrifice, atonement and eternal reward and punishment, and it demands impossible rules to be obeyed and tasks to be accomplished.[60]

Hitchens identifies creation myths as responsible for unscientific conceptions of reality.[61] Human sacrifice was used to placate non-existent wrathful deities.[62] The monotheisms prohibited human sacrifice, but with them came widespread animal slaughter.[63] This bloodlust, according to Hitchens, is a manifestation of religion's proclivity for homicide. As an example, Hitchens refers to massacres such as the pogrom at Hebron during the Arab revolt of 1929 and the mass shooting of Muslims by Dry Baruch Goldstein at the Cave of Machpela.[64]

The Christian doctrine of the atonement Hitchens denounces as immoral itself.[65] That it is deemed necessary for an innocent man to die for other's sins is ethically wrong.[66] Moreover, Hitchens neither wishes to be told that his sins are responsible for Christ's death when that death took place before he was even born;[67] nor does he like the notion that if he rejects Christ's offer of atonement, he will be forever punished.[68]

Religion requires people to obey rules that are impossible to obey either because they demand a level of goodness that is too strenuous, or require

---

58. Ibid.

59. This axiom we have already noted is one of the four key objections Hitchens raises against religion. See Hitchens, *God is Not Great*, p. 4.

60. Ibid., p. 205.

61. Ibid., pp. 205-206.

62. Ibid., p. 206

63. Ibid., pp. 206-207.

64. Ibid., pp. 207-208.

65. Ibid., pp. 208-210.

66. Ibid., p. 209.

67. Ibid.

68. Ibid.

obedience to immoral rules.[69] That religion requires obedience to what cannot be performed is the essence of totalitarianism which keeps people in perpetual terror at their failures.[70] As evidence of these impossible rules, Hitchens cites the injunctions which say that if a man merely looks at a woman desirously, he has committed adultery (Matt. 5:27-30), and the command to love one's neighbor as oneself (Matt. 5:43-48; Luke 6:27, 28).[71]

The Evil Teachings of the Old Testament

The sacred books of Judaism and Christianity are deeply flawed morally according to Hitchens. His attack on the moral teachings of the Old Testament begins with the Decalogue which he discerns as the centerpiece of Old Testament morality. Hitchens has no problem with the prohibition of murder, theft, adultery, and false witness, but condemns the text for failing to condemn the ill-treatment of children, rape, slavery and massacre.[72] The reason for this he deduces is that those crimes are sanctioned by the Old Testament. Rules are given governing the purchase and sale of slaves and the sale of daughters. The death sentence pronounced on witches later inspired Christendom's massacre of women suspected of witchcraft. Orders are given for the expulsion of the Canaanites and a massacre of three thousand men is later described as perpetrated by Moses against those Israelites who made an idol.[73]

The Evil Teachings of the New Testament

In the eighth chapter of *God is Not Great* which concerns the New Testament, Hitchens identifies what is wrong about its moral teachings.[74] Hitchens is critical of Christ's ethics. His most serious objections are to the doctrines of the atonement and hell.[75] As Hitchens' denunciation of the doctrine of atonement has already been covered, I shall focus on his repudiation of the doctrine of hell. According to Hitchens, the Old Testament does not teach that there is everlasting torment for those who have disobeyed God.

69. Ibid., pp. 212-215.
70. Ibid., p. 212.
71. Ibid., pp. 212-213.
72. Ibid., p. 100.
73. Ibid., p. 100.
74. Ibid., pp. 109-122.
75. Ibid., p. 118.

It is the New Testament that introduces the idea that people will forever suffer for their finite transgressions. Hitchens finds such a sentence grossly disproportionate to the temporal crimes these people have committed and cruelly ironic in that it is the supposedly loving Jesus who teaches us about the hell. The phenomenon of hell is also evidence that God is a totalitarian, for there is no reprieve from hell.[76]

Religion Cannot Make People Better

According to Hitchens, believers make the point that religion improves people's behavior when they have run out of arguments. Once they have conceded that miracles do not happen and that their faith is unhistorical, they fall back on the moral argument.[77] Hitchens' evidence for his argument that religion cannot make people better morally is the focus of the thirteenth chapter of *God is Not Great.* [78] Hitchens examines the life of the moral giant, Dr. Martin Luther King.[79] Hitchens denies that King was a Christian and hypothesizes that King used the story of the Jewish Exodus from Egyptian slavery as a metaphor for the Civil Rights' struggle because it was a story that his supporters knew and would give them hope in the midst of their struggles.[80] King was therefore a very good man whose moral stature was achieved without religious conviction.

How Religions Make People Much Worse

If religion cannot make people better, Hitchens asserts, it is because it makes them far worse than they would have been had they not been religious, and it ruins morally even the best. [81]

Religious people may make false claims which they genuinely believe are true, but Hitchens sees religion also as fraudulent where religious figures make claims they know are not true, but which give them power and influence over Christianity's rank and file. For example, he labels colorfully Oral

---

76. https://hitchensdebates.blogspot.co.uk/2010/08/hitchens-vs-kresta-ave-maria-radio.html (accessed 26 November 2015 at 08:24 am).

77. Hitchens, *God is Not Great*, p. 184.

78. Ibid., pp. 173-193.

79. Ibid., pp. 173-184.

80. Ibid., p. 173.

81. Griffiths, ed., *Hitchens vs. Blair*, pp. 9-10.

Roberts, Jim Bakker, Ted Haggard and Jerry Falwell as conmen and accuses Mother Teresa of mere pretense of concern for the sick and dying poor.[82]

Religion is also, according to Hitchens, responsible for racism. The Dutch Reformed Church provided the theological justification for apartheid whilst the ruling National Party used the book of Exodus to define the Afrikaners' 'right' to their promised land. Racism, Hitchens declares, is a totalitarian way of thinking because it makes a person into a permanent victim and destroys his/her dignity.[83] Catholicism has perpetuated anti-Semitism. The Jesuit Order, until the twentieth century, would only admit men who had no Jewish blood for several generations; the Vatican has held the Jews responsible for deicide.[84] Despite *rapprochement* between the Catholic Church and Jewish people,[85] Hitchens remains deeply concerned that there is a revival of anti-Semitism among some Catholics.

Hitchens works with the view, as most people do, that there is a spectrum of evils with their specific features and textures. As we have seen, Hitchens regards totalitarianism as the greatest wickedness. Child abuse he describes as most repellant and by it he means not only sexual abuse, but all the varieties of ill-treatment children receive.[86] It is the prevalence of religious people among those who commit crimes against children that Hitchens believes legitimizes anti-theism and anti-religionism further.

Religion is a murderous phenomenon on a staggering scale according to Hitchens as it is dangerously talented at exacerbating ethnic rivalries.[87] At the heart of Hitchens' argument that religion kills is the most infamous of all contemporary terrorist outrages, the '9/11' tragedy. Hitchens describes the terrorists as completely sincere.[88]

The greatest potential religion has for violence is its capacity to cause a nuclear war. Hitchens cites Professor Pervez Hoodbhoy of the University of Islamabad who claims that there are Bin Ladenists among those working on Pakistan's nuclear programme. Hitchens is of the view that the religiously-motivated Middle East conflict could tip the world over the edge into nuclear immolation.[89] People might find it hard to believe that religious fanatics countenance nuclear annihilation but Hitchens states that it is the

82. Christopher Hitchens, 'Faith-Based Fraud', *Slate*, 16 May 2007.

83. Hitchens, *God is Not Great*, p. 251.

84. Ibid., pp. 250-251.

85. Rory Carroll, 'Pope says sorry for sins of church', *The Guardian*, 13 March 2000.

86. Christopher Hitchens, 'John Paul II's Other Legacy', *Slate*, 1 April 2005.

89. Hitchens, *God is Not Great*, p. 36.

88. Ibid., p. 32.

89. Ibid., pp. 24-25.

end of the world which religions look forward. The religious have contempt for this world because they have paradise in the next to look forward. The source of this attitude is the infantile delight in smashing things up which religion somehow preserves. What provokes greater excitement is the belief that one will be spared this nullification and taken to heaven where, like Tertullian expected, one will be able to watch the torment of the wicked.[90]

Hitchens and the East

According to Hitchens, the eastern religions are no better morally than the Middle East and the West's monotheism. Chapter fourteen of his *God is Not Great* attempts to prove this.[91]

Politically, Hindus and Buddhists have shown themselves as ready as Christians and Muslims to engage in violence and impose dictatorships, thus giving the lie to their reputations as pacifists. During the Sri Lankan Civil War, for example, the Hindu Tamils waged war with the Buddhist Sinhalese and atrocities were committed by both sides. The Dalai Lama demands Tibetan independence from China, which in Hitchens' view is a good demand. However, the Dalai Lama's form of government in his Indian enclave is a dictatorship where severe punishments are imposed on offenders and dissenters.[92]

Catholicism allied with Fascism; so too did Buddhism ally with Japanese imperialism. In 1938, the Nichiren sect devoted themselves to Imperial Way Buddhismin which the object of adulation was the Emperor of Japan. Japanese Buddhists welcomed the invasion of Manchuria as the end of Caucasian dominance in China and the beginning of Asian hegemony. The alliance with Nazi Germany and Fascist Italy was a means of liberation theology from European colonialism and a holy war to establish eternal peace in East Asia. The consequence was a bloody Pacific war with the United States.[93]

The Hitchens' Challenge

Though well known for his verbosity, Hitchens is also adept at creating concise formulations of his ideas. What might be termed the 'Hitchens' Challenge' is Hitchens' pithy, rhetorical way of summarizing his view of the

---

90. Ibid., p. 219.
91. Ibid., pp. 195-204.
92. Ibid., pp. 199-200.
93. Ibid., pp. 201-203.

effects of religious morality. The Challenge can be expressed as follows: Can you think of any good deed a religious person performs that an unbeliever could not? Now, can you think of an evil act that only a religious person could perform?[94] By asking these two questions, Hitchens is not only aiming to establish the proposition that people can be morally good without the influence or supervision of religious belief, but also to propose that religion actually causes people's morality to degenerate to the lowest level.

Hitchens' Normative Ethics

So far much has been made of what Hitchens does not like about religious morality, but it is now apposite to ask of what his normative values consist. If Hitchens were to draw up a moral code, what would it look like? We have already noted above that his most fundamental value is personal and socio-political freedom. All that totalitarians deny people, such as freedom of thought, opinion, speech, assembly and movement and personal privacy, are of the highest value to Hitchens. His normative values are liberal, democratic, and secular. It is no surprise that he chose to immigrate to the US and take on US citizenship.

Hitchens has identified personal qualities and virtues he most and least admires when responding to the *Proust Questionnaire*, a series of questions that Hitchens' colleagues at *Vanity Fair* would ask of a celebrity once a month. When asked what quality he most admired in a man and in a woman, he replied, courage. When asked what his favorite virtue was, he said, a liking of irony. His last favorite virtue unsurprisingly was faith.[95]

Conscience is at the heart of Hitchens' moral praxis for it is the motivation to do good which makes divine compunction irrelevant.[96] Hitchens rejects the Golden Rule, or the law of reciprocity in which people are called on to treat others as they would wish to be treated themselves. Although Hitchens calls the Rule a common sense principle which is simple enough to be taught to a child and attainable by any atheist,[97] he rejects it as too demanding for mere human beings to achieve.[98]

94. For the use of the Challenge in debate, see e.g., 'Christopher Hitchens vs John Lennox Is God great' [sic], You Tube, 8 May 2015 at https://www.youtube.com/watch?v=sHiGsL4bzmM (accessed 3 September 2016 at 13:50).

95. Hitchens, *Hitch 22*, p. 334.

96. Hitchens, *God is Not Great*, p. 213.

97. Ibid., p. 213.

98. Ibid.

Hitchens' normative values therefore rest on the axioms that humans are innately self-centered, yet they have rights and obligations to others. Rather than condemning self-centeredness, Hitchens' morality works round this by arguing that moral precepts must therefore be possible to keep. As a humanist, Hitchens sees humans as intrinsically valuable, and so they have their rights. Therefore, no harm is to be done to them, whether by causing them great and egregious suffering or by causing them irritation. The mutual respect of rights is how each one's obligations to others are fulfilled. It is a way of balancing the importance of the self with the importance of others. Other beliefs lie in the foundations of Hitchens' normative ethics. The principle of equality sees humans as equally valuable and equally endowed with rights. Hitchens' support for civil rights demonstrates this.[99] Hitchens' normative values are therefore those of a contemporary secular liberal democrat with an environmental conscience and a secular confidence that morality can exist separately from religion.

Hitchens' Metaethics

Hitchens' ethics rest on four metaethical foundations: His belief in free-will which means people can be held culpable for the wrongs they commit, his view that morality is objective and that what is morally right and wrong is the case regardless of what people might think or feel, his conviction that morality's source lies within human evolution rather than in divine command, and his opinion that follows on from his belief in morality's evolutionary origins that with the exception of the small minority of psychopaths, most people possess a conscience and incline towards the good. It is these axioms that make Hitchens confident that if religion disappears, moral goodness will not.

If human beings are not capable of freely choosing between right and wrong, they cannot be held morally responsible for the wrong they do. X is responsible for the wrong s/he does in the sense that it is X who did the wrong and not some other person, but it is hard to see how X can be punished as being morally responsible. S/he can be identified as the cause of the wrong and corrected for the wrong s/he has done, perhaps by some sort of therapy, but not blamed. Hitchens' writings, however, are suffused with demands for justice. He appears to take it for granted that the great majority of people, except for psychopaths, can choose whether to do right or wrong. This chapter has delineated in detail the crimes for which he holds believers guilty and there is no sense in what he writes or says that he considers

99. Ibid., p. 173.

those responsible as having no free choice; rather they are perpetrators who have freely chosen the wrong. Whether it be jihadists, Catholic child abusers or theocrats, all are guilty of gross crimes and ought to be brought to justice. Though Hitchens never explicitly explores the issue of free-will, his language demonstrates that his moral outlook is premised on the axiom that humans have free moral choice.

Hitchens has no time for moral relativism. When he condemns God as a totalitarian, he does so because he believes that such an authority style is wholly wrong even though many people appear to him to welcome such a God. When Hitchens denounces Islamism and praises civilized Islam as epitomized by the Grand Ayatollah Sistani who forgave those Islamists who tried to assassinate him,[100] he is expressing the opinion that certain views are morally excellent and others are morally bankrupt, and this is the case regardless of what anyone may think.[101] When Hitchens speaks of the war between faith and civilization,[102] he seeks the triumph of civilization rather than a relativistic accommodation of the two. When Hitchens calls for a new secular and liberal Enlightenment in which the proper study of mankind is humanity and people are free to enquire,[103] he is presenting his view of what values constitute the best type of society. When Hitchens calls al Qaida and the regimes of Saddam Hussein, Kim Jong-Il and Mahmoud Ahmadinejad evil, he is using an adjective that he intends to transcend all moral variations between cultures and ethical disputes to identify a certain type of political organization and government that all good, right-thinking people ought to agree is superlatively wicked.[104] Hitchens therefore adheres to a moral code that he expresses in an objective way and which he takes as being self-evident despite conflicting moral codes. He has the firm conviction that something is right or wrong regardless of what people think. It is this sense of being morally right that makes Hitchens such a determined opponent of alternative religious moralities.

As Hitchens argues that the origins of morality lie within human evolution and that humans therefore know what is right and wrong without having to be told by a deity, it brings him into a direct collision with the moralistic argument. Arguably, the moralistic argument has two parts: the epistemological argument and the psychological argument. According to the epistemological argument:

100. Christopher Hitchens, 'Stop the Masochistic Insanity', Slate, 23 May 2005.

101. Ibid.

102. Hitchens, God is Not Great, p. 280

103. Ibid., p. 283.

104. Hitchens, 'Simply Evil', Slate, 5 September 2011.

1. humans only know the difference between good and evil if God tells them.

2. humans know the difference between good and evil.

3. therefore God exists.

According to the psychological argument:

1. humans only do the good and not evil if and only if God demands the good of them.

2. humans do good and avoid evil.

3. therefore God exists.[105]

It is very important to Hitchens that he rebuts these arguments as they argue that moral knowledge and behavior are dependent on God, which makes His existence attractive.

Hitchens agrees with premise two in both the epistemological and the psychological arguments. He denies premise one in both arguments and the conclusion of both arguments by deploying what J. L. Mackie terms the naturalistic argument.[106] According to this argument, humans know what is right and wrong and do it, not because of a divine supervisor, but because morality is encoded within humans by evolution and natural selection. As evidence, Hitchens states that societies that permitted immoral acts do not survive.[107] The knowledge of what is right and wrong, and the desire to do what is right, such as the Golden Rule,[108] is therefore natural to humans with the exception of psychopaths.[109] As a personal example of altruistic behavior that appears innate and therefore intrinsically satisfying, Hitchens refers to how he donates blood.[110]

Hitchens therefore takes humanist offence at the moralistic argument. If evolutionary forces have encoded within humanity a knowledge of and a

---

105. It is Elizabeth Anderson who calls this argument the moralistic argument. See Elizabeth Anderson, 'If God is Dead, Is Everything Permitted', ed. Hitchens, *the Portable Atheist*, p. 335.

106. J. L. Mackie, 'Conclusions and Implications', in ed. Hitchens, *the Portable Atheist*, p. 259.

107. Ibid., p. xvi.

108. This is usually taken to mean treat others as you would wish them to treat you.

109. Hitchens, ed., *the Portable Atheist*, p. xvii.

110. Ibid., p. xvi.

desire to do what is right, then surely it is an assault on human dignity to say that humans cannot be morally good without a deity's supervision?[111]

Religion is Irrational

Hitchens' approach to religion's belief is to cut it away with what has come to be known as 'Hitchens' Razor'. The Razor, like Ockham's razor, is an epistemological one, and it is double-edged. First, the Razor establishes that the burden of proof in a debate is on the person who makes the bigger claim. If the person with the burden of proof is not prepared to accept that s/he has this burden, his or her argument can be ignored. Second, once the burden of proof is established and accepted, if the 'prover' has no evidence for his or her propositions, but simply asserts them, then his or her arguments can be dismissed. [112] Hitchens' razor appears to make short work of religion: The religious have the greatest burden of proof for they make the greatest claim of all, which is that God exists; therefore the burden of proof is theirs. As they cannot adduce any evidence for their maximal proposition, their religion can be dismissed immediately.

The Hitchens' Razor is not, however, an original idea. Hitchens' assertion that what can be asserted without evidence can be dismissed without evidence has been in circulation since the early 19th century.[113] The principle it expresses is as old as human logic itself.

Hitchens' Materialism

Materialism holds that matter is the fundamental substance of the world and that all phenomena are material interactions. Materialism therefore denies the existence of things such as God, spirits, and souls. Evidence of Hitchens' materialism is plentiful in what he wrote. One example from the many is his approving inclusion of Lucretius' *De Rerum Natura* in *the Portable Atheist*.[114]

The gist of Hitchens' materialism is that super-material explanations of the universe arose during humanity's pre-scientific intellectual infancy, and that with the advance of science's material explanations, super-material

---

111. Ibid., p. xvi.

112. Hitchens, 'Mommie Dearest' and Hitchens, *God is Not Great*, p.150.

113. Jon R. Stone, ed., The Routledge Dictionary of Latin Quotations: The Illiterati's Guide to Latin Maxims, Mottoes, Proverbs and Sayings (London: Routledge, 2005), p. 101.

114. Hitchens, ed., *the Portable Atheist*, pp. 2-6.

explanations have been demonstrated as false.[115] On the basis of this evidence, it is far more probable that the world is material rather than also super-material, and appeals to super-material explanations are irrational and lacking evidence.

The Argument Against Revelation

One piece of evidence that religion is irrational is its reliance upon revelation. Hitchens sees strong arguments against the argument from revelation. Revelation has supposedly been given to a wide variety of seers in diverse times and places. Original revelations are in the Christian tradition supplemented by later revelations. In other cases, the original revelation remains in force, but the person to whom it was delivered is lost in time. Hitchens' conclusion is that since inconsistent revelations cannot all be true, some must therefore be false. Hitchens therefore countenances the possibility that one might be true, but why might that revelation be believed when religious wars are fought over which revelation is true? A further difficulty exists in the fact that the revelations that birthed the monotheisms were given in the cultural desert of the ancient Middle East.[116] The recipients therefore were of an irrational and uncultured frame of mind and so prone to eccentric claims.

Biblical Untruth

Hitchens declares the Old Testament as untrue based on the absence of archaeological evidence. Hitchens refers the reader to the work of Israel Finkelstein and Neil Asher Silberman at Tel Aviv University. After extensive digs, the two men concluded that there was no evidence for the historicity of the books of Exodus and Joshua. What does show in the archaeological record is that Jewish communities were native to Palestine from thousands of years ago.[117]

Hitchens finds it is as irrational to trust the New Testament as it is the Old as the New Testament also does not synchronize with what is known by ancient historians. The Gospels say that Christ was born in the year that Caesar Augustus ordered a census for taxation and that Herod ruled Judaea and Quirinius was the Syrian legate. The truth is that Herod died four years before Christ was meant to have been born and during his reign there was no governor of Syrian called Quirinius. No Roman historian refers to

115. Hitchens, *God is Not Great*, p. 64.
116. Ibid. pp. 97-98.
117. Ibid. pp. 102-103.

Caesar's census. A Jewish historian, Josephus, mentions one, but it took place six years after Christ's birth.[118]

The case of the Virgin Mary is for Hitchens the best proof that the Gospels are legends. According to the Gospel texts themselves, Jesus makes no mention of his mother having been a virgin when He was born and fails to show her respect when she turns up to see how he is getting on. Mary appears not to recollect the Archangel Gabriel's visitation and is surprised at her Son's precocity, even though she is supposed to have conceived him supernaturally.[119]

To give further substance to his chapter, Hitchens turns to the work of Bart Ehrman, the New Testament scholar. Ehrman started his academic career as a champion of evangelical Christianity but could not reconcile his Christianity with his knowledge. His argument is that some of the most famous narratives of Jesus' life were added long after Jesus had died, thus calling into question the historicity of Christianity.[120]

The Metaphysical Arguments

What of the philosophical arguments for the existence of God? Hitchens' response to these arguments constitutes one of the shortest chapters in *God is Not Great*. The brevity of his argument possibly demonstrates that Hitchens thinks that metaphysical arguments are so poor, they can easily be dismissed. The thesis of this chapter is that religion is irrational for it posits a metaphysical worldview that is no longer possible in the light of the advances of knowledge in natural science. According to Hitchens, the religious answers to the metaphysical question of the nature of reality were formulated during the primitive early stages of humanity,[121] when little was known scientifically and natural events such as eclipses caused terror. Supernatural beings were invented to account for events that are now explained scientifically. Hitchens concedes that some eminent scientists have held religious and superstitious beliefs, such as Newton, but is convinced that religious explanation has been made redundant by scientific explanations.[122]

The version of the cosmological argument with which Hitchens contends is the *kalam* cosmological argument which argues that as everything

118. Ibid. pp. 112-114.

119. Ibid., pp. 116-117.

120. Hitchens, *God is Not Great*, p. 120.

121. Ibid., p. 64.

122. Hitchens, *God is Not Great*, p.70.

that comes into existence has a cause, the universe must therefore have a cause too. This cause would be pre-existent to time and space, therefore eternal, and of enormous intelligence. Hitchens sees two problems with this argument. First, why does there have to be a first cause if an infinite chain of causes is not impossible and second, if God is the creator, who created God? For these questions, Hitchens does not believe religion and theology have an answer.[123] Hitchens adds three further objections to the cosmological argument in his debate with William Lane Craig at Biola University in 2009. First, he argues that the existence of a Creator does not imply the truth of theism. The Creator may have made the universe but that does not mean that He therefore feels any sort of loving attachment to it and its occupants or that He wishes to intervene miraculously or be incarnated in it. At most, the argument for a Creator from the *kalam* cosmological argument leads to deism. Second, there is confusion as to whether God worked with pre-existing material to create the universe or created it *ex nihilo*. Third, Hitchens refers his audience to the myriad of collapsed suns and failed galaxies which speak not of a great, benevolent Designer but either of a capricious and cruel deity, an incompetent creator, or matter acting randomly in the absence of a divine supervisor.[124]

The Argument from Design

Hitchens begins his argument against the argument from design by establishing where he believes the argument from design comes from. Those who argue that the universe was created for human benefit argue on the basis that God cares for human beings individually.[125] This Hitchens regards as a manifestation of human solipsism because it is the belief that God is intensely focused on humanity and that our existence's conditions can be changed through weird rituals.[126]

The arguments from design Hitchens divides into the macro and the micro and he deals with them in that order. He begins with a simple summary of William Paley's famous argument that the world and all that it contains is designed on the basis that if one concludes that a watch has been designed for a purpose, the world ought to be considered so because it too

123. Ibid., p. 71.

124. 'Does God Exist? William Lane Craig vs. Christopher Hitchens-Full Debate [HD]', You Tube, 28 September 2014 at https://www. https://www.youtube.com/watch?v=otYm41hb48o (accessed 8 April 2017 at 19:43).

125. Hitchens, *God is Not Great*, p. 74.

126. Ibid.

contains the marks of design. Hitchens' attempt at rebutting Paley is not a philosophical argument but a biological one. He makes no use, for example, of Hume's four criticisms of the argument from design.[127] Hitchens tells us that things such as eyes and ears have not been designed but exist because they are the product of adaptation and selection.[128] Equally challenging to the intelligent design and creationist camp is the absence of design as evidenced by the confusion of the cosmos.[129] This for Hitchens is hardly evidence of design.

In micro terms, intelligent design exponents and creationists use the human eye as evidence that evolutionary adaptation through natural selection has not occurred. Their argument is that the eye is too astonishing to be the consequence of chance. Hitchens refers his readers to Michael Shermer who describes the stages of the eye's development from an initial eye-spot of light sensitive cells to the complex eye now found in modern mammals such as humans. The eye also calls into question the Master Designer hypothesis for according to Shermer it is built upside down and backwards.[130]

Hitchens' chapter progresses to an analysis of religionists who accept the fact of evolution but see in evolution evidence of a directing Mind. Though Hitchens cannot deny that it is indeed a logical possibility that evolution is God's mechanism for bringing forth life, it is an argument that reduces God to a blunderer who has taken vast tracts of time and much wasted biological matter to produce life forms which though adapted, are defective.[131] It also reduces God to a cruel and capricious deity. Hitchens states that 98% of all species have gone extinct during the evolutionary process.[132] With regards to human evolution, Hitchens poses two questions to theistic evolutionists. First, humans are very violent, therefore why would a Designer create such a rapacious species as humanity? Second, if human beings are the intended goal of evolution of a caring God, why is their existence so contingent?[133] As an example, Hitchens refers his audience to a cataclysmic event of global warming that occurred 180,000 years ago which

---

127. A helpful summary of Hume's criticisms is given by T. J. Mawson in his book, *Belief in God: An Introduction to the Philosophy of Religion*, p. 134.

128. Hitchens, *God is Not Great*, p. 79.

129. Ibid. p. 80.

130. See Michael Shermer, *Why Darwin Matters: The Case Against Intelligent Design*, p.17.

131. Hitchens, *God is Not Great*, p. 85.

132. Ibid., p. 91.

133. Ibid., p. 92.

reduced the human population down to near-extinction levels of 30-40,000. This according to Hitchens counts against theistic evolution.[134]

Theists argue that organisms at their most simple are still too complicated for evolution to explain how they came into existence in the first place. What Intelligent Design proponents call the argument from irreducible complexity, Hitchens dismisses as laughable.[135] He refers to a study made by the University of Oregon in April 2006 which demonstrated how basic protein molecules, using trial and error, switched hormones on in a time before life had emerged from the oceans and the evolution of bones.[136]

The Nonsense of Miracle Claims

Hitchens deploys Hume's skeptical arguments against miracles. According to Hume, a miracle is an interruption in the regular, established course of things and if you believe you have witnessed a miracle, you have two options: either you believe that the natural laws have been suspended or that you are mistaken, or even deluded. The likelihood of the latter being the case is far greater than the first. If reports of miracles come second or third hand or even after many generations with no independent corroboration, such as was the case with the claims that Christ was raised from the dead, the chance of the miracle having happened is close to zero.[137]

The Epistemic 'Wickedness' of Religion

Though Hitchens does not use the term virtue epistemology, his eighteenth chapter of *God is Not Great* asserts that religious belief lacks it.[138] Virtue epistemology states that knowledge is true belief acquired through the operation of reliable epistemic virtues or cognitive faculties.[139] An epistemic virtue is a personal quality that makes a person more likely to discover and understand the truth.[140] As an example, the philosopher Duncan Pritchard

---

134. Christopher Hitchens, 'Does God Exist?', You Tube (accessed 8 April 2017 at 19:48).

135. Hitchens, *God is Not Great*, p. 87.

136. Ibid. p. 87. For the study, see Jamie T. Brigham, Sean M. Carroll, and Joseph W. Thornton, "Evolution of Hormone Receptor Activity by Molecular Exploitation", *Science* 312:5770, 7 April 2006, pp. 97-101.

137. Hitchens, *God is Not Great*, p. 141.

138. Ibid., pp. 253-275.

139. Ibid., p. 183.

140. Duncan Pritchard, *What is this thing called knowledge?*, p.173.

gives conscientiousness.[141] This quality describes a person who will take the trouble to check what is true in a thorough way and therefore is by virtue of such a trait more disposed to finding out the truth than someone who lacks it or possesses it to a lesser degree.[142] On this definition, a person who possesses an epistemic virtue is one who regularly deploys this virtue in truth-seeking activities rather than occasionally or rarely.

In his eighteenth chapter of God is Not Great,[143] Hitchens identifies the use of reason[144] as an epistemic virtue which leads to disbelief[145] in God and religion. Contrary to the Psalmists' statement that 'The fool has said in his heart there is no God' (Ps. 14:1; Ps. 53:1), it is the fool who believes there is a God and accepts the teachings of organized faith. The believer, therefore, is one who is irrational whereas the atheist is the one who is epistemically virtuous.

Religion's greatest epistemic iniquity according to Hitchens is that it teaches its adherents to accept uncritically the dogma of religious leaders. The epistemic virtues of doubt and skepticism are absent from the religious mind. What intensifies the iniquity of religion is that it often has and frequently still does punish those who refuse to think in the way that it does.[146] For Hitchens, reasonable people therefore stand in contradiction to organized religion and religion's irrationality is also a form of immorality.

Mother Teresa

The first book length denunciation of religion by Hitchens came in 1995 with the publication of The Missionary Position: Mother Teresa in Theory and Practice. What is important about this book is not only does it demonstrate how consistent Hitchens' anti-theism has been over time, but also because his criticism of her marries his view that religion is immoral and irrational and reveals that his target is not only religion generally, but prominent religionists also.

Hitchens' accusation that Catholicism accommodated itself to Fascist regimes before and during the Second World War is repeated in this book. In the introduction, Hitchens presents evidence of Mother Teresa's close connection to the Duvaliers who were at the time Haiti's dictators. Hitchens

141. Ibid., p. 173.
142. Ibid.
143. Hitchens, God is Not Great, pp. 253-275.
144. Ibid., p. 255.
145. Ibid., p. 255.
146. Ibid., p. 254.

is not sure what the connection was, but Mother Teresa is in his mind guilty of something by association at least.[147]

Hitchens deploys the testimony of those who have worked with Mother Teresa to reveal that rather than alleviate suffering, she promotes it because she believes that through suffering people share in Christ's sufferings.[148] For example, Hitchens quotes Mary Loudon, a former volunteer, as saying that her first impression of Mother Teresa's Home for the Dying was that it resembled a Nazi concentration camp.[149]

Hitchens debunks Malcolm Muggeridge's claim that a miracle happened whilst he was visiting Mother Teresa's orphanage in Calcutta to make a documentary about her work in 1969. According to Muggeridge, the cameraman Ken MacMillan was certain that the House of the Dying was too dark to film, but tried anyway, and when the film was processed, a beautiful, soft light could be seen which Muggeridge claimed was a divine light.[150] Hitchens presents MacMillan's prosaic explanation which was that he had used a newly invented Kodak film which was responsible for the clear pictures.[151]

Hitchens' imputation that Mother Teresa received donations from dictators, fraudulently claimed to alleviate suffering and encouraged claims that miracles were part of her ministry reveals, according to Hitchens, how the immoral and irrational forces of religion meet within the person and work of a Catholic celebrity.[152]

The Future of Religion

Contrary to Dawkins, Hitchens does not think that religion will disappear, or at least not for a very long time. Whereas for Dawkins, religion is like the small pox virus, which is hard to eradicate, but will eventually be expunged by science,[153] for Hitchens, religion will remain, for it was engrained in humans by natural selection.[154] Faith, Hitchens believes, replicates too

---

147. Hitchens, *The Missionary Position*, pp. 3-7.

148. Ibid., p. 44.

149. Ibid., p. 42.

150. Ibid. p. 25.

151. Ibid. p.27.

152. 'C4 Right to Reply - Christopher Hitchens vs Mother Theresa', You Tube, 7 May 2016 at https://www.youtube.com/watch?v=DWSU9Y2Fa8E (accessed 21 March 2017 at 15:10 pm).

153. Richard Dawkins, 'Is Science a Religion?', *The Humanist*, Jan./Feb. 1997, p 26.

154. Hitchens, 'The God Squad'.

quickly to die out, even when it is cut down.[155] Hitchens also sees religion in Freudian terms: The will to believe in God or the gods is caused by the fear of death and the desire for eternal life. Hitchens' conclusion is that the likelihood of this is very small.[156]

Hitchens' Secular Manicheanism

If religion will not go away, what does Hitchens propose to do with it? Regarding theocratic fascism Hitchens seeks its overthrow.[157] His view is a secular Manicheanism for it interprets history and the future as the struggle between theocracy and religious fanaticism on the one hand and the forces of civilization on the other. This is therefore not a struggle with private, responsible religion, but with an imperialist faith that seeks control.[158] It is a struggle between good and evil, though not between gods, but between flesh and blood.

In this struggle with religious extremism, Hitchens is no pacifist. This has led him into political alliances that no one suspected he would make. In an article titled 'Bush's Secularist Triumph: The left apologizes for religious fanatics. The president fights them',[159] Hitchens salutes the American President at the time, George W. Bush, for taking on jihadism militarily. Hitchens regards those who commit acts of terrorism as enemy combatants and the deployment of forces against them is justified. American success against the Taliban, al-Qaida and the radicals in Iraq are great advancements for non-fundamentalist Muslims in many countries.

Does Hitchens believe the war with extremism will ever be won? Hitchens believes it can, but he also believes the war must be waged permanently to keep extremism suppressed. Hitchens is not a utopian who believes that humans can be perfected; instead, he regards human flaws as ineradicable and therefore understands history as tragic.[160] Religious fanatics will always be there and appeasing them is of no use. War with them is unending.[161] Hitchens' vision of the future is therefore not one of liberal confidence in the

---

155. 'The Four Horsemen-Hitchens, Dawkins, Dennett, Harris', YouTube, 23 July 2012 at https://www.youtube.com/watch?v=n7IHU28aR2E (accessed 21 February 2016 at 17:17 pm).

156. Hitchens, *God is Not Great*, p. 247.

157. Hitchens, 'The God Squad'.

158. Ibid., p. 280.

159. Christopher Hitchens, 'Bush's Secularist Triumph: 'The left apologizes for religious fanatics. The president fights them', *Slate*, 9 November 2004.

160. Steven Pinker, *The Blank Slate*, (London: Allen Lane 2002), p. 338

161. Christopher Hitchens, 'In Defense of Endless War', *Slate*, 19 September 2011.

linear march of progress and he warns his audiences that perhaps there will
come a time when civilization will seek to appease its foes rather than fight
them. But it is one of Hitchens' aims in joining the ranks of the New Atheists
to stimulate civilization's response to the forces of theocratic darkness. Hope
therefore is not lost according to Hitchens.

Old Right and Neo-Conservative Influences

Though his assessment of human nature can be optimistic, Hitchens never
denies the powerfully inherent and universal moral flaws of humanity.
This is possibly a leftover of his Christian upbringing but also a result of
his understanding that such imperfections have been encoded in humanity through natural selection. Religion, as we have seen, was one of those
imperfections. His experiences as a journalist reporting from oppressed
and war-scarred regions of the world no doubt underline his pessimism. In
asserting that humans are flawed with ineradicable weaknesses, Hitchens
demonstrates the influence of the Old Right on his anthropology. Traditional conservatives have viewed human nature as beset with moral weakness and politics is therefore the means of creating societies that restrain
and reduce the effects of such imperfections. The root of this philosophy is
the Augustinian doctrine of original sin.[162]

But Hitchens also manifests the influence of the utopian Right, or neo-
conservativism, which has emerged recently in the US. Unlike liberals who
seek to spread the free market peacefully, American neo-conservatives wish
to impose their capitalist and democratic values and if necessary by force.[163]
Hitchens welcomes the neo-conservative struggle against Islamic theocracy
and though an opponent of the First Iraq War, he supported the overthrown
of Saddam Hussein in the Second War. Hitchens argues that Saddam Hussein was a Muslim dictator, not a secular one, because he festooned his regime with the trappings of Islamic piety and jihadism and added the caption
'Allah Akhbar' to the Iraqi flag. Hussein also ordered the construction of the
largest mosque in the region which contained a Koran written in what he
claimed to be his own blood.[164]

Further evidence of his conviction that the Second Iraq War was about
the implantation of secular values into a region formerly dominated by Islamic theocracy is found in Hitchens' description of his holiday in Iraqi
Kurdistan at Christmas 2006. One of the many benedictions Hitchens sees

162. John Gray, *Black Mass*, p. 44.
163. Ibid. p. 45.
164. Hitchens, *God is Not Great*, p. 25-6.

in this territory's liberation is the creation of the American University of Iraq which provides a secular education.[165]

Keeping Moderate Religion Tame

Like his New Atheist colleague, Sam Harris, Hitchens distinguishes between extremist religions and moderate religions.[166] Of moderate religion, Hitchens asserts he is no persecutor. As evidence, he condemns one of his favorite writers, George Orwell, for his insouciance to the destruction of churches during the Spanish Civil War. Hitchens assures us also that he removes his shoes when he enters mosques and covers his head when he visits synagogues.[167]

However, though Hitchens assures us that with regards to moderate religion he is respectful,[168] he is not prepared to accept the form that religion takes in contemporary American society, which is religious pluralism, whereby all religions are accorded the same respect.[169] Some forms of moderate religion therefore are deserving of less than the maximum of respect he says he has for it more generously elsewhere. When dealing with the absurd, pompous elements of faith, Hitchens advises mockery.[170]

Hitchens argues that if religion is to take the moderate form that can be tolerated within secular societies, then secular societies must render it harmless.[171] To achieve this, there ought to be a separation of state and religion in which religious convictions play no part in the running of society or in its public discourse but retreat to the private sphere. This would permit a new Enlightenment to happen in the public sphere.[172]

As well as a separation of state and religion, according to Hitchens, this process of disarming religion is achieved through the restrictions and prohibitions the democratic, secular state would place upon what religious people can and cannot do, and the right of the state to intervene where religious attitudes and behavior are wrong and dangerous. The secular state

---

165. Christopher Hitchens, 'Holiday in Iraq', *Vanity Fair*, 12 March 2007.

166. Harris, *The End of Faith: Religion, Terror and the Future of Reason* (London: The Free Press, 2006), p. 108

167. Hitchens, *God is Not Great*, p. 11.

168. Hitchens, ed. *the Portable Atheist*, p. 207.

169. Hitchens, 'The God Squad'.

170. 'The Four Horsemen-Hitchens, Dawkins, Dennett, Harris', YouTube, 23 July 2012, (accessed 21 February 2016 at 17:18 pm).

171. Christopher Hitchens, 'Free Exercise of Religion? No, Thanks', *Slate*, 6 September 2010.

172. Hitchens, *God is Not Great*, p. 283.

therefore operates from an independent moral base to that of religion, though the two may coincide, and it is the state's moral code that has the final word on what is permitted.[173]

A Greater Heresy

It has been seen that Hitchens does not think that religion will disappear in the way that Dawkins anticipates it will but Hitchens deviates even more radically from New Atheist orthodoxy when he asserts that he does not wish to see moderate religion disappear. There are certain religious beliefs that are useful such as the idea that humanity does not know everything[174]and the belief in a Creator which prevents human hubris.[175] Hitchens is impressed by the eloquence of the King James Translation of the Bible (though this is not heretical as Dawkins shares this admiration)[176] and recognizes that the religious impulse inspired great works of art such as poetry.[177] Hitchens surprises his New Atheist colleagues by arguing that he wants the argument with religious people to continue because by arguing with others it is possible to learn from them and because it is enjoyable.[178]

There is another reason why Hitchens does not wish the demise of moderate religion. At the end of the documentary DVD *Collision* made about Hitchens' series of debates with Pastor Douglas Wilson, Hitchens speaks of the meeting in his apartment in Washington between the New Atheist leaders. He narrates to Wilson part of the dialogue that Hitchens does not think was captured on camera. Hitchens recalls that he said the following: If he had managed to convince everyone in the word of the falsity of religion and there was only one person left to convince, he would not do it. He would not expunge religion from the world. When Dawkins asked why, Hitchens said he had no explanation. At that point, *Collision* suddenly ends.[179]

Though Hitchens on that occasion could not give the reason for his desire to preserve religion, we already know that he values the debate with the religious. Another reason is possible, knowing what we do about Hitchens'

173. Christopher Hitchens, 'Free Exercise of Religion? No, Thanks'

174. 'The Four Horsemen-Hitchens, Dawkins, Dennett, Harris', YouTube, 23 July 2012, (accessed 21 February 2016 at 17:13).

175. Ibid.

176. Ibid.

177. Ibid.

178. Ibid.

179. Hitchens and Wilson, *Collision: Is Christianity Good for the World*, (LEVEL 4: 2008).

worldview. As an anti-totalitarian, Hitchens is unable to act the totalitarian and abolish religion, albeit through persuasion rather than violence. Hitchens is aware of how utopias and total solutions have led to appalling bloodshed.[180] One of the criticisms Hitchens makes of totalitarians is that they seek to control their subjects' private lives and in extinguishing religion, that is what Hitchens would be doing.

Hitchens in Context

This chapter has identified what constitutes Hitchens' anti-theism and anti-religionism and how it fits within and deviates from New Atheism generally. Hitchens, however, exists within other contexts and under other influences. Bernard Schweizer identifies Hitchens as standing within an anti-theist tradition that stretches back to the nineteenth and early twentieth centuries Russian anarchism.[181] Hitchens recognizes his lineage by including an essay from 1916 by the Russian anti-theist Emma Goldman called 'The Philosophy of Atheism' in *the Portable Atheist*.[182] Goldman regards the idea of God, as does Hitchens, to be the result of primitive humanity's attempt to explain terrifying and mysterious natural forces.[183] Like Hitchens, Goldman presents the problem of evil as an insurmountable argument against the existence and goodness of God.[184] On the question as to whether the irreligious can be virtuous, Hitchens agrees with Goldman for she regards atheists as torchbearers of the highest values. The religious on the other hand are immoral.[185]

Blackburn defines the Enlightenment of the 18th century as a time in history when European thought was characterized by rational and liberal ways of thinking.[186] Even the term anti-theist was a product of the Enlightenment. According to Reza Aslan, the first recorded use of the term anti-theist in the English language was 1788.[187]

Blackburn's definition of the Enlightenment almost captures Hitchens' worldview. Hitchens' dismissal of religion as superstitious irrationalism that

---

180. Hitchens, *God is Not Great*, p. 153.

181. Schweitzer, *Misotheism*, p. 76.

182. Emma Goldman, 'The Philosophy of Atheism', ed. Hitchens, *the Portable Atheist*, pp. 129-133.

183. Ibid., pp. 129-130.

184. Ibid., p. 131.

185. Ibid. p. 133.

186. Simon Blackburn, *Oxford Dictionary*, p. 115.

187. Reza Aslan, 'Sam Harris and the "New Atheists" aren't new, aren't even atheists', *Salon*, 21 November 2014.

fails to provide evidence for its propositions demonstrates the fundamental importance of rationality and empiricism to his anti-theism and anti-religionism. His suspicion of authority which took the form of Trotskyism in his youth and his contrarian style of journalism in his maturity shows Hitchens' suspicion of established authority. Hitchens also is a materialist: There is no non-material dimension to the universe and humans do not survive death. Like Enlightenment ethicists, Hitchens is a utilitarian when he says that moral values endure based on whether they are useful to human survival. Where Hitchens deviates from the Enlightenment message is in the poorer measure of optimism he feels about the possibilities of human progress and his ethical views. As we have seen, Hitchens believes that the war against extreme religion is one that will last as long as democracy is prepared to stand up for itself, a statement which suggests that there is a possibility that democracy might give up the fight. However, despites these differences, Hitchens' commitment to a rational, empirical, anti-religious and materialist worldview is synonymous with Enlightenment thinking.

Anti-postmodernism

Postmodernism accommodates religious worldviews in ways that New Atheism cannot and therefore New Atheism is a reassertion of modernist, Enlightenment epistemology against postmodernism's tolerance. Nietzsche, one of the greatest postmodern philosophers, saw all worldviews as perspectival. Everything that is stated depends on a point of view which is no more an accurate picture of reality than any other point of view.[188] Enlightenment epistemology, on the other hand, sought evidence for what is exclusively true.

Hitchens, however, proceeds on the basis of evidence and cuts away at postmodernism's relativism with his 'Razor'. There is for Hitchens truth and falsehood and not a range of relatively true perspectives. But Hitchens demonstrates his anti-postmodernism in other ways. According to the later Wittgenstein, no statement has a single meaning, but is understood only within the context, or word game, in which it is used.[189] Hitchens contrarily understands language to correspond with reality and can be understood out of its original setting. Thus, for example, when discussing the Decalogue, he writes on the assumption, that these ancient laws can be understood by someone reading the text in the 21st century in the same way as they were understood by the ancient Jews.[190]

188. Sire, *Naming the Elephant*, pp. 39, 40.
189. Orr-Ewing, *Why Trust the Bible*, p. 18.
190. Hitchens, *God is Not Great*, p. 99.

Postmodernism denies the existence of overarching narratives or myths that explain existence. One would expect that Hitchens with his deep loathing for totalitarianism would agree but Hitchens operates from the standpoint of metanarratives. Chapter eighteen of *God is Not Great* is devoted to how atheism and antitheism are superior worldviews to religion because of their use of science.[191] Chapter seventeen extols the virtues of secularism as a bulwark against totalitarian government on the belief that it is better to be politically free than oppressed.[192] The most fundamental proposition of Hitchens' critique of religion is that there is no God or gods, and that their non-existence is a welcome fact. There are therefore ways of accounting for the world that are true such as scientific knowledge and there are ways that are false such as religions' mythologies.

Foucault regards knowledge as the imposition of truths on others by the powerful as a means of controlling them.[193] In the case of religion, Hitchens would agree. But Hitchens regards rational and empirical knowledge not as a means of subjugating people but as the means of liberating them from religion's superstitions to enjoy the fruits of intellectual and artistic achievement. One of the most spectacular examples of this liberation in Hitchens' writings is the consequences of the end of Jewish ghettoization. Once Jews could play their part in European society, the sciences, art and literature were transformed.[194]

Conclusion

This chapter began by describing how Hitchens defines himself. He is an atheist, but a specific kind of atheist: He is an anti-theist who detests the idea of God because if God did exist, He would be the total totalitarian and human freedom would be impossible. We have drawn a logical distinction between anti-theism and anti-religion in the sense that it is possible to be an anti-theist without being an anti-religionist and *vice versa*. Hitchens is both an anti-theist and an anti-religionist who condemns religion for being immoral and irrational. In terms of his metaethics, Hitchens assumes that humans have moral freewill, that morality is an objective thing which has emerged during human evolution and which makes humans naturally good. The collapse of religious morality is therefore not to be feared, for people are good without needing to be religious and in fact are morally better for not being religious. Hitchens denounces religion for its irrationality and for attempting to prevent people

191. Ibid., pp. 253-275
192. Ibid., pp. 229-252.
193. Orr-Ewing, *Why Trust the Bible*, p. 20.
194. Hitchens, *God is Not Great*, p. 273

from challenging that irrationality. In contrast, science provides the rational standard for humanity by its search for evidence, something that religion cannot provide. Hitchens' view of the immorality and irrationality of religion is best summed up by his Challenge and his Razor.

Though Hitchens' criticism of religion is wide-ranging, he does not think religion will disappear because it is ingrained in humanity through evolution. Against extremist religion, Hitchens advocates armed struggle which will unfortunately be unending as human flaws are ineradicable. In this Hitchens demonstrates he is not a liberal utopian who believes in inevitable progress but a secular Manichean. As moderate religion will no less disappear than extremism, it ought to be accommodated within secular civilized society but only if it remains a private pursuit and is tamed through laws. If Hitchens could erase moderate religion, he would not do so for that would mean playing the totalitarian himself. The argument with moderate religion is also entertaining and a means of defining what is secular and civilized.

Within the context of the history of thought, Hitchens' anti-theism stretches back to anarchist thinkers such as Goldberg and the Enlightenment. Hitchens' anti-theism is therefore counter-cultural in its reassertion of rationality and empiricism *contra* postmodernism's relative worldview ensemble. Hitchens is neither a moral nor an epistemological relativist, but a moral objectivist and foundationalist, something that ironically, he shares with his Christian opponents.

3

A Review of the Critical Literature

Introduction

THE PURPOSE OF THIS chapter is to summarize and evaluate the best and most representative critical responses made by Christians to Hitchens. Atheists and agnostics have also been very critical of New Atheism and I have chosen to include some of their criticisms to demonstrate not only a further range of inadequacies in Hitchens' worldview but to show that the debate with Hitchens is not simply one between him and believers. I will explore critically both the Christian and others' counter-arguments by presenting their strengths and commenting on weaknesses. I will consider Christian and other criticism separately, for the integral differences within their core beliefs usually lend their criticism a different emphasis and line of attack.

Grounds for Debate

As established in chapter two, Hitchens is an anti-postmodernist; so too are the other leading New Atheists. As most Christian believers and theologians are not postmodernists,[1] a debate is possible between the two over such things as what is true and what is good. John Lennox, the Christian

---

1. Postmodernism is a feature of some theologies, but postmodernism among all theologies seems to be a minority position. James C. Livingston and Elizabeth Schussler Fiorenza identify four theologies as representative of postmodernism: those of Kaufmann, Altizer, Taylor and Marion; but the great majority of theologians and theologies they chronicle in their history of twentieth century theology are seeking the objective truth. See Livingston *et al.*, *Modern Christian Thought*, pp. 494-506.

mathematician, finds New Atheism's objectivism revivifying.[2] According to Lennox, the New Atheists accept the law of the excluded middle: Either God exists, or He does not. This means that debate is possible with them because they believe there is such a thing as truth.[3]

Is New Atheism in Any Sense New?

Christian apologists have asked what is new about New Atheism. It is an important question because the adjective 'new' makes something like an ideology or a product attractive. In the introduction it was established that Hitchens' anti-theism proposes nothing new in terms of content, but what is new is a new confidence about atheism and a new set of enemies. Hitchens himself admitted in an interview for *The Guardian*, that there was nothing substantially new about New Atheism[4] except that new scientific discoveries have given New Atheists greater confidence and warrant in criticizing religion.[5] In the same interview, Hitchens sees New Atheism's novelty as consisting also in terms of its struggle against Islamism.[6] Conquest in the name of religion is as old as religion itself but an ecumenical sympathy between the monotheisms is relatively new; so too is the global reach of Islamist terrorists. Thus, New Atheism has new opponents. What is also new is the urgency of the secularizing response of the New Atheism to the irruption of fundamentalist violence. Dawkins identifies the 9/11 disaster as the event which destroyed his view that religion was benign.[7] Hitchens agrees that 9/11 was a major turning point in attitudes to religion but his turning point came nearly twelve-and-a-half years earlier when a *fatwa* was issued against the novelist Salmon Rushdie by the Ayatollah Khomeini. Hitchens' warning is chilling: religious fanatics are planning the destruction of civilization.[8]

For Christians such as Alister McGrath and John Lennox, what is new about the New Atheists is not their doctrine but their tone. According to McGrath, New Atheism is characterized by rage against religious belief.[9] Lennox suggests also that New Atheism is more vocal than its predecessors

2. Lennox, *Gunning for God*, p. 20.

3. Ibid.

4. Andrew Anthony, 'Christopher Hitchens: You Have to Choose Your Regrets', *The Guardian*, 14 November 2010.

5. Ibid.

6. Ibid.

7. Dawkins, *The God Delusion*, p. 28.

8. Hitchens, *God is Not Great*, p. 13.

9. McGrath, *Why God Won't Go Away*, p. 25.

and more belligerent.[10] There is much evidence that anger is an important feature of New Atheism, though its adherents would argue it is a righteous anger. It is also important to acknowledge that the New Atheist leaders come across as angry in varying degrees. Dawkins is arguably the New Atheist with the greatest reputation for being angry about religion.[11] Outrage is routine on atheist forums when anyone challenges the party line. When the atheist Julian Baggini dared to suggest accurately in an article for *Fri Tanke*[12] that reason and evidence play an important part in religious belief, the atheist bloggers subjected him to revilement. Harris comes across as urbane when he is speaking, even when confronted with forceful religious apologists. Dennett too appears restrained when he is debating Christians. Hitchens is the most charismatic of the New Atheist leaders, but it is true that Hitchens too can lose his temper. Incensed at Reverend Jerry Falwell for his claim that American immorality was the cause of the 9/1 atrocity, Hitchens decried him in a CNN interview as a fraudster.[13] On Fox News, Hitchens mordantly asserted that if Falwell were administered a laxative, no more than a matchbox would be needed to bury him.[14]

Christian apologists ask why therefore are the New Atheists are so angry? Two causes have been identified: First, the fact that religious belief in the West has not died out as it was predicted to do in the Sixties but has shown remarkable resilience and continues to be embraced around the world. Second, atheists are held in low esteem, particularly in the USA.

According to William Lane Craig, the prediction of the death of religion was a confident expectation of secular intellectuals in the 1960s.[15] Within academia, positivism's message that religious propositions were meaningless let alone true or false had left philosophers of religion, as Anthony Kenny observes, feeling defeated.[16] Church attendance in the Western

10. Lennox, *Gunning for God*, p. 16.

11. Dawkins is famous for a paragraph of invective indicting God for the worst crimes imaginable. Dawkins, *The God Delusion*, p. 51.

12. Julian Baggini, 'Nyateismen virker mot sin hensikt', *Fri Tanke* 2009/1, March 2009, pp. 42-3.

13. 'Classic: Christopher Hitchens on The Death Of Jerry Falwell', You Tube, 16 January 2008 at https://www.youtube.com/watch?v=iq939cZv2Uc (accessed 20 February 2017 at 16:22).

14 'Christopher Hitchens on Hannity & Colmes about Rev. Falwell's Death', You Tube, 17 May 2007 at https://www.youtube.com/watch?v=doKkOSMaTk4 (accessed 20 February 2017 at 16:19).

15. William Lane Craig, 'The Resurrection of Theism', *Truth Journal*, updated 8 August 1997 at www.leaderus www.leaderus.com/truth/3truth01.html (accessed 20 February 2017 at 16:23).

16. Anthony Kenny, 'The Wisdom of Not Knowing', *The Philosopher's Magazine*,

democracies, which had been declining since the end of the First World War, continued to decline in the Sixties and there was no sign of that being arrested or reversed. Humanists, secularists, and atheists therefore believed they were on the verge of a golden age of reason. This grand expectation, however, never came to pass. Positivism was shown by its own criteria to be meaningless and was declared a mistake in the early seventies by one of its greatest exponents, A. J. Ayer.[17] Religious propositions were now regarded as meaningful after all and the God-hypothesis was once more a legitimate and significant subject of study. Philosophers began to put life back into religious questions and some of them were Christians. For example, Alvin Plantinga, at the height of Sixties' radicalism, wrote in a book called *God and Other Minds* that if belief in other minds is considered a rational view, then so too is belief in God.[18] A counter-movement was now underway.[19] The atheist philosopher, Quentin Smith, estimates that currently 25% to 33% of philosophy professors are theists, and most of them identify as Christians.[20] Smith has no reason to exaggerate for he regards such a development as plunging academia back into barbarism[21]

On the broad front of popular opinion, religious belief has survived in the West and is thriving outside of it. In an article for *The Telegraph*, Raziye Akkoc reports the findings of a survey by WIN/Gallup International which involved polling nearly 64,000 people in 65 countries. Britain is found to be one of the least religious countries in the world with only 30% of British people saying they are religious compared with 53% who say they are not.[22] However, there is enough in the survey's results to provoke the New Atheists' wrath. The worst news of all for New Atheism is that the researchers predicted that atheism across the world would decline in 35 years with the exception again of the West, the least populous part of the world.

Atheists suffer from low status and a poor image. The evidence for this is particularly strong in the USA. The University of Minnesota in 2006 carried out a survey that revealed that atheists were most distrusted out

Issue 37, 1st quarter 2007), pp. 38-39.

17. A. J. Ayer, *The Central Questions of Philosophy*, pp. 22-34.

18. Alvin Plantinga, *God and Other Minds*, p. 271.

19. Peter S. Williams, *A Sceptic's Guide to Atheism: God is not Dead*, p. 17.

20. Quentin Smith, 'The Metaphilosophy of Naturalism', Philo Vol. 4, Number 2, 5 January 2002 at www.philoonline.org/library/smith_4_2.htm (accessed 14 January 2016 at 11:00).

21. Ibid.

22. Raziye Akkoc, 'Mapped: These are the world's most religious countries', at https://www.telegraph.co.uk/news/worldnews/11530382/Mapped-These-are-the-worlds-most-religious-countries.html (last accessed 14 January 2016 at 14:39).

of all groups within American society.[23] The *American Sociological Review* discovered in 2006 that it is acceptable within American culture to be intolerant of atheists.[24] In response, the New Atheists are going on the attack to build atheist self-respect. Dawkins describes one of the tasks of *The God Delusion* as being to show that it is possible to be a contented atheist.[25] Another term New Atheists are being encouraged to use to bolster their poor self-image is the word 'brights'. Dennett writes that the word brights is not a declaration of intellectual arrogance, but a sign that atheists are curious about the world.[26]

Hitchens is angry with religion not because it has not disappeared for that is something he does not think will happen. Neither does he desire it to happen. Hitchens' ire is provoked by religions' irrationalism and immorality, and yet despite this, it is privileged within society and sidesteps the law.[27] Hitchens is therefore angry also that atheists do not receive the same privilege and are treated as inferior, but he certainly does not personally feel inferior. On the contrary, he believes the religious ought to be ashamed of their beliefs. Enjoying such self-confidence, it is no surprise that Hitchens rejects the use of the term 'bright' as an embarrassing strategy. He writes of how annoyed he is with Professors Dawkins and Dennet for their conceited self-nomination as brights.[28] Hitchens is right to take this position. Those who are not a 'bright' would be forgiven for thinking that therefore they are 'a dim' which is not wise when one is trying to convert people to the New Atheist cause.

Apologists recognize there are other elements about New Atheism that make it new. New Atheism is evangelistic for it seeks to convert people in a much more determined way than Old Atheism ever tried, using the power of the modern Media. All four Horsemen spend a lot of time seeking publicity for their views. (Part of this no doubt is at the behest of publishers seeking to gain an audience for their books.) Dawkins presented in January 2006 a television documentary for Channel Four called *Root of All Evil?*[29] He was

23. Tina Beattie, *The New Atheists: The Twilight of Reason and the War on Religion*, p. 6.

24. David Aikman, *The Delusion of Disbelief*, p. 5.

25. Dawkins, *The God Delusion*, p. 23.

26. Daniel Dennett, 'The Bright Stuff', at https://www.the-brights.net/vision/essays/dennett_nyt_article.html (accessed at 20 February 2017 at 16:24).

27. 'Christopher Hitchens versus Al Sharpton-Is God Great', YouTube, 28 September 2015 at https://www.m.youtube.com/watch?v=pHVpQIZqHPo (accessed 23 December 2017 at 18:00).

28. Hitchens, *God is Not Great*, p. 5.

29. 'Religion—the "Root of all Evil?"' at https://humanism.org.uk/2006/01/05/news-194/?desktop=1 (accessed 20 February 2017 at 16:29).

one of the sponsors of the atheist bus campaign in 2009 in which London red buses carried an advertisement telling people to live as happy atheists.[30] Sam Harris undertook in 2014 a series of live events in Los Angeles, New York and San Francisco to publicize his new book, *Waking Up: A Guide to Spirituality Without Religion*.[31] Of all the four Horsemen, it is Hitchens who arguably has the largest exposure to the general public through his print journalism and frequent appearances on news producers in the USA such as CNN and Fox News. Whether Hitchens can be described as evangelistic in his anti-theism is another matter. Certainly, when Hitchens had written his book *God Is Not Great*, he took his message to the Bible-Belt. He certainly would not have been unhappy if his arguments persuaded someone away from their superstition. But Hitchens appears to enjoy the argument more than the possible conversions to his cause and the attention he receives when debating. Moreover, his agenda appears to be a defensive one: To preserve the secularity of the American Republic through the separation of state and church.[32]

Though its leaders have much media exposure, according to McGrath the core of the movement is online communities that are easily accessed across the globe. In February 2010 the forum hosted by the Richard Dawkins Foundation for Reason and Science reached 85,000 members worldwide, and was the world's largest online atheist community.[33] As to whom the New Atheists are trying to reach, Dawkins is very clear: It is not the incorrigibly religious, but those whose minds remain open to persuasion.[34] Websites have been established for Hitchens by admirers and their internet addresses can be found in the bibliography. Hitchens, however, is ubiquitous on the Internet and it is likely that it is through this medium that he is most frequently encountered rather than through his books now that we live in the Internet age.

But the New Atheists have a more unpleasant agenda: A derisive lack of respect for religious belief and believers. According to Albert Mohler, the New Atheists seek to stigmatize religious observance.[35] Dawkins' tac-

---

30. Riazat Butt, 'Atheist bus campaign spreads the word of no God nationwide', *The Guardian*, 6 January 2009.

31. https://www.samharris.org (accessed 16 January 2016 at 07:47 am).

32. 'Christopher Hitchens-Mr Jefferson Build Up That Wall', You Tube at https://m.youtube.com/watch?v=WV5mWfDFE9A (accessed 23 December 2017 at 16:12).

33. McGrath, *Why God Won't Go Away*, p. 27. This dependence on technology is not only literal, but also metaphorical: the machinery of surveillance and propaganda in modern totalitarianisms is Hitchens' metaphor for God's rule.

34. Dawkins, *The God Delusion*, p. 28.

35. Albert Mohler, 'The New Atheism?' at https:// www.albertmohler.com/commentary_read.php?cdate=2006-11-21 (accessed 10 January at 09:50).

tic to achieve this is ridicule. If the religious were to retaliate, Dawkins is confident that the atheists would win as they have so much more to be contemptuous about and are so much better at it, and he cites Hitchens and Harris as atheism's satirical geniuses.[36] As already seen in the case of the late Jerry Falwell, Hitchens can be scathing. Hitchens has other sneers up his sleeve. For example, he has compared the former Archbishop of Canterbury to a sheep for suggesting permission ought to be granted to Muslims to practice sharia law in Britain.[37] Hitchens also advocates mockery not only of religious leaders but their congregations for believing what their leaders have taught them.[38] But there is more to Hitchens' way of interacting with religious apologists than ridicule. Hitchens counted religious people among his friends, one of whom was Timothy Rutten, the Catholic journalist and with whom Hitchens had a cordial exchange of views.[39]

Problems with New Atheism's Understanding of Religion and Faith

One of the fundamental attacks made by Christian apologists is to highlight how New Atheists have committed factual errors. One of the problems is their misuse of terms. McGrath has raised an important objection regarding the New Atheist use of the term religion: there is no adequate definition of what religion as a term means within New Atheist literature.[40] Therefore, when the New Atheists attack religion, they mean only to attack God (gods)-believing religion; they fail, probably through ignorance, to make the distinction between theism and those religions where there is no God. This realization immediately blunts their criticism, for there are religious beliefs that lay beyond the scope of their attack and their generalization fails to account for individual differences between the religions.

36. https://www.theguardian.com/commentisfree/andrewbrown/2009/apr/30/religion-atheism-dawkins-contempt (accessed 15 January 2016 at 08:04 am).

37. Christopher Hitchens, 'To Hell With the Archbishop of Canterbury: Rowan Williams' dangerous claptrap about "plural jurisdiction"', *Slate*, 18 February 2008. It is impossible to disagree with Hitchens' opposition to sharia law being established in British society. A legal system that sentences apostates to death has no place in a liberal democracy. Williams, for all his intellectual acumen, was acting naively in the matter.

38. 'The Four Horsemen-Hitchens, Dawkins, Dennett, Harris', YouTube, 23 July 2012, (accessed 23 December 2017 at 17:58).

39. '#9 Debate-Christopher Hitchens vs Tim Rutten-God Is Not Great-2007', YouTube, 4 June 2007 at https://m.youtube.com/watch?v=wNW4DeM6ZVo (accessed on 30 December 2017 at 17:48).

40. McGrath, *Why God Won't Go Away*, p. 44.

Faith is another word that the New Atheists fail to deploy correctly according to the critics. The New Atheists define faith as irrational because it is belief without evidence. Dawkins sums up the position well when he criticizes faith as belief without supporting evidence.[41] Faith therefore lacks epistemic and moral virtue. Hitchens agrees. Epistemologically, Hitchens defines faith as irrational for it disregards evidence. For him, faith is mere wish-thinking.[42] It is the antithesis of reason.[43] But faith is also immoral in Hitchens' eyes. Faith is that habit of mind, or emotion, which prevents intellectual freedom[44] with all the consequences that that has for the advancement of human knowledge and civilization.

Terry Eagleton provides one of the richest responses to the New Atheist definition of faith. He distinguishes between faith and knowledge. He gives the following example: If God one day were to write across the sky that He exists, it might make no difference to faith in Him as people might acknowledge His existence, but choose to ignore Him. Therefore, it is possible to have knowledge without faith.[45] What then is faith according to Eagleton? Faith is synonymous with trust[46] in the character of God. Faith is not the evidence or the belief in the evidence, but the stage of behavior that follows once the evidence has been accepted. But trust, though essential to Eagleton's definition of faith, is more than trust but also love.[47] Eagleton presents one further dimension of faith. Knowledge is made possible by faith, for by relationship with God, in whom reason is rooted, one comes to a full attainment of it.[48] Eagleton's definition of faith, which is a biblical one, does not of course provide justification for believing the proposition that Christianity is a true worldview, but it does demonstrate that faith is a relationship with God based on trust once the evidence has been examined, rather than an irrational assent to baseless propositions.

41. Richard Dawkins, *The Selfish Gene*, p. 198.

42. Hitchens, *God is Not Great*, p. 4.

43. Ibid.

44. Ibid., p. 5.

45. Terry Eagleton, *Reason, Faith, and Revolution: Reflections on the God Debate*, p. 113.

46. Ibid.

47. Ibid., p. 120.

48. Ibid., pp. 120-121.

Other Factual Errors

Hitchens wrote *God is Not Great* at high speed and in the process made factual errors. Mark Roberts points out Hitchens' many errors when it comes to the New Testament, an area of study for which Roberts holds a PhD from Harvard University. In a series of blog posts, inspired by his radio debate with Hitchens, Roberts explains Hitchens' errors. Roberts asserts that he can find 15 factual errors relating to the New Testament and 16 misunderstandings or distortions of evidence. Some of the errors are not significant in terms of their content but they reveal carelessness. Other errors are a serious misreading or ignorance of the texts Hitchens deems himself to be expert enough to elucidate. One such example is Hitchens' assertion that the New Testament is not a historical record and that the writers of the Gospels cannot agree on anything of importance.[49] Roberts replies that even the most skeptical of scholars see the Gospels as in some sense a historical record. He also lists 15 of the 33 points of agreement between the Gospels that he includes in his book, *Can We Trust the Gospels?*[50]

The Hitchens' Challenge Answered

The emotional force of Hitchens' criticism of Christianity very much emanates from his lambasting of its morality. To demonstrate this, Hitchens, as we have seen in chapter two, liked to challenge audiences with what I have called the 'Hitchens' Challenge'. It has come to light through the testimony of his brother, Peter Hitchens, that Hitchens withdrew this challenge at the end of his life because he had thought of an answer to it. He confided to his brother that there was at least one thing he could think of that only a religious believer could have done, and that was the creation of the trade union Solidarity by the Catholic Lech Walesa and his resistance of Polish communism and Soviet military power which stood behind it. Presumably such an action required the sort of fearless courage that only belief in a God and an afterlife might give.[51]

49. Mark D. Roberts, 'Is Hitchens a Reliable Source of "Facts"?', 7 June 200 at https://markdroberts.com/?p=94 (accessed 18 January 2016 at 17:09), p. 111.

50. Mark D. Roberts, *Can We Trust the Gospels: Investigating the Reliability of Matthew, Mark, Luke and John* (London: Crossway, 2007).

51. Peter Hitchens made this statement during a radio debate on Premier Radio with the present author and Ed Turner, an atheist blogger and admirer of Christopher Hitchens. The debate was titled 'Unbelievable? Was Christopher Hitchens right about religion?' It took place on 20 February 2016 and can be found at https://www.premierchristianradio.com/Shows/Saturday/Unbelievable/Episodes/

The Goodness of Biblical Morality

Much can be said and has been said in riposte to Hitchens' view that the Old Testament is immoral[52] and the New Testament is wicked.[53] For the sake of concision, I shall first examine how Alister McGrath has dealt with what is in Hitchens' view one of religion's worst features: Its violence. Second, I shall turn to John Lennox's apology for the Old Testament. Both McGrath and Lennox have done a great service to Bible-believing Christians who might have been very troubled by Hitchens' criticism of some of the more puzzling verses in Scripture.

McGrath argues that Christian morality provides grounds for pacifism. For Christians, God's nature is revealed in Christ. It is important to note that Christ demonstrated a non-violent response to His opponents. Christ was the victim not the perpetrator of violence. He taught that those who are wronged are not to take revenge. As an example of how Christian non-violence works out in practice, McGrath refers to the Amish Schoolhouse Killings of October 2006. A gunman, who was filled with hate for God, opened fire in an Amish school in the village of Nickel Mines in Pennsylvania and killed five school-girls. As the Amish repudiate retaliation and violence because of Christ's teachings, they urged forgiveness. The widow of the mass murderer was deeply grateful for this reaction.[54]

With reference to the Old Testament, John Lennox has provided an exhaustive rebuttal of Hitchens (and Dawkins).[55] Again, for the sake of brevity, I shall provide an overview of Lennox's argument and select how Lennox deals with the New Atheist accusation that God commands genocide during the invasion of Canaan.

Lennox's argument is based upon two propositions: that the New Atheist view of God is inaccurate, and that the morality proposed by the New Atheists is remarkably like the Ten Commandments. In the debate he had with Hitchens at the Edinburgh Festival, Hitchens accuses God of being a browbeater.[56] But Lennox dismisses this for the New Atheists have not noticed that God is presented as being benevolent in many ways in the Old Testament.[57] Lennox's

---

Unbelievable-Was-Christopher-Hitchens-right-about-religion-Peter-Hitchens-Ed-Turner-Peter-Harris-plus-Unbelievable-2016-announced (accessed 20 February 2017 at 15:34).

52. Hitchens, *God is Not Great*, p. 97.

53. Ibid., p. 109.

54. McGrath, *Why God Won't Go Away*, pp. 48.

55. Lennox, *Gunning for God*, pp. 117-142.

56. Ibid., p. 118.

57. Ibid.

conclusion is that the New Atheists have inaccurately or selectively (which is a form of inaccurate reading) read the Old Testament.

The invasion of Canaan in which many died and during which the inhabitants of the land were driven out by the Israelites[58] is a major stumbling block for skeptics. Lennox points out that the campaign was exceptional. On no other occasion were the Israelites commanded to expel whole populations from their homeland. The rules of war commanded in Deuteronomy 20 restricted the violence.[59] The invasion was also God's judgement against the Canaanite nations. Judgement was necessary against civilizations that practiced child sacrifice (Deut. 12; 31; 18:10). Thirdly, God had given these civilization four centuries to repent (Gen. 15:16). Fourthly, the Israelites were warned against regarding themselves as morally superior to the people they had driven out (Deut. 9:4). Finally, the Israelites were warned that if they committed the same crimes as the Canaanites, they too would forfeit the land (Deut. 8:19-20). This is indeed what happened, as Lennox reminds us. Israel went into Assyrian exile and the Judeans went into Babylonian captivity.

Lennox turns to Nicholas Wolterstorff to explain the ostensibly chilling statement that Joshua and his troops massacred Israel's enemies with 'the edge of the sword'(Josh. 10:32). Wolterstorff argues that this is a formulaic expression which is synonymous with the declaration of having scored a great victory over another nation, rather than the utter extirpation of its people.[60] Lennox adds an observation of his own: if cities such as Debir and Hebron had been completely exterminated during Joshua's campaign, why do the tribes of Judah and Benjamin have to re-conquer them again in the Book of Judges?[61]

At the heart of both Old and New Testament biblical morality is the atonement of the cross. Without the sacrificial death of Christ, no forgiveness of sins is possible. Hitchens, however, has questioned whether it is possible for God to forgive the sins done by one person to another, when it is the victim who alone has the right to forgive. Surely God cannot absolve someone of the wrong they have done to another?[62] Lennox's response is to point Hitchens to the fact that Christ was not only a human being, but God also. Sin is ultimately against God as it is His laws that are violated when X

---

58. Hitchens, *God is Not Great*, p. 101

59. Lennox, *Gunning for God*, p. 127.

60. Nicholas Wolterstorff, 'Reading Joshua', presented at the conference *My Ways Are Not Your Ways* at the University of Notre Dame, 10-12 September 2009.

61. Lennox, *Gunning for God*, p. 129.

62. Hitchens, *God Is Not Great*, p. 211.

mistreats Y. God therefore has the right to forgive for it is His laws which have been transgressed.[63]

The Use and Abuse of History

If the New Atheist movement is to win the argument that religion has been to the grave detriment of humanity, it requires an historian who can furnish the data. But Hitchens, who is the closest the quartet of New Atheist leaders has to an historian, is by ignorance or by design selective in what historical data he uses. There is much historical fact incorporated in *God is Not Great*, but there is much that is left out that would give a much different picture of Christianity (and other religions). It is David Bentley Hart who has done excellent work in exposing New Atheism's myths. Bentley Hart refutes on a case by case basis the accusations of New Atheists over such things as the unparalleled ability of religion to incite war,[64] the persecution of Galileo,[65] witch-hunts[66] and the Spanish Inquisition.[67] There is not room here to present a comprehensive exploration of how Bentley Hart does this; rather, the focus shall be upon the broader, fundamental lines of argument he presents for the unmatched benevolence of the Christian Revolution and the foolishness of the notion that once there was an Age of Faith, characterized by superstition and violence, which suddenly gave way to the Age of Reason.

In contrast to Hitchens' spiteful hyperbole that all religion poisons all things, Bentley Hart draws our attention to the Church's charitable work over two millennia.[68] Of course, Hitchens has responded to such kindnesses by saying that they are ruined by the Church's teaching that all are miserable sinners. With such a view in the background, it is hard to enjoy the Church's tender mercies. But Bentley Hart makes the point that the relationship to God is more than the awareness of sin. It is also the experience of God as love and of the sense that one ought to love one's neighbor as oneself.[69]

The idea that the Middle Ages, which was a time of great religiosity, ought to be characterized as an idea of ignorance and superstition is a travesty according to Bentley Hart. He argues that the Renaissance was

---

63. Lennox, *Gunning for God*, p. 158.

64. David Bentley Hart, *Atheist Delusions: The Christian Revolution and Its Fashionable Enemies*, pp. 4, 5, 12, 13.

65. Ibid., pp. 62-66.

66. Ibid., pp. 76-83.

67. Ibid., pp. 84-86.

68. Ibid., p. 9.

69. Ibid., p. 17.

a product of the vibrant scholarship of the medieval period stimulated by the cultural importations from Byzantine civilization. According to Bentley Hart, few historians of science deny the continuities of science's development from the Middle Ages through to the modern period.[70] The catastrophist theory that the Enlightenment erupted as a revolutionary response to the ignorance of the age of faith, a revolution that the New Atheists think they are re-enacting through their media-savvy appeals and rhetorical savageries, therefore is untenable in the light of evidence. The implication is that rational and empirical inquiry was an essential part of religious civilization as it was and is within a secular one.

Secular Dictatorships

Peter Hitchens, Christopher Hitchens' brother, has presented an important counter argument to Hitchens' assertion that secular dictatorships were religious states. P. Hitchens argues that just as Christians must admit that faith has led to extraordinary levels of persecution, so too must atheists confess that atheist governments have killed believers en masse.[71] P. Hitchens recognizes a predictable outcome to the rise of revolutionary atheist states: Once established, they become vicious in order to build the utopian society they desire. As examples, P. Hitchens lists the French Revolution, Bolshevism, Chinese Communism, the Khmer Rouge and Cuban Communism.[72] In contrast to the end of civil wars and persecutions within Christendom, P. Hitchens believes that violence are integral features of revolutionary atheism.[73] P. Hitchens rightly scorns the argument that if atheist regimes committed crimes against their subjects, it is only because they took on the character of religion. That atheist regimes took on the external features of the religion with which their populations were required to worship the leaders and hold to the revolution's ideas as sacred ideals does not negate the fact that the internal nature of these regimes was atheistic. The specifically antireligious and anti-Christian nature of Stalinism, for instance, demonstrates the truth of this.[74] P. Hitchens develops his argument with the observation that for such regimes to demand the worship of their leaders, they would have to be atheistic. Without a belief in God, Stalin and Kim Il Sung were

70. David Bentley Hart, *Atheist Delusions: The Christian Revolution and Its Fashionable Enemies*, pp.33-35.

71. Peter Hitchens, *The Rage Against God*, p. 153.

72. Ibid., p. 154.

73. Ibid., p. 155.

74. Ibid., p. 155.

able to substitute themselves as human idols. They were also able, as in the case of Bela Kun, the Hungarian atheist leader, to declare themselves arbiters of morality and that the only test of what was good and bad was whether it benefited the proletarian state.[75]

The Cosmological and the Teleological Arguments

Not all Christian philosophers are enamored with the cosmological and teleological arguments. Peter Mawson, for example, is one such philosopher.[76] William Lane Craig, however, is the contemporary Christian apologist perhaps best associated with making the case for these classical arguments for God's existence and does so in his debate with Hitchens at Biola University.[77] William Lane Craig opens the debate by using the *kalam* cosmological argument which takes the logical form of:

1. whatever comes into existence has a cause.

2. The universe came into existence.

3. Therefore, the universe is caused.[78]

Craig proceeds to ask what entities that pre-existed the universe could have caused the universe. His answer is that there are only two possibilities: abstract entities such as numbers and a Personal Mind. As abstract entities cause nothing to happen, the cause of the universe is a Personal Mind.[79]

In response to Hitchens' objection during the debate that there is confusion as to whether God created out of nothing or worked with pre-existent material, Craig argues that the universe sprung from nothing because space and time came from a singularity before which nothing existed.

Craig also presents the teleological argument from fine tuning which argues that the universe is set up with great precision to create intelligent life. Craig describes how if the laws of the nature are expressed mathematically, one notices that there are constants such as the gravitational constant which

---

75. Ibid., p. 157.

76. For Mawson's objections to the cosmological and teleological arguments, see T. J. Mawson, *Belief in God*, pp. 133-162.

77. 'Does God Exist? William Lane Craig vs. Christopher Hitchens–Full Debate [HD] at https://www.youtube.com/watch?v=otYm41hb48o (accessed 8 April 2017 at 12:20).

78. J. P. Moreland and William Lane Craig, *Philosophical Foundations for a Christian Worldview*, p. 468.

79. 'Does God Exist?', You Tube, 28 September 2014 (accessed 30 December 2017 at 18:45).

are not determined by the laws of nature themselves and arbitrary quantities such as the balance of matter and anti-matter in the universe on which the laws of nature originally operated. All these constants and arbitrary quantities fall within a very narrow range of life-giving quantities and if they were altered by an almost infinitesimally small amount, life would cease. Craig argues that the logical explanation for the universe is design.[80]

In response to Hitchens' argument that the immense wastefulness of evolution and the certain end of the universe make the argument from fine-tuning preposterous, Craig rejoins that the efficiency of something is not the mark of whether it has been designed. As for the end of the universe, Craig states that the limited duration of something is not proof that it was not designed.[81]

As for Hitchens' response to the argument that the positing of a Creator begs the question who created the Creator and who created the creator of the Creator and so on which sets up an infinite regression, Keith Ward provides a lucid response.[82] In order to help people understand how God can be the final cause of the universe, Ward asks what that final cause would have to be like to be such a cause. Things in the universe exist in time and they have causes. If we can think of caused things in time, one can think of something not being in time. Such a thing would be eternal, and therefore uncaused, for causation belongs to the temporal universe. Eternal things can be the cause of things in time, for example, contemporary physics regards time as caused by a super-temporal reality such as a vacuum state. Ward identifies God as the eternal cause of the universe and that He is therefore uncaused.[83]

Both Craig and Ward make arguments from natural theology plausible. It is possible to have knowledge of God from purely scientific and philosophical premises. With reference to Hitchens, they expose his ignorance of the philosophical arguments for God and his lack of sophistication when discussing them. Hitchens has dismissed these arguments for God's existence as disproven and yet fails to see that progress within scientific understanding has breathed new life into the cosmological and teleological arguments. The questions of what caused the universe and why it seems to be so precisely set up for life remain powerful ones.

80. Ibid., (accessed 30 December 2017 at 18:46).

81. Ibid.

82. Keith Ward, *Why There Almost Certainly is a God*, pp. 51-52.

83. Ibid., p. 52.

Faith, Science, and the Christian Response

If Hitchens' assertion that materialism is true is questionable, so too is his use of science for the New Atheist cause. Hitchens uses science in a way that is typical of all the New Atheist leaders: He regards science's explanations as true in contrast to false metaphysical explanations which science has rendered redundant. Religion is on the side of irrationalism whereas science is the operation of reason.[84] Religious explanations for the physical world's existence and behavior are for Hitchens the result of the thinking done when humans were at their most primitive. It is for this reason according to Hitchens that the relationship between science and religion can only be one of conflict and attempts to reconcile faith with science will ineluctably fail.[85] In this matter, Hitchens' opinion is orthodox New Atheism.[86]

Though in awe of science and ready to use it to attempt to disprove theism, it cannot be argued that Hitchens subscribes to scientism, which Dawkins wishes to advance.[87] This is a very significant difference between Hitchens and the other members of the New Atheist Quadrumvirate and it is not something that has been noticed by Christian apologists. Hitchens does believe that the origins of morality, rational inquiry and religious belief can be explained through the process of natural selection and that science is the best discipline by which to understand the material world's workings. Yet though human evolution can explain why humans ask questions, there are questions of ultimate meaning that Hitchens accepts cannot be answered by science. These questions, however, cannot be answered either by religion according to Hitchens for it is too backward a way of thinking. Hitchens' preferred repository of wisdom on matters of meaning and value is the classics of literature rather than barbaric religious books.[88]

The Christian response has refuted Hitchens' binary opposition of science and religion. Alister McGrath has been at the forefront of challenging Hitchens and his response begins with demonstrating that there are many scientists who are also religious believers. He refers his reader to two surveys of religious belief among scientists: one taken in 1916 and one in 1997.

84. Hitchens, *God is Not Great*, pp. 63-72.

85. Ibid., pp. 64-65.

86. Dawkins regards the struggle between science and religion as a bitter life or death struggle. See Dawkins, *The God Delusion*, pp. 279-86.

87. Alister McGrath, *The Dawkins Delusion*, p. 16.

88. Hitchens, *God is Not Great*, p. 5. This is the view of some scientists also. Sir Peter Medawar, a Nobel prize winner for medicine, has argued that certain questions cannot be answered by science, such as 'what is the point of living?' and 'what are we all here for? See Medawar, *The Limits of Science*, p. 66.

In both surveys, 40% identified themselves as religious believers in a personal God who answered prayer. If the scientists questioned had been asked if they believed deistically in a God, the number of believers might have been higher.[89] Admittedly, 40% may be lower than the population generally, but the view that real scientists doing academically credible work cannot be believers in God is demonstrated as ludicrous in the face of this statistic. McGrath also points to what may surprise many Christians: That Roman Catholicism accepts the theory of evolution though rejects the materialist arguments drawn from it.[90]

The historical argument that religion and science are enemies is also justifiably dismissed by McGrath who refers to a prominent historian of scienceas describing the conflict theory of the historical relationship between science and religion as a refuted stereotype.[91] McGrath does not identify his source, but in his bibliography, he references Ian G. Barbour, the late American historian of science, and his *When Science Meets Religion*.[92] Barbour's contribution to the study of science and religion's relationship does indeed challenge the gross simplifications of Hitchens *et al*. According to Barbour, the relationship between science and religion is not a case simply of conflict in which religion's empire of delusion is being rolled back by the assaults of reason but is characterized by a typology that adumbrates four relationships: conflict, independent co-existence, dialogue and integration.[93]

McGrath also references John Hedley Brooke, the Cambridge historian of science, who presents the relationship between science and religions as a three part typology of conflict, complementarity and interrelationship.[94] Hedley Brooke fascinatingly describes how A. N. Whitehead hypothesized that the seventeenth century assumption among natural philosophers that the universe is structured and therefore knowable may have been derived

---

89. McGrath, *The Dawkins Delusion*, p. 20-21. McGrath cites the physicist, Paul Davis as an example of an important scientist who accepts that the evidence points to some kind of god or supreme spiritual principle.

90. McGrath refers to John Paul II's address to the Pontifical Academy of Sciences on 22 October 1996 in which he offered support for the general notion of biological evolution. See McGrath, *The Dawkins Delusion*, p. 26.

91. Ibid. pp. 23-24. This is McGrath's paraphrase of what the historian said rather than a quotation from him.

92. For the bibliographical reference, see McGrath, *The Dawkins Delusion*, p. 78.

93. 'Barbour's Typologies' at https//serc.carleton.edu/sp/library/sac/examples/barbour.html (accessed 14 April 2017 at 15:03).

94. For the reference to Hedley Brooke's contributions to the history of science, see McGrath, *The Dawkins Delusion*, p. 78. For John Hedley Brooke's typology, see *Science and Religion: Some Historical Perspectives*, pp. 2, 4 and 5.

from medieval theology.[95] He also cites the sociologist, R. K. Merton, who is of the opinion that Puritan values assisted the rise of science in the seventeenth centuries.[96] Lennox refers to C. S. Lewis' view that science was born from the expectation that because the universe had a lawgiver, there were natural laws to be discovered. [97] It is transparent that Hitchens' characterization of science and religion solely as one of conflict fails to describe what is really the case and therefore appears either to be ignorance, or worse, a refusal to countenance what specialists in the field are saying.

The Rationality of Christian Belief

Hitchens' view that Christianity is an opponent of scientific progress is a consequence of the broader belief that religion is always to be found on the side of irrationality. Again, Christian apologists have rebutted this nonsense. McGrath responds to this conclusion by demonstrating that the New Atheist worldview, like all worldviews, is in part irrational.[98] Lennox and Williams respond by demonstrating from the Bible the rationality of Christianity.

McGrath says that rationality is less concerned about the starting point of one's reflection and more concerned with the process by which one arrives at one's conclusions. All worldviews go beyond what can be proved by reason by standing on unfounded foundations and reaching for unprovable ends. Human beings regularly live with views that have no evidence and yet remain trustworthy, for example, the belief in other minds. The New Atheists demand that believers give up their irrationality and yet their view that to be rational one must exclude belief in God requires the adoption of values, assumptions, and indemonstrable starting points about what is real which cannot be verified by reason.[99] Hitchens' anti-theism rests on moral values that cannot be proven by reason, therefore his 'beliefs' are indeed beliefs.[100]

Peter S. Williams provides a convincing argument that Christian belief is rational. He gives twelve examples from both the Old and New Testaments where evidence and reason are valued. Two examples from Williams' list, one from the Old and one from the New, will suffice to demonstrate his case. According to the Old Testament prophet Isaiah, God invited Israel to reason with him regarding their appallingly sinful state

95. Hedley Brooke, *Science and Religion*, p. 5.

96. Ibid., p. 5.

97. John C. Lennox, *God's Undertaker: Has Science Buried God?* p. 21.

98. McGrath, *Why God Won't Go Away*, pp. 56-71.

99. Ibid., p. 58.

100. McGrath, *Why God Won't Go Away*, pp. 60-61.

(Isa. 1:18). In the New Testament, Christ urged His disciples to believe in Him on the evidence of His miracles (John 14:11).[101] God is revealed not only in Scripture but through the natural workings of the world. Either to perceive God, or to derive evidence for His existence from an examination of the world, is called Natural Theology.[102] Though the atheist cannot accept the conclusions drawn about God's existence from the world, s/he cannot deny that Natural Theology is a rational way of approaching the existence of God.

Problems with Materialism

Hitchens is a scientific materialist. An anti-theist does not necessarily have to be a materialist or a naturalist, for it is possible to argue that non-material entities exist without believing that any of these entities is a God. Though it is not controversial to Christians, or ought not to be, that science is the best discipline by which to study the material world, Hitchens' belief that matter is all there is, is a belief system that is simplistic rather than justifiably reductionist, is unable to account for the phenomenon of consciousness, makes impossible the assertion of truth and moral culpability, and rules out moral objectivism. It is therefore no exaggeration to say that Hitchens' atheism and moral judgements of religious people cannot get off the ground of materialism on which it is based fails.

Hitchens must be conscious to make his claim that the world's properties are exclusively material, but materialism struggles to give an explanation as to why there is such a phenomenon as consciousness. Peter S. Williams lists eleven atheist and anti-theist thinkers who admit that consciousness cannot on present knowledge be explained by a study of the brain.[103] These eleven thinkers, that include the New Atheists Dawkins, Grayling and Harris, most likely believe that the problem will eventually be solved to the physicalists' satisfaction, but there is a significant problem in closing the gap between the brain's nervous activity and the subjective experience of having thoughts, memories and sensations. In contrast to the eleven thinkers quoted, Williams advances the argument of the agnostic James Le Fanu who says that rather than continue unprofitably in seeking a way of reconciling

---

101. Peter S. Williams, A Sceptic's Guide to Atheism: God is Not Dead (Milton Keynes: Paternoster, 2009), p. 74.

102. Ibid., p. 75.

103. Peter S. Williams, *C.S. Lewis vs the New Atheists*, pp. 95-96.

physical activity with subjective experience, why not accept that the two cannot be reconciled.[104]

Materialism undercuts the ability to state what is true in a second way. Williams quotes C. E. M. Joad who argues that if materialism is true, then the individual is only and nothing more than his or her body. If this is the case, the individual's reasoning is a bodily functioning, like blood pressure, which bears no connection to facts external to the body, but only to the bodily conditions of which it is a function. As materialism makes statements about facts external to the body as well as making statements about individual bodies, if on materialism statements cannot make statements that connect to external facts, it has undermined itself.[105]

Hitchens holds religious people culpable for the crimes they commit in the name of their religion, but they can only be held guilty if they have freely chosen to do the deeds of which he accuses them. Materialism makes free will impossible. Again, it is Joad who provides the reason why. Joad argues that if the individual is all and nothing more than his or her physical body, his or her behavior is ultimately explainable in terms of the same laws that govern the motion of molecules. A person therefore has no choice but to be determined by these laws which operate regardless. If that is the case, religious terrorists and theocrats are merely obeying physical laws and so cannot be held guilty, as Hitchens holds them to be, of freely choosing to murder others.

There is no evidence anywhere in Hitchens' *oeuvre* that he considered any of these arguments against materialism. When confronted with one of the problems that beset materialism by Douglas Wilson during their debate at Westminster Theological Seminary, Hitchens did not respond to the question. Wilson asked how if thoughts were only pieces of matter, what reason could there be to think that any thought is true, including the thought that thoughts are only pieces of matter? Wilson stated that he would continue asking for Hitchens' response until he received an adequate answer. He never did.[106]

The Argument from Desire

Hitchens conceives of the relationship between God and humans in only one way: that of dictator and slave. Those who obey God, according to Hitchens, do so from terror, or from masochistic self-abnegation. His view

104. Ibid., p. 97.

105. Ibid., pp. 93-94.

106. 'Christopher Hitchens vs. Douglas Wilson Debate at Westminster,' YouTube, 30 November 2011 at https://www.youtube.com/watch?v=g6UU9C-WmvM (accessed 20 February 2017 at 16:40).

is appallingly impoverished because it fails to recognize that the relationship between the Christian God and His people is one of love. The Old Testament captures well the desire for God when it describes: 'As the deer pants for the water brooks, so pants my soul for You, O God' (Ps. 42:1). There is desperation in the Psalmist's words which communicate the most fundamental need for God. Augustine famously argued that humans only find true peace once they have a relationship with God.[107] Hitchens no doubt would dismiss these sentiments as further evidence of Christian masochism, but the Argument from Desire (AFD) demonstrates how humans have certain desires that only God can satisfy. This is not therefore a form of masochism, but a form of self-nourishment through finding satisfaction of these desires in God.

Peter S. Williams summarizes the AFD in two ways: deductively and inductively. Deductively, the argument runs like this:

1. for every natural desire exists a satisfaction.
2. there exist desires in humans that God alone can satisfy.
3. God, therefore, exists.[108]

Inductively, the AFD would argue that it is probably the case that for every human desire there is a fulfillment of that desire,[109] therefore there is probably a God who is the satisfier of those desires.

The AFD therefore is deductively or inductively an argument for the existence of God. Though this book asserts that the best explanation for the universe, mind and morality is God, it is not the direct purpose of this book to argue for the existence of God. Its purpose is to demonstrate that Hitchens' anti-theism and anti-religionism in relation to Christianity perspective are untrue, for they misunderstand the way Christians understand the nature of God and the character of the Christian religion. But the AFD is still useful to our present purposes because the AFD presents God's existence as desirable in that there are certain desires that only God can satisfy. The question then becomes what are those desires that only God can satisfy? John Haldane writes of the Christian desire to live eternally with God.[110] C. S. Lewis uses the German word *sensucht* which means nostalgic yearning that cannot be satisfied in this world, but only in an afterlife.[111] The Christian may enjoy living in this world, but senses that s/he belongs to another place, a transcendent place, where God is waiting for his or her return.

107. Augustine, *Confessions*, p. 201.
108. Williams, *C. S. Lewis vs the New Atheists*, p. 63.
109. Ibid.
110. John Haldane, *Atheism and Theism*, p.247-8.
111. C. S. Lewis, *Mere Christianity*, p. 113

How different are these ways of speaking about the relationship with God to those of Hitchens! The Psalmist, Augustine, Lewis, and Haldane speak of God with the same intensity as that of romantic love where the beloved desires not to subjugate herself masochistically to the lover's control but seeks the blessings of the lover who possesses them in eternal abundance. In chapter four, we shall return to the theme of God the lover through an analysis of the Song of Songs, a book that Hitchens never refers to and which does much to destroy his views that God is a dictator and that Christianity at best tolerates human sexuality.

Cultural Criticism

New Atheism seeks to present an objective view of reality and yet some critics, under the influence of Christian socialism, have discerned in it a racial and cultural supremacy. Terry Eagleton claims to see in New Atheism a white Western fear of what it regards as Black zealotry.[112] Religious terrorism is something that comes into the West from the so-called uncivilized world outside. New Atheism also is a racist revival of white Western cultural arrogance[113] in which the West believes it is growing nicer and more civilized in distinction to the rest of the world. Therefore, those outside of the West again require the civilizing effect of Western culture, not this time through imperial colonization, but through economic and cultural control. New Atheism, which is originally a Western phenomenon, therefore seeks to teach Black, Middle Eastern and Asian people how to behave by calling on them to abandon their terrorist religions.

The accusation of racist cultural supremacy is a very serious one, but one of which Hitchens is not guilty. Hitchens' membership of the International Socialists and his trip to Cuba under Castro reveals that he has been prepared to seek models of Marxism's application in countries outside of the West, even if he came to reject Castro's Marxism. That Hitchens regards secular liberalism as the best form of government has nothing to do with the historical fact that this form of society originated in the West. He regards it as the best form of government regardless of its provenance, and where similar types of pluralist societies characterized by religious toleration have emerged outside of the West, such as in Bombay, Hitchens has eulogized them.[114] Hitchens is as scathing of Western liberalism's attempt to appease Islamism as he is of

112. Terry Eagleton, 'Faith, Knowledge and Terror' in John Hughes (ed.), *The Unknown God: Sermons Responding to the New Atheists*, p.7.

113. Ibid., p. 8.

114. Hitchens, *God is Not Great*, p. 20.

Islamism's terror,[115] and he reserves as much censure for Serbian genocides in the Balkans as he is does for the Rwandan genocides.[116] Finally, Hitchens' close friendships with people from outside of the West, such as Rushdie, whose life Hitchens' helped to protect,[117] clear him of xenophobia.

A Christian Feminist Critique

Tina Beattie's voice within the debate brings to our attention the gender prejudices of New Atheism which intersect with Eagleton's charge that New Atheism is a neo-colonialist revival.[118] Beattie's desire is to broaden the debate by contextualizing the New Atheists as the products of white male intellectual culture.[119] According to Beattie, those theologians and apologists who debate with the New Atheists, such as Keith Ward and Alister McGrath, are part of this intellectual elite also, for their defense of Christianity is on the grounds of the preoccupations of the elite such as Christianity's rationality and compatibility with science.[120] The implication of such contextualization is that the New Atheist and Western male theology's understanding of reality is a perspective among a range of perspectives which have been excluded from the debate. Beattie therefore invites into the debate the voices of women's theologies[121] and the philosophies of civilizations that run parallel to the West.[122] Beattie interprets Western science, or scientific rationalism, as not simply an intellectual endeavor to understand the natural world, but also as a means of control of women and nature that comprise chaotic and irrational forces.[123] Science is therefore not wholly objective in the way that the New Atheists describe, but is value-laden as much as the religions that they impugn.[124]

As a writer who is a white middle-class male (and something for which I do not apologize) whose focus is partly to assert the rationality of Christianity, my thesis might be vulnerable to the charge that I am focusing

115. 'Christopher Hitchens responds to a Jihad sympathizer', YouTube, 20 August 2009 (accessed 30 December 2017 at 18:48).

116. Hitchens, *God is Not Great*, p. 21.

117. Ibid., pp. 28-30.

118. Tina Beattie, *The New Atheists: The Twilight of Reason and The War on Religion* (London: Darton, Longman and Todd, 2007).

119. Ibid., p. 5.

120. Ibid., p. 9.

121. Ibid.

122. Ibid., p. 7.

123. Tina Beattie, *The New Atheists*, p. 60.

124. Ibid., pp. 19-56.

on the preoccupations of an historical elite to the exclusion of women. My response is that I am doing nothing of the sort! I do not see rationality as the preserve of the white male elite but as a distinguishing feature of all human beings who are *compos mentis*. Beattie states the historical and cultural truth that women and parallel civilizations have been excluded from the white male rational sphere and have been marginalized by being characterized as irrational, passive and dependent.[125] This illogical and unempirical characterization of women and people from parallel civilizations has enabled males to create their rational identity by asserting their difference from 'others'. Yet, the assertion of the rationality of Christianity is the assertion that all human beings are capable of being rational because all human beings are fashioned in the image of God, both men and women, and people across the globe without exception. To cede the rational and scientific spheres to New Atheism, as Beattie appears to want to do, is therefore both unnecessary and undesirable and may itself be a form of racism and sexism in that such a cession denies the capacity of women and parallel civilizations to act and think rationally. Rationality *per se* is not a problem for it is an extraordinarily important feature of the human mind. Human civilization would be impossible without rational thought modes. Beattie's own response to New Atheism consists of rational argument which demonstrates that she as a woman is rational. Rationality is the enemy of discrimination and prejudice. The problem has been not so much rationality as the political appropriation of rationality as a characteristic of an elite to the detriment of the majority, which itself is an irrational act. The Indian female philosopher is as rational as her Western white male counterpart. Though God is known irrationally through revelation and art, He is the God of mathematics and physics also. It is time to claim rationality as a universal language rather than evacuating it on the grounds that it has been used as a gender and race weapon, or that it is seen to be synonymous with New Atheism.

Hitchens' Atheist Critics

New Atheism is the object of effective criticism from within the atheist camp. There are four lines of riposte discernible in the atheist critique of New Atheism. First, there are those who wish to dissociate themselves from the New Atheists' aggression and misunderstanding of religion. This camp includes people such as Michael Ruse, Julian Baggini and Camille Paglia, but it also includes a new generation of young atheists whom Theo Hobson calls the

---

125. Ibid., p. 40-41.

New New Atheists.[126] A second form of criticism comes from thinkers such as Alain de Botton who think that many religious practices are worth preserving and adapting to a secular life. His work is a direct refutation of Hitchens' proposition that all religion poisons all things. A third criticism comes from atheist feminism that like Christian feminism deems New Atheism as an exclusive white man's club. Finally, there are John Gray and Alex Rosenberg who argue that rather than having eliminated Christianity from their thinking, the New Atheists retain much of the intellectual inheritance of Christianity and therefore have failed to take their atheism to its logical conclusion.

To understand how moderate, intelligent atheism has censured New Atheism for its viciousness towards religion, one might profitably turn to Camille Paglia as representative of this view. Paglia is skeptical, yet deeply intelligent and generous in her attitude towards religion. She is unequivocally an atheist and yet she respects religion very much because it has produced more insightful beliefs about the nature of reality than liberalism.[127]

This contrasts with Hitchens' view that religion is an impoverished vision of the world when compared to science's wonders and an immoral system when compared to liberal values such as democracy and secularism.

Paglia sees several other problems with New Atheism. She condemns its propensity to jeer at religion. She also condemns it for a lack of knowledge of religion and regards God is Not Great as a sham in which the unscholarly and badly researched content of the chapters do not live up to their titles.[128] Paglia epitomizes a form of atheism that is far more persuasive to believers than New Atheism can ever be with its snarling mockery. One is more likely to accept the arguments of someone who respects one's position than someone who takes one for a fool.

Alongside the 'Old Atheist' voices of Baggini, Ruse and Paglia are those younger atheists whom Theo Hobson has recognized as the latest wave of atheism. In an article called 'Richard Dawkins has lost: meet the new new atheists',[129] Hobson hypothesizes that the high tide of New Atheism that began over ten years ago is now over and that Richard Dawkins is seen as

---

126. Theo Hobson, 'Richard Dawkins has lost: meet the new new atheists', *The Spectator*, 13th April 2013.

127. David Daley, 'Camille Paglia takes on Jon Stewart, Trump, Sanders: "Liberals think of themselves as very open-minded, but that's simply not true!"', at https://www.salon.com/2015/07/29/camille_paglia_takes_on_jon_stewart_trump_sanders_liberals_think_of_themselves_as_very_open_minded_but_that%E2%80%99s_simply_not_true/ (accessed 17 February 14:31 at 14:01).It is my opinion that Paglia is one of the most intelligent of contemporary feminists.

128. David Daley, 'Camille Paglia takes on Jon Stewart, Trump, Sanders.'

129. Theo Hobson, 'Richard Dawkins has lost: meet the new new atheists'.

a comic figure. Hobson's evidence is those younger atheists who reject New Atheism's simplistic view of religion. Hobson describes how Douglas Murray recently recounted debating alongside Richard Dawkins and was embarrassed by Dawkins' bellicose approach. Young feminist, atheist writers, such as Zoe Williams, resist the temptation to dismiss all of religion as a patriarchal system. Tanya Gold ridicules the idea that religion is only a force of evil and incapable of good. Andrew Brown of *The Guardian* who is an agnostic has contempt for New Atheism's crudities and admits he is attracted to religion. These emerging New New Atheist and agnostic voices clearly demonstrate a far greater accuracy and fairness in their description of religion than the New Atheists whose one-dimensional thinking ought to make them ashamed.

The New New Atheists not only refuse to demonize all religion, but seek to preserve certain features of it which they admire. Alain de Botton provides the most developed version of this view in his book *Religion for Atheists*. De Botton's thesis is that secularization is not only about getting rid of bad religious ideas and practices, but holding on to the good ideas also.[130]

He proceeds to identify the following nine attitudes and practices embedded within religion as being of value to a secular society: the creation of community, the expression of kindness, education as character development, the expression of tenderness, honesty about the human condition, seeing our lives from a cosmic perspective, using art to teach values, using architecture to improve behavior, and using institutions to provide strength to ideas. De Botton demonstrates in each chapter how a secular society might create its own versions of these worthy things. Whether de Botton's secular alternatives can satisfy the hunger for the transcendent is another issue, but de Botton, like Paglia, Ruse and Baggini, is more persuasive to believers for he begins from a position of respect for their beliefs.

Another line of criticism that has emerged is that of feminist atheists who though in full agreement with the anti-theism of New Atheism criticize it for being an exclusively white men's club. Like the Christian feminist Tina Beattie, Monica Shores' is surprised there is a lack of female participation in New Atheism considering the hostile attitude of religion to women. It is Shores' hypothesis that it is the sexism within the leadership and the rank and file of New Atheism that deters female atheists from becoming involved. She singles Hitchens out for his misogynistic statement that females are less funny than males and websites such as the 'Top Ten Sexiest Female Atheists' as evidence.[131]

---

130. Alain de Botton, *Religion for Atheists*, p. 17.

131. Monica Shores, 'Will "New Atheism" Make Room for Women?', *Ms Magazine*, 1 November 2010.

My focus is on Hitchens' anti-theism and anti-religionism rather than whether he and the New Atheist movement are misogynistic. However, the feminist critique of Hitchens does raise the question as to what extent Hitchens' anti-theism and anti-religionism are inspired by religion's ill-treatment of women. Though Hitchens did assert that men are more humorous than women,[132] which gave rise to the accusation of misogyny, there is very good evidence that Hitchens is a feminist and that it is one of the reasons why he is an anti-theist and anti-religionist. Hitchens speaks up for women and denounces their subjection by religion frequently. Of the many, here are some examples. Hitchens applauds Ireland's decision through a referendum to defy the Catholic Church and legalize divorce which allows women to escape abusive marriage partners and start their lives again.[133] He praises the women from Bengal for their swift embrace of polio immunization for their children in contrast to the male Muslim extremists who spread the nonsense that the vaccination was a Western plot to spread disease.[134] Hitchens declares the Mormon practice of polygamy as evil.[135] The Ten Commandments Hitchens censures for failing to prohibit rape.[136]

Hitchens in turn charges religion with sexism, but is that true of Christianity? Amy Orr-Ewing examines this question in her text *Why Trust the Bible: Responses to 10 Tough Questions*. Though she is not writing in response to Hitchens, Orr-Ewing is writing in response to the view that the Bible is a sexist document, a view that Hitchens would share. Orr-Ewing's hypothesis is that though the Bible was written during times when women did not have equality with men, the Bible throughout presents many women in complimentary and empowering ways.[137] Among the many examples she gives, Orr-Ewing refers her readers to the fact that Christ chose women to be His disciples[138] and the example of the Wife in Prov. 31 who is a successful business person.

Hitchens accuses religion of sexist oppression but fails to recognize the tradition of Christian feminism. Christian feminism is a necessary response to the patriarchal nature of historical Christianity and in certain ways, Hitchens is right to criticize the Church for undervaluing women. But two things need to be made clear at this point: The poor behavior of certain

132. Christopher Hitchens, 'Why Women Aren't Funny', *Vanity Fair*, 1 January 2007.

133. Hitchens, *God is Not Great*, p. 17.

134. Ibid., p. 44.

135. Ibid., p. 51.

136. Ibid., p. 100.

137. Orr-Ewing, *Why Trust the Bible*, p. 80.

138. Ibid., pp. 80-81.

members of the Body of Christ must be distinguished from the God who created both women and men as equals and the fact that some Christian feminists make a case for equality from the Bible demonstrates that authentic Christianity is egalitarian.

One such feminist is Elizabeth Schussler Fiorenza who believes that Christianity ought not to be rejected as incorrigibly patriarchal but is capable of feminist reform through the earliest traditions of Christ and the Church.[139] Her method to achieve this is to apply a feminist hermeneutic to the Bible.[140] One example she gives is Mark 15:41 where many female disciples are present at Christ's crucifixion. Schussler Fiorenza concludes that these women were the authentic disciples for their presence at the crucifixion demonstrates that they were the true witnesses of his ministry of service.[141]

Though it cannot be denied that the Church has been a source of oppression of women over the centuries, this oppression was contrary to God and His revealed will in Scripture. With women of the stature of Beattie, Schussler Fiorenza, and Orr Ewing speaking for women in the Church, reform in the direction of equality is already well underway because Christianity itself mandates it. To dismiss Christianity as sexist as Hitchens does is simplistic to say the least.

The Christian Heritage of New Atheism

One of the most interesting voices of criticism to have emerged among atheists is that of John Gray. Gray ironically notes that far from having eliminated Christianity from their thinking, Dawkins and Dennett are very much influenced by their Christian context. Dawkins' view that humanity alone can transcend evolution's influences on its behavior is an equivalent of the Christian doctrine that humans are unique among God's creation. Dennett's life's labor of attempting to reconcile free-will with materialism is a Christian project, for the notion of free-will is one that only became a serious philosophical concern with the rise of Christianity.[142] I would argue that these observations apply to Hitchens and I am sure Grey would not disagree. Humans are distinguished by their rationality, moral conscience and free-will according to Hitchens which are the exact same qualities that Christians traditionally have identified as being the specialness of humanity.

139. Livingston *et al.*, *Modern Christian Thought*, p. 425.
140. Ibid., p. 425.
141. Ibid., p. 426.
142. John Gray, 'The Atheist Delusion', *The Guardian*, 15 March 2008.

Pure Atheism

What then might New Atheism look like if it took its atheism to its logical conclusion? It would look like Alex Rosenberg's atheism which I shall call 'pure atheism'. Though Alex Rosenberg does not direct his text specifically at the New Atheists, his form of atheism does raise serious questions as to why the New Atheists do not adopt his stance on the matter of morality. The New Atheists are a very moral group in that their dislike of religion is a moral rejection of what they consider to be primitive codes of conduct, particularly those of the three monotheisms. Though Richard Dawkins at his most deterministic has said that human behavior is dictated by their DNA, the New Atheists' moral discourse assumes a universal set of values that are right or wrong regardless of what individuals may prefer to do and assumes also that people can choose to what is right and wrong and are therefore blameworthy for the things they do wrong. Rosenberg, however, takes materialism to its logical conclusion by denying the existence of objective morality and of free-will.[143] According to Rosenberg, the universe is nihilistic[144] because there are no intrinsic values in the godless universe which justify certain ethics and condemn others.[145] What is fortunate is that most human beings are committed to a core morality which has been embedded in our species because they have beneficial consequences for our survival and reproduction.[146] Free-will does not exist according to Rosenberg because science has disproved humans can act freely.[147] As possible evidence he describes the findings of Bernard Libet's experiment which appears to demonstrate that humans decide what to do before their conscious mind makes a decision.[148] Hitchens and his New Atheist accomplices use the argument that morality has its origins in human evolution rather than divine purpose which puts them outside of the Christian camp, but their objective morality and the blame they attach to religious people for their crimes demonstrates they have not escaped the Christian heritage of intrinsic worth and free-will. They are using the tools of a Christian worldview to condemn all religion, which is a contradiction. Rosenberg conversely has the courage to take his atheism to its logical conclusions.

143. Alex Rosenberg, *The Atheist's Guide to Reality: Enjoying Life Without Illusions*, (New York: Norton, 2011), p. 3.

144. Ibid., p. 95.

145. Ibid., p. 98.

146. Ibid., p. 102.

147. Ibid., p. 293.

148. Ibid., pp. 152-4.

Conclusion

This chapter has presented the arguments used specifically against Hitchens by Christians, atheists, and agnostics. It has examined their arguments against New Atheism in general for Hitchens is a member of this cultural movement. The counter-literature that has risen in response to Hitchens and the New Atheists is incisive and multi-componential. New Atheism is defined by its critics as new, not in the sense of adding new arguments to the debate, but in terms of its aggressive tone and its media-savvy methods of evangelizing its ideas. What makes the debate possible is that neither New Atheism nor Christian apologetics are post-modernist ways of thinking. Both believe the truth can be known and deny that the other knows the truth about God. Hitchens has focused most of its efforts on attempting to prove the immorality of religion and this has resulted in a counter-defense of biblical morality and a reassertion that though secular dictatorships might operate theocratically, they are still atheist at their heart, hence their persecution of religious believers. Hitchens' other accusation of Christianity is that it is irrational as it demands faith in rather than evidence of its propositions. The Christian response has been to argue that Hitchens and his allies have been guilty of inaccurately using the terms 'religion' and 'faith'. It is impossible to group all religions together under the term 'religion' as they are so diverse. Faith is trust in God based on evidence rather than blind. The Christian critique has also identified the contradiction between Hitchens and the New Atheists' belief in free-will and rationality and their materialist dogma. Much good work has been done by scientists who are Christians in demonstrating that there is no contradiction between having a Christian faith and being a scientist. What has been interesting to note is how there are good historical arguments that Christianity created the cultural conditions which made science possible. This chapter too has explored the cultural criticism of New Atheism that it is Western-centric, white-centric and even misogynistic, and has argued that on neither of these counts is Hitchens guilty. It has also evaluated Peter Williams' confrontation of Hitchens and New Atheism with the Argument from Desire and found it wanting as evidence that God exists. Finally, what has been established is that New Atheism does not speak for all atheists. Atheists of older generations and the New New Atheists have distanced themselves from the bellicose tone of New Atheism and assert (as Hitchens does himself) that there are aspects of religion that if secularized are important to retain. Feminist atheists have rejected the patriarchal nature of New Atheism's leadership. Older critics such as John Gray and Alex Rosenberg point out rightly that Hitchens and New Atheism are influenced by Christian philosophy for they retain a belief in human free will and rationality which on a truly atheist view of the world do not exist.

The response to New Atheism has therefore been powerful and in many places decisive, but the argument with Hitchens is not finished. What makes this dissertation possible is that there are lines of argument against Hitchens that need development and there are new arguments that are possible. It is on the basis of these two propositions, as well as the well-known fact that Hitchens enjoyed disputation immensely and would not want the argument to end, that we shall proceed.

4

Why the Christian God
is not a Totalitarian

Introduction

HITCHENS DECLARES THAT THE God of theism is by nature a totalitarian. A being, such as the Christian God, who has all power, is eternal or everlasting, has complete knowledge and is present everywhere, is the total totalitarian who would nullify or at best seriously circumscribe human freedom. For Hitchens, the struggle against theism is the most important, for it is the struggle between liberty and dictatorship.[1] Refuting Hitchens' charge that God is a totalitarian is a refutation of his most important objection to religion and therefore the most important means of undermining his worldview.

The present refutation of Hitchens' accusation that God is a totalitarian rests on seven counter-propositions:

1. The Christian God is unchangeable; He is not therefore capricious, which for Hitchens is an essential feature of totalitarianism.

2. Totalitarians make impossible laws. On the contrary, God has provided humanity through Christ with the means of being called righteous without having kept His law and the means through regeneration and glorification to obey His law.

3. Though God is omnipotent, because of His love and His desire to be loved, God has created human free-will, for it is impossible to love another unless one does it freely.

1. Hitchens and Wilson, *Is Christianity Good for the World?*, p. 11.

82

4. That God has provided the means of liberation from the greatest of totalitarians: the law of sin.

5. That the doctrine of hell, which Hitchens regards as evidence of God's totalitarianism, is in fact evidence of human freedom.

6. That God the Son in His incarnation as Jesus of Nazareth is presented in the Gospel narratives as suffering, yet triumphing, over earthly totalitarianism. (The Church as a target and liberator from totalitarianism will feature in chapter five as evidence that Christianity is not, or should not be, the friend of dictatorship.)

7. That God also loves with the intensity of a lover who rather than commanding His people, woos them (not seduces or manipulates) and becomes metaphorically their husband. The evidence for this view of God is the superb erotic and romantic Old Testament poem, *Song of Solomon*.

God is Not Capricious

One essential feature of the totalitarian according to Hitchens is that s/he is capricious so that his/her subjects never know whether they have broken the law or not and therefore are perpetually in a state of terror. Yet, one of the incommunicable traits of God is His unchangeable nature.[2] Grudem provides many scriptural examples that God's immutability is at the heart of the Judeo-Christian definition of God. One piece of scriptural evidence that particularly shows that God is not capricious can be found in Numbers 23:19: 'God is not a man, that He should lie, nor a son of man, that He should repent. Has He said, and will He not do? Or has He spoken, and will He not make it good?' God is therefore a God of His word and not a being that changes His mind at a whim. He therefore does not possess one of the defining features of the totalitarian.

God Does Not Make Impossible Laws

For Hitchens, God is a totalitarian because His laws are impossible to keep and yet He demands that humans obey them. The Bible indeed describes humanity as having failed morally. According to Paul, all are 'under sin' (Rom. 3:9) and 'all have sinned' and have 'fallen short of the kingdom of God' (3:23). The solution that God has provided for human turpitude is righteousness through faith, not good works, in the saving power of the

2. Grudem, *Systematic Theology*, p. 163.

Cross and Resurrection of Christ. In the same epistle that Paul describes human immorality, he describes how Abraham was declared righteous not through his good works, for that was impossible for Abraham was a sinner like the rest of mankind, but through his faith or belief in God (4:1-4). Righteousness has therefore appeared not through keeping the law, but through faith in Christ whose death is the propitiation for sin (3:21-26).

Christ's atoning death makes it possible for humans to be saved by faith and not by good works. Chapter two has already explicated Hitchens' objections to the Atonement and John Lennox's excellent response. A further response can be made to Hitchens. It is not the case that God forgives people their sins and ignores the wishes of the offended party. God forgives the sins of the truly repentant, but gives people the choice as to whether they will forgive or not those who have injured them. God's forgiveness does not therefore override the victim's prerogative to forgive and declare someone forgiven or not. God forgives the injury done to Him through the transgression of His law and the injury done to one of His human creations, but the victim him/herself still retains the choice to forgive or not what has been done to him/her.

Scripture illustrates this point very clearly. In the Parable of the Unforgiving Servant, the King forgives an enormous debt owed by one of his servants. This servant, however, assaults one of his own debtors for not paying a much smaller debt and demands immediate repayment. The King therefore refuses to cancel the servant's enormous debt on hearing what he has done and commands that he pays back all he owes (Matt. 18:21-35). It is a sobering story, for it makes clear that each person has the capacity to forgive or condemn which is separate to God's power to forgive. The story, however, warns us of what happens when we seek God's forgiveness without being ready to forgive ourselves.

Obtaining God's forgiveness does not absolve a person from his or her responsibilities to the person or people against whom s/he has sinned. Repentance means to change and repudiate sin.[3] Repentance, therefore, is an acknowledgement of one's moral responsibility to God's laws, but also to other people, for in changing one's attitude and behavior for the better, one is changing not only for God and for one's own sake, but for the sake of others who have suffered at one's hands. The New Testament provides an excellent example of restitution following repentance. Zacchaeus the avaricious tax collector informs Christ that he will give half of his goods to the poor and will compensate those he has extorted goods from fourfold.

---

3. W. E. Vine, Merrill F. Unger and William White Jr., *Vine's Complete Expository Dictionary*, p. 525.

Christ approves because He declares that "'Today salvation has come to this house'" (Luke 19:1-10).

Hitchens impugns God for imposing impossible laws on humanity, but Christianity teaches there is divine power to keep the law. When Nicodemus, a prominent Pharisee, secretly visited Christ, he was told by Christ that unless a person is born again, "'he cannot see God'" (John 3:3). To be born again, a person's physical birth is not repeated, but s/he is born of the Spirit (v. 6). This means that Christians now have a new nature which consists of the capacity to walk according to the Spirit (Rom. 8:1) and to set their minds of things of the Spirit (v. 5). It is by the power of the Holy Spirit that Christians can 'put to death the deeds of the body' which in fact means to cease to sin (v. 13). The extent to which a Christian can live a life free of sin is a matter of debate, but what is not for debate is whether Christianity posits impossible rules. It does not for it is the presence of God the Holy Spirit who makes holiness possible. It is also important to repeat that if a Christian fall short of God's standards, there is forgiveness for him/her through the blood of Christ (Col. 1:14).

God's Freedom and Human Freedom

Hitchens argues that God, whether He is immutably evil or good, cancels out through His very existence human free-will. If He is evil, He will enforce His evil will and if He is good, He will do us good whether we like it or not, which is an evil thing to do. Christians, of course, do not describe God as immutably evil, but as immutably good (Ps. 52:1). The first problem with Hitchens' argument is that it seems nonsensical for an evil dictatorial God who wants complete obedience from humans to create them with free-will. Would such a God not create humans who are automatons in the first place? It could be argued that God has created humans with free-will which He then enjoys frustrating by imposing His will. It could also be argued that God has created humans with free-will and therefore the capacity to be disobedient to enjoy punishing them. Hitchens believes that this is how Christians do indeed see God for he notes that Tertullian, the Roman Christian, describes heaven as a place from which the torments of the evil might be viewed with sadistic glee.[4] If Tertullian could enjoy the prospect of watching the evil suffer, surely his God would too? But other questions arise in relation to this, for example, surely such an evil God would enjoy punishing those who do obey His laws as well as those who do not? The obedient ones would also find themselves in hell and there would be no people like Tertul-

---

4. Hitchens, *God is Not Great*, p. 219.

lian in heaven. If God is a tyrant according to Hitchens, He is capricious, and so capable of suddenly deciding to punish whomever He choses. If on the other hand God is a benevolent dictator, why would He sentence people to hell for disobeying Him if He were good? Hitchens does not provide an answer for this, but Christianity does, for it believes in a good God, though not a benevolent dictator, and explains why hell exists.

Hitchens argues that it is wrong to give people what is good for them whether they want it or not, but if God does override someone's free-will to do him/her good, it is not always the case that it is an evil thing to do. R might not wish to be hospitalized for his severe delusions which means he believes that people wearing spectacles are hostile aliens from Mars who must be killed, but when he has been treated with anti-psychotic medicines, he may very well be glad that he was confined against his will in a mental hospital to receive treatment before he harmed anyone wearing spectacles. We also do well for ourselves whether we like it or not. X might resent deeply the diet she has decided to follow, but she follows it because she wishes to avoid the chronic health problems that are incurred through obesity.

In a situation where S overrules T's good choice and instructs her to choose a better choice is problematic. Imagine if T, who does not have much money and wishes to shop as cheaply as she can, is shopping and has placed in her trolley bananas that have been reduced in price only for S to take those bananas out of her trolley and replace them with another set of bananas that are as good and of the same quantity and weight, but are being sold even more cheaply. If T has not given S permission to act like this, then S's actions would seem impertinent and unwarranted, even if they were well-meaning. We would expect S, if she wishes to do T good, to tell her where she might find cheaper bananas and let her decide whether she will take up this offer. If T does not take up this offer that might strike us as irrational in the light of her desire to save money, but we would respect her decision. If S regularly does this, and not only in the matter of bananas, but in more serious choices, then we would worry that T's freedom has been impinged wrongly by S. We would also perhaps question how S is benefitting from such a strange scenario. This is how Hitchens sees God: a do-gooder who is forever meddling in His creation's choices on the basis that He knows what is best for them regardless of their preferences. The problem with this description of God is that it is not the God that Christians believe in. If free-will were a good thing, and both Hitchens and Christians would agree that it is, then if God were maximally good and can only act in accordance with His nature, which is what Christians say He is and does, He is by definition incapable of patronizing behavior and claustrophobic supervision that keeps humanity in a state of moral infancy, for such behavior is not good. As

God is maximally good, the relationship between His freedom and human freedom is the very best that it can be for both freedoms whether or not that relationship can be understood or defined.

Another way of understanding how the Christian God can create a free humanity without compromising through His existence their freedom is divine love. Hitchens is unable to conceive of a genuinely loving God other than in the form of an irritating, eternal paternalist, but God is defined as 'love' by the New Testament' (1 John 4:8). The word love in this context means that God's essence is love[5] and it is manifested toward us in the gift of Christ (v. 9) which is unmerited favor, or grace (v. 10). God's love is not therefore that of a meddler who cannot resist interfering in the lives of His children, but a sacrificial love that cost His Son His life. By giving up His Son for our redemption, God demonstrates that He desires people. He has taken the initiative by sending Christ because it was while people were sinners, and therefore incapable of loving God, that Christ came and died for them (Rom. 5:8).

But if God has the initiative, how is it possible for humans to be free? David Ford discusses several responses made by theologians to this question. Some have accepted that there is competition between divine and human freedom and have identified separate spheres in which they can operate. Other theologians have described God as creating a world which is autonomous. Others have allowed for divine encouragement, persuasion, and advice, but nothing that might undermine human freedom. Theologians such as Barth and Rahner have asserted that divine and human freedoms are non-competitive.[6] One way of understanding the non-competitive relationship between God and people is the analogy of love between people.[7] When people come together, each person cannot do whatever s/he likes, so there is an inevitable reduction of freedom to make human society function. But if there is love between these people, they will respect each other's freedom and initiative. They will choose to protect and maximize each other's freedom without destabilizing the society of which they form a part or the relationship that they have with each other. Therefore, without the love of others, it is not possible to attain certain freedoms.

The problem with this analogy is that it requires one to think of God as just another person, which of course He is not, for He is transcendent and radically different to us. His freedom cannot be placed in the same category as ours. Ford suggests one theological approach to this problem which is

5. Vine *et al.*, *Vine's Complete Expository Dictionary*, p. 381.
6. David F. Ford, *Theology*, p. 59.
7. Ibid.

the idea of dependent or secondary freedom. As created beings, humans owe their freedom to God and their desire to be free of God is the wrongful desire to be gods. Humans are free to respond to, or reject, God's initiatives which gives them enormous scope of possible action. They are at their best when their desires harmonize with those of God which is to love God, one another, and creation.[8]

One way in which one can understand the relationship of God's and human freedom is through Friedrich Gogarten's theology which speaks with great significance into the debate with Hitchens on the matter of political freedom. Hitchens declares the Stalinist and Hitlerite regimes as theocratic because they demanded worship of the state and of the dictator, yet Gogarten calls this a secular form of idolatry.[9] Whereas Hitchens sees the separation of state and church as the solution to theocracy, Gogarten regards secularism as a form of idolatry in that it promotes trust in human-made governments rather than a humble dependence upon God. Like Paul, Gogarten warns against focusing on the created order of which the state is part.[10] Gogarten promotes a religious form of secularism instead. This he defines as humanity's maturity in which humans are free from but responsible for the world.[11]

Gogarten takes us back therefore to the Garden of Eden whose narrative poses substantial problems for Hitchens' view of God the dictator. Whether we interpret this narrative as an historical description with a moral message or as a parable, the lessons drawn are the same: Human beings are created in the image of God (Gen 1:27). While this phrase can be interpreted in many ways, it is a plausible argument that it refers to human sovereignty over God's creation whilst remaining accountable to God for the way in which that sovereignty is exercised.[12] Therefore, rather than Christianity reducing human beings to the level of sycophantic myrmidons of a celestial despot, human beings are called to exercise a degree of authority and care over God's creation. Humans are therefore endowed with a creative freedom that has a global reach and through the exercise of that creative freedom attain to self-actualization which is the manifestation of the greatest freedom.

8. Ibid., p. 60.

9. Livingston *et al.*, *Modern Christian Thought*, p. 86.

10. Friedrich Gogarten, *The Reality of Faith*, trans. Carl Michelson *et al.*, p. 15.

11. Livingston *et al.*, *Modern Christian Thought*, p. 86.

12. Walter Brueggemann, *An Introduction to the Old Testament*, p. 35.

Freedom from the Law of Sin

In the discussion above of the power of the Spirit to enable Christians to live in a holy fashion, we have already touched upon the way God liberates humans from the tyranny of sin. It is important to the argument with Hitchens to emphasize the fact that it is not God who is the totalitarian above all totalitarians, but the law of sin which no one can resist by their own strength and which enslaves the human will. As love can only be exercised freely, God has created humans with sufficient free-will to love Him, thus freely choosing the greatest good, which is to love and be loved by God. Yet, free-will entails the possibility of choosing the greatest evil, which is to reject the love of God for the love of sin. Sin is defined in a multitude of ways in the Old and New Testaments and by understanding its definitions, one can understand why it is the greatest and wickedest totalitarian force in existence.

In the Old Testament, the overview of sin is that it is wicked, causes suffering to the victim and perpetrator alike and makes the perpetrators guilty.[13]

Perhaps most memorably, the power of sin is seen in the ramifications of Adam and Eve's decision to eat from the Tree of the Knowledge of Good and Evil (Gen. 3:1-7). Eve is told that childbirth will be painful and difficult, and she will be dominated by her husband though she will seek to control him. Adam is cursed with unproductive ground from which he will eke a living by great labor and that he will die, a death which, of course, Eve will share (vv. 16-19).

The Old Testament is aware of sin's capacity to capture humans in its power and hold them to a life of sin. When Cain became envious of God's pleasure in Abel's sacrifice, God warned Cain that 'sin lies at your door. And its desire is for you, but you should rule over it.' Cain never mastered sin and murdered his brother. His punishment was that he would be a fugitive and vagabond for the rest of his life (Gen. 4:1-12).

In the New Testament, the Greek word for sin is *hamartia* which can literally be translated as missing the mark. The sinner therefore has failed to meet God's righteous standards. The phrase missing the mark appears to rob sin of its seriousness, but it is of great importance to the Christian apologist who wishes to demonstrate that sin and not God is the great totalitarian. *Hamartia* is used to describe sin's causative nature. It is powerful in the way that the law is, but instead of restraining evil, it causes humans to do evil. The consequence is spiritual and physical death.[14]

---

13. Vine *et al.*, *Vine's Complete Expository Dictionary*, pp. 230-232.

14. Ibid., pp. 576-577.

God is the One who liberates humans from their sinful status and the yoke of sin. It is this proposition that is central to the Christian description of the relationship between God and humankind. Paul expounds this by first describing the wrath of God which is revealed against all types of sin committed by those who 'suppress the truth' about the nature of God and have chosen to worship idols fashioned in the images of 'birds, four-footed animals and creeping things (Rom. 1:18-23). God's response to this has been to give humans over to all forms of unrighteousness, the types of which he lists in gruesomely honest detail, beginning in his list with sexual immorality and ending with lack of mercy (1:24-32). Paul denies humanity any exculpation or mitigation for humanity commits sin in the full knowledge of the righteousness of God and that their actions deserve death (1:32).

God's righteousness is revealed through His Law, which humanity willfully and knowingly transgresses. Paul's saddening conclusion is that 'all have sinned and fall short of the glory of God' (Rom. 3:23). The 'good news' is that God's righteousness is available 'through faith in Jesus Christ' to all who believe (v. 22). Paul's theology can be understood through a series of essential terms he uses: 'justified' (v. 24), 'redemption' (v. 24), 'propitiation' (v. 25), 'faith' (4:5), 'grace' (5:17), 'gift' (v. 17), 'reconciliation' (5:10) and 'love' (v. 5). God justifies those who believe on Christ because he has deemed them to be right.[15] Those who are justified have been redeemed which in Romans 3:24 means they have been expiated or delivered from their sin guilt.[16] This redemption is made possible because Christ has propitiated, or satisfied, God's wrath caused by sin, by dying in the place of sinners (5:6). Those who believe that Christ has achieved salvation for them and know that they can perform no works which can contribute to their own justification are the ones whose 'faith' is 'accounted for righteousness' (4:5). Salvation is by grace, or unmerited favor; there is nothing the sinner can do to merit such a 'gift'. Its consequence is that the relationship between God and man is restored; for though man was the enemy of God in his sin, he is now 'reconciled' to God and God can pour out His love in the hearts of His children by the Holy Spirit who has been given to them (5:5).

Sin seeks control of human beings; its power is great and deadly, and its reach is universal. Hitchens would deny the existence of sin, though he would not deny the existence of evil. Sin is a theological term with reference to God's law and therefore rejected by Hitchens, whereas evil describes human wickedness without the parallel belief in a God who hates that wickedness and therefore is acceptable to Hitchens. That sin does not exist in

15. Ibid., p. 339.
16. Ibid.

Hitchens' worldview means that the notion of God as a liberator from sin is an empty one. If Hitchens, however, is prepared to use the Christian or theist description of God as a means of defining God as a totalitarian and explaining theocracy's authoritarianism without believing that Christian and theist descriptions of God refer to anything, it is legitimate for Christians to use their descriptions of God as a means of defending God against Hitchens' accusations and demonstrating that Christian cultures ought not to be tyrannical, (though conceding that some have been).

The Doctrine of Hell

Hitchens condemns Christianity for its doctrine of hell and asserts that this doctrine is evidence that God is an unspeakable tyrant. Though Christianity has presented several interpretations of what hell is like, the concept of hell that Hitchens condemns is the traditional Christian view that hell is a place where the damned are subjected to eternal torture.[17] Lost souls therefore remain conscious after death and really suffer. This is the worst fate of all, for there is neither respite nor reprieve from Christianity's hell.[18] Hell demonstrates that God punishes finite, temporal wrongdoing in the most absolute and final of ways. Hell is another reason why Hitchens is so pleased that God does not exist, for without God there is no hell. Hell is therefore the invention of human sadists.[19]

It is a weakness in Hitchens' argument that he does not consider alternative Christian doctrines of hell which present less harsh hells or have no belief in hell. Annihilationism teaches that the damned will be annihilated by God and therefore there is no kind of hell. Some annihilationists do assert that God puts the damned through some temporary punishment for their wrong-doing before removing them from existence, but this temporary hell is nothing like the hell Hitchens describes. Universalists, on the other hand, believe that all people will go eventually to heaven. According to necessary universalism, it is impossible for anyone to be separated from God. According to contingent universalism, it is possible for people to reject God, but none will do so. Most universalists nevertheless believe that sinners will undergo a temporary form of post-death punishment or purgatory before being admitted to heaven.[20]

17. Hitchens, *God is Not Great*, p. 220.

18. Ibid., p. 219.

19. Ibid.

20. C. P. Ragland, 'Hell' at http://www.iep.utm.edu/hell/ (accessed 14 January 2017 at 10:31).

None of these alternative models would satisfy Hitchens and one can imagine his response to them. Annihilation perhaps is preferable to eternal torment, but it is evidence nevertheless that God is a totalitarian, for it is a form of total punishment for finite transgressions. The fate of all souls on universalism is to go to heaven, but that does not placate Hitchens either for heaven is a boring place[21] where God is praised everlastingly. This for Hitchens is a form of torture itself.

The traditional view of hell is of an eternal place of conscious torment. This is the view too of the present writer. There are good scriptural reasons for belief in everlasting conscious suffering. In Mark 9:48, Christ describes hell as a place for the condemned where their 'worm does not die, and the fire is not quenched.' In Matt. 25:31-46, the damned will 'go away into everlasting punishment,' which is 'the everlasting fire prepared for the devil and his angels.' In the parable of Lazarus and the rich man (Luke 16:19-31), the rich man dies and is in torment in Hades (v. 23). A great fixed gulf separates the rich man from heaven which no one can cross from either side (v. 26) and which suggests that an individual's fate is unalterable. How is it possible from the traditional perspective on hell to answer Hitchens' charge that hell is excellent evidence that God is an evil totalitarian?

The strongest defense of hell against the libertarian Hitchens is to use the very free-will in which he believes. This interpretation teaches that the purpose of hell is not to punish sinners, but is God's way of honoring the decision of sinners to reject Him wholly. God has not created humans with the capacity to choose freely in the way that He can. Quite clearly, I cannot choose to fly by flapping my arms. But God has created us with the capacity to love or reject Him and each other, but people can only love if they are free to do so. Those who are forced 'to love' another cannot be said to be in love. Some people therefore will exercise their free choice and reject God's love which God will honor, for He will not override the freedom that He has given humans.[22] The source of people's free-will is therefore God's desire that they love Him.

At this point we might ask why the choice of relationship with God is cast as either one of love, or of rejection. Why is it not possible to have another kind of relationship with God such as one of mutual respect and acquaintance? The answer lies in the nature of God and how God has created humanity. God is love and it is through love that God seeks to know humans and to be known by them (1 John 4:16). Such a relationship is superlative because of the nature of love. According to the Apostle Paul, love:

---

21. Hitchens, *God is Not Great*, p. 219.
22. Ibid.

'suffers long and is kind; love does not envy; love does not parade itself, is not puffed up; does not behave rudely; does not seek its own, is not provoked, thinks no evil; does not rejoice in iniquity, but rejoices in the truth; bears all things, believes all things, hopes all things, endures all things. Love never fails' (1 Cor. 13: 4-8).

A loving relationship on such terms is the very best relationship that God can offer humans and therefore as God only wants the best for humans, any relationship with Him is a loving one. No other is possible. What makes the relationship one of love is that God is eminently loveable. Therefore, the only two choices a human can make with regards to God is to love and be loved by God or reject Him. This does not mean that there are no variations in the extent to which God is loved or rejected by individuals, but the choice is the same: love or rejection.

To know the extent to which humans have been gifted with free-will is not necessary to know; it is sufficient to state that God has given humans moral free-will in the sense that they can love or reject Him. It is necessary, however, to affirm that the free-will defense of hell is not a compatibilist defense, but a libertarian one. On a compatibilist view of human free-will, human choices would ultimately be predetermined, but the causal steps to-wards the choice would run through human will and intellect. On this view, God could determine that all choose His Kingdom, but as the Scriptures teaches, some will not make this choice, and so therefore on a compatibilist view, God is the ultimate cause of some going to hell, which is a conclusion that would suit Hitchens very much. But a libertarian defense exculpates God, because it is the view that humans are free to love or reject Him in that they are the ultimate cause of their choice. In other words, the agent decides, and that decision is determined by nothing external or internal to the agent other than the agent's own causal powers. As Craig and Moreland state it, a person of libertarian free-will is one who is and is alone the cause of their deeds.[23] Some humans therefore ultimately choose to reject God and their fate is hell whilst others choose to embrace salvation and their reward is the Kingdom of God.

The libertarian view is very controversial (but so too are the compati-bilist and determinist accounts) and it is not within the scope of this disser-tation to present a full-blown defense of the view. Instead, I shall suggest a line of reasoning by which the ability of humans to love or reject God might be understood as truly free in a way that avoids compatibilism. According to Christian anthropology, humanity is made in the image of God. This myste-rious declaration yields many possible lines of interpretation, but it suggests

23. Moreland and Craig, *Philosophical Foundations for a Christian Worldview*, p. 270.

that humans resemble God in some way or ways. God is a first mover, or unmoved mover. No event or sufficient cause determines His actions. He acts only in accordance with His nature, but His nature is not a prior cause of His actions, for they are spontaneous. To use another term, God is wholly sovereign in that He is wholly free in His decisions and actions and nothing constrains His choice other than His own nature. Though humans are constrained in many ways, for example, the limitations of their bodies and their intellects, other people and institutions and the natural world and have nowhere near the same level of capacity for action that God possesses, it is plausible that they too possess the capacity to act as first movers within the sphere of their capacity to choose to love or reject God. In this, among other resemblances, they bear the image of God. Though human bodies are subject to the laws of the universe, that they possess spirit means they transcend the deterministic physical world and can make the decision to love or reject God caused by nothing but themselves. Though humans are sinful, the image of God in them has not been completely erased..[24] Therefore, the liberation of God's people from the tyranny of sin is a restoration of that part of the image of God which pertains to freedom. Of course, Hitchens would never accept this account as He does not believe there is a God in the first place, but if the Christian God exists, and it is the contention of this dissertation that He does, then His gift of His image to His human creation contains elements of His own nature, and one of those elements is His capacity for uncaused action. Those humans who merit hell therefore are the sole originators of their decision and are responsible for their destiny.

If we argue that humans have the capacity for uncaused action in their response to God, we could be arguing that they are sovereign in this in that no other can interfere or suppress their choice. Now it is clear that human free-will can be manipulated or suppressed. Humans can be deceived and coerced into doing things they would not wish to do. In these matters, humans are not sovereign. But in the most important decision, that of loving or rejecting God, humans are sovereign, for what is at stake is their everlasting destiny. Now if this is the case, it is the case that not even God can override the choice to reject Him, though He desires human love without needing it, for if humans are sovereign in this matter, their choice cannot be interfered with. It might be objected that this means God is not omnipotent in that there are human wills in this universe that are not under His control when it comes to the question of loving or rejecting Him. But it is important to emphasize that the freedom that we are talking about is the freedom that is necessary if humans are to love God, for love is by definition freely chosen.

24. Vine *et al.*, *Vine's Complete Expository Dictionary*, p. 318.

God therefore is willing to create humans as free for the sake of something even greater, which is the love of humans, for love must be a wholly free choice, otherwise it is not love.

The above view of the sovereignty of human free-will meets the objection that if the fate of being in hell is so horrifying, why would not God override the choice of rejecting Him and be content at saving people from hell without receiving their love? People derive satisfaction from saving others' lives without expecting their love in return. If I send money to UNICEF to feed starving children, I do not expect those children to love me in return. This seems a plausible response and if correct, would render the sending of people to hell a grave injustice on God's part. The answer is that God cannot override human sovereignty otherwise humans would not be sovereign. But even if it were possible for God to intervene against the will of those rejecting Him, it would mean the destruction of the personal identity of the person being transformed. The person who was now being admitted to heaven would not be the same person as the wicked person he was before being transformed. Perhaps an omnipotent God could transform a wicked person gradually over time so that his/her personal identity was preserved, but those who adhere to the free-will defense of hell would argue that the loving attitude of the transformed person would not be his or her own, but something imposed upon him/her by God.[25] If Hitchens denounces the benevolent dictator God for doing good to humans whether they like it or not, he could not agree to such a transformation, unless he is prepared to admit that hell is so awful, which it is, that God ought to make an exception for it and override human free-will in order to prevent humans from freely choosing to go there. Hitchens never considered such an option in his writings or public speeches but argued against the necessity of hell in the first place. But to do so fails to see how those who freely reject God must be somewhere, and as they do not wish to be in God's presence, they must be in a God-less place which because there is nothing of God there is a place of immense self-inflicted suffering.

A number of decisive questions arise at this point if the free-will defense of hell is true. First, would the unrepentant really choose to go to hell rather than the Kingdom of God? In the light of human self-preservation, the notion of humans choosing hell over the Kingdom seems preposterous. Second, is being in hell an everlasting state of being, or is there a possibility that some or all might in the light of their suffering ask to be saved and God would respond by saving them? And finally, why does God give the vicious

25. Raglan, 'Hell' (accessed on 30 December 2017 at 19:07).

an afterlife at all: Would it rather not be more merciful or God to remove them from existence as annihilationism suggests He does?

That some will choose hell over heaven seems impossible, but it is in fact not inconceivable. It is not improbable that some will prefer their autonomy to the obedience of the godly in the Kingdom, even though their suffering is great. For them, the presence of God is a source of greater suffering than hell. There seem to be only two reactions to God: One of attraction and love and one of aversion and hate. Paul states this when he teaches that Christians are for those who are perishing 'the aroma of death leading to death' and to those being saved 'the aroma of life leading to life' (2 Cor. 2: 15, 16). If we examine the Gospels, there are only two reactions to Christ: Either one of attraction, or of aversion. There is a hatred of God in human hearts that can explain their choice of hell. One example from the Bible demonstrates this. Before Christ appeared before the Sanhedrin, he was mocked and tortured by the guards who had arrested Him in Gethsemane (Luke 22:63-65). There was no reason for this other than sadistic animosity. It is believable that there are people whose hatred for God is so great they will prefer separation from God over His presence. People therefore might suffer in hell greatly, but despite their sufferings, they will prefer their decision to remain apart from God. God in turn cannot interfere with that choice if humans are free to choose or reject Him and must leave them to the consequences of it.

Is hell therefore forever for those inside it? Christ's teachings reveal that it is. Earlier it was noted that He warns that hell is the place where the worm does not die and the fire is not quenched (Mark 9:44, 46, 48). If those in hell have in a libertarian sense chosen hell and God has honored their choice, the everlasting existence of hell demonstrates that its inhabitants are incorrigible in their choice and God is correspondingly incorrigible in His acceptance of their choice. But might it not be true that there could be people who have chosen hell, but who later choose to repent and are rescued from the 'worm' and the 'fire' by God? There is nothing in Scripture that gives such hope and therefore hell can justifiably be seen, if the free-will defense is true, as a place where people go who will forever choose to be there.

Why might God not put the unrepentant out of their misery once they have been punished for their sins by annihilating them? One response is that non-existence might be more horrifying to some than living even in great suffering, for existence, albeit a tortuous one, is better than not existing at all. This does not mean that all would agree, and it is plausible on the basis of people who choose to die rather than endure suffering that there are people for whom non-existence would be preferable to hell. But hell may very well be a place populated by those who are unrepentant in their rejection of God and who prefer existence to non-existence. God therefore does not annihilate them, for that is not their desire, but confirms them in the manner and mode of their freely chosen post-mortem existence, which is to live on forever without God.

One last point needs to be considered. The free-will view of hell regards the fact that people are in hell not as a punishment, but as God's confirmation of their choice. It can be argued nevertheless that God's decision to honor the decision of those to reject Him is a form of punishment according to scriptural data. Matt. 25:31-46 teaches that when Christ returns, He will separate His people from those who have rejected Him. Christ's people will be rewarded with their inheritance of His kingdom. Those who have rejected Him will be told to depart into 'the everlasting fire prepared for the devil and his angels' (v. 41). If the fate of the righteous is their reward, the fate of the unrighteous is their punishment. The theme of reward is therefore balanced by the theme of punishment in this narrative. Moreover, to allow someone to suffer the consequences of his or her actions is a form of punishment. Nothing more is added to the punishment other than what ensues from the decision to reject Christ.

Christ and the Tyrants

When Hitchens labels with horror God as the greatest totalitarian, he does so without realizing that Christians believe that God the Son suffered at the hands of three absolutisms: the Herodian dynasty, Israel's theocracy, and the Roman Empire. Christianity therefore ought to be an opponent of political and religious absolutism and where the Church has collaborated with Fascism, it has betrayed itself.

The first occasion in which Christ came close to being a victim of a dictator is Herod the Great's purge of baby boys in Bethlehem. According to Matthew, wise men from the East arrived in Jerusalem to worship 'the King of the Jews'. This troubled King Herod who feared political rivals and so he gathered the chief priests and scribes and asked them where the Christ was prophesied to be born. They told him that Christ's birthplace was Bethlehem. Herod asked the wise men to let him know where the Child was once they had found him, so he could worship Him too. The wise men found Christ, worshipped Him, and presented their gifts, but were warned in a dream not to return to Herod, but return to their country by a different route. Joseph, the father of Jesus, took his wife and Son to Egypt after having been warned also in a dream of Herod's intentions to murder Christ. Herod, when he had discovered the wise men's deception, was enraged, and ordered the killing of all boys in Bethlehem of two years and under (Matt. 2:1-17).

Matthew is the only ancient writer who provides this grisly narrative, but he considered it important enough an event to devote the whole of His Gospel's second chapter to the story. Doubt however has been cast on the historical truth of Herod's massacre of the infants and most of Herod's most recent biographers deny he gave such an order.[26] Perhaps such an instruction was too heinous even for Herod to issue. More importantly, the lack of objective historical evidence suggests the infanticide did not happen. Matthew's readiness to denounce debased authority may have led him to believe a fantastical story that Herod was an infanticide.[27] As a Jewish writer, Matthew's inclusion of Herod's barbarism reflected widespread Jewish antipathy for Herod whose Hellenism[28] and collusion with the Romans outraged Jewish sensibilities. Perhaps Matthew included the infant Christ's survival as a narrative device to prove the invincibility of God in the face of human machination. Another reason for skepticism is that Josephus, the most important source for the history of Herod's reign, does not refer to the story, though Josephus was prepared to report other atrocities that Herod perpetrated.[29]

However, Herod cannot be exonerated. Josephus may have been ignorant of the killing or he may not have considered it significant enough to report in comparison to Herod's greater executions because of the insignificance of Bethlehem and by the fact that the number of infants killed would have been small. Though Bethlehem has great cultic significance in Jewish history and faith,[30] in first century Palestine it was a small village and the number of children who would have been killed would at most have numbered a dozen.[31]

As for what is known of Herod's reign, there is unanimity among historians that Herod was capable of extraordinary cruelty against his enemies, rivals, and members of his closet family. Bo Reicke, for instance, describes

---

26. Ibid.

27. Matthew labels the Pharisees hypocrites fourteen times: 6:25, 7:5; 15:17; 22:18; 23:13, 15, 23, 25, 27, 28-29; 24:15.

28. H. Conzelmann and A. Lindemann, *Interpreting the New Testament*, p. 126.

29. Herod the Great's reign is chronicled by Josephus in his *Jewish Antiquities* and *The Jewish War*. See William Whiston's translation *The New Complete Works of Josephus*, pp. 492-670.

30. Bethlehem was the burial place of Jacob's second wife, Rachel, who was the mother of two tribes-Joseph and Benjamin. It was the home town of King David and of Boaz. Most importantly, Micah the prophet had declared it was to be the Messiah's birthplace.

31. Ben Witherington III, *New Testament History*, p. 72.

Herod as stifling rebellions savagely.[32] According to Elwell and Yarbrough, Herod's reign was characterized until his death in 4 B.C. by war, insurrection and murder.[33]

Herod was ruthless in removing rivals against his rule from within his family and if he was not prepared to spare his wife and his sons, it is easy to see how he might not spare other's children. Perhaps his readiness to destroy those closest to him on the grounds of suspected treason was the consequence of his father's assassination. Herod had married Mariamne, a princess from the Hasmonean dynasty, whom the Jews preferred as their rulers for their heroics in winning Jewish autonomy from the Syrian Seleucids in 142 B.C.[34] Herod presumably hoped that by marrying into the Hasmonean dynasty, he would improve his relationship with his Jewish subjects, but this proved not to be the case, for his building of pagan temples in his Gentile dominions was to the Jews unforgivable. When Mariamne I produced two sons who bore traditional Hasmonean names, Aristobulus and Alexander, they became popular with the people which caused Herod to suspect they might overthrow him. Consequently, while they were still young boys, Herod executed their mother on suspicion of treason; both boys met the same fate later. Herod also executed his other son, Antipater, on suspicion of treachery.[35]

With advancing age, Herod became more paranoid and vicious. It was a pain-wracked and deranged Herod[36] who imprisoned in the hippodrome in Jericho hundreds of Jewish aristocrats on suspicion of treachery and ordered their execution once he was dead.[37] The command was never carried out for in order to secure the people's support for the accession of Herod's son Archelaus, Herod's sister Salome and her husband Alexis released the Jewish captives.[38] The Bethlehem infanticide, which was carried out not long before Herod died was therefore, as David Stern concludes, the sort

---

32. Bo Reicke, *The New Testament Era*, trans. David E. Green, p. 91.

33. Walter A. Elwell and Robert W. Yarbrough, *Encountering the New Testament*, p. 49

34. F. F. Bruce, *New Testament History*, p. 5.

35. Ibid., pp. 22-23.

36. Josephus describes vividly the symptoms of the illnesses that may have contributed to Herod's growing paranoia and mental instability in his final days. According to Josephus, Herod suffered from among a number of things a high temperature, a painful stomach and his genitals were rotting away. See Josephus, *The Jewish War, Book 1*, Chapter 33, 5. 656, trans. William Whiston, *The New Complete Works of Josephus*, p. 726.

37. Ibid., pp. 565-6.

38. Ibid., p. 570.

of horror of which Herod was capable.[39] and one which Paul L. Maier states Herod was sufficiently evil to do.[40]

To suggest that Herod could never have given an order for the execution of infants not only demonstrates an ignorance of his reign, but a failure to recognize that atrocities against children are not uncommon in human history. A recent case is that of the Rwandan genocide of 1994. This slaughter was perpetrated by the ruling Hutu majority against the Tutsi minority who had risen in rebellion against Hutu violence and oppression. According to Human Rights Watch, children numbering in their thousands were butchered.[41] Physicians for Human Rights uncovered a mass grave in Kibuye Province and calculated that 44% of the bodies discovered were those of children under fifteen, and 31% were under ten.[42] The most infamous genocide, the Nazis' Holocaust, efficiently and remorselessly sent children and babies to the gas chambers with their mothers.

Christ also suffered at the hands of Israel's theocracy. Though a Roman province, Jewish domestic and internal government was led by one man, the High Priest, who was chosen from a governing body called the Sanhedrin. He was called the High Priest, but this man was as much a political leader as he was a religious leader for he was Israel's representative to the Roman Empire.[43]

There is evidence that suggests that the High Priests and their families ruled in an oppressive manner. A satirical chant found in the Talmud demonstrates that they used violence to back up their commands.[44]

When Christ entered Jerusalem, adulated by large crowds as the Messiah (Matt. 21:1-11; Mark 11:1-11; Luke 19: 28-40; John 12: 12-19), He immediately came into direct conflict with the theocratic oligarchy who saw Him as a rival to their power. Unnerved by His popularity and incensed at His expulsion of the money changers and dove sellers from the Temple, the chief priests, scribes, and elders demanded by what authority He did such things. Christ's response was defiant: He did not directly answer their question but asked them whether the baptism from John was from heaven or from men. When his interrogators would not answer, he refused to tell them the source of his authority. Christ's counter-question exposed the bankruptcy of their theology. If the theocrats had said that John's authority had come from God,

---

39. David H. Stern, Jewish New Testament Commentary, p. 9.

40. Josephus, The Jewish War, Book 1, p. 567.

41. 'Children Targeted in the Genocide' at https://www.hrw.org/reports/2003/ rwanda0403/rwanda0403-03.htm (accessed 3 March 2018 at 20:38).

42. Ibid.

43. Bruce, New Testament History, p. 63.

44. TB Pesahim 57a quoted in Bruce, New Testament History, pp. 67-68.

Christ could then have claimed the same source; if the theocrats had denied John's divine commission, it would have been impossible to explain why so many responded to John's call to repent. (Matt. 21:12-17; 23-27; Mark 11:15-19; 27-33; Luke 19: 45-48; 20:1-8).

An attempt was made by the ruling class to arrest Christ after He preached a parable about vinedressers in which he declared that Jewish unbelievers would not inherit the kingdom of God. Christ escaped on this occasion because the accompanying crowds venerated him as a prophet and would have resisted his arrest (Matt. 21: 33-46; Mark 12:1-12; Luke 20: 9-19). Christ's teachings continued to provoke, particularly His passionate denunciation of the scribes and Pharisees as hypocrites (Matt. 23:1-36) and His prediction that the Temple would be destroyed (Matt. 24:1, 2; Mark 13: 1). Therefore, the Sanhedrin called a crisis meeting at Caiaphas' palace. They were concerned that Christ would win over many people and the Romans would react by deposing them and dispersing the Jewish people. They concluded that Christ had to die, and they began to plot this (Matt. 26:3-5; John 11:47-53). The opportunity to arrest Christ came when one of His disciples chose to betray Him. Judas Iscariot, motivated probably by avarice, approached the chief priests and the captains of the Temple and in return for thirty pieces of silver, agreed to inform the leaders where Christ could be arrested secretly (Matt. 26:14-16; Mark 14:10, 11. Luke 22: 22:3-6). Consequently, Christ was seized at night whilst praying in the Garden of Gethsemane by a combination of Jewish and Roman troops which suggests co-operation with the Romans by the Jewish authorities as how best to deal with Christ (Matt. 26:47-56; Mark 14:43-50; Luke 22:47-53; John 18:1-13).[45] After being questioned by Annas, the former High priest (John 18:19-24), and then by his son-in-law, Caiaphas, who was the High Priest, Christ was found guilty of blasphemy for claiming to be the Messiah (Matt. 26: 57-68; Mark 14: 53-65; Luke 22:66-71; John 18:24). To secure Roman permission for his execution, Christ was presented to Pontius Pilate, the Roman Governor, as guilty of sedition. When Pilate declared Christ to be innocent, the Jewish leaders pressurized him into passing the death sentence by threatening to riot and accusing him of treason if he did not execute Christ (Matt. 26:47-27:56; Mark 14:43-15:41; Luke 22:47-23-49; John 18:1-19:30).

When Christ was given over to the Roman soldiers to be crucified, he suffered at the hands of another absolutism-that of Roman imperialism. In 6 A.D. Augustus had reduced Judaea to the status of a Roman province which because of its religious and nationalist turbulence was governed by a prefect

---

45. Bruce, *New Testament History*, pp. 195, 196.

who had the authority to act with the full *imperium*.[46] Judaea bore a great financial burden under Roman rule. Rome exacted a tribute from its provinces and used force, if needed, to collect it. Already obligated to pay the Temple tax, the Judeans also had to pay Rome's tribute. Neither the Romans nor the Temple leaders were prepared to reduce their tax in the light of the other. It is likely that pious Jews paid the temple tax willingly as an act of devotion to God. The imperial tribute, however, was deeply unpopular and the ruthless means by which it was extracted made it hated more. It has been estimated that between 30 and 40% of Jewish incomes were taken by the combined demands of the Temple and Rome's taxes which discouraged economic activity and therefore made the exactions proportionately worse.[47]

The governor of Judaea was Pilate whose behavior was often tyrannical. He was appointed in A.D. 26 and quickly demonstrated on several occasions disregard for Jewish sensitivities. His attempt to dedicate some gilded shields in the Temple met with strong Jewish protests and the situation was only resolved when Emperor Tiberius instructed Pilate to remove the shields to the temple of Augustus in Caesarea.[48] On another occasion Pilate brought military standards bearing the emperor's image into Jerusalem under the cover of night which precipitated sustained Jewish protest. When the threat of military force did not dissuade the Jews, to avoid a popular uprising Pilate removed the images.[49] A violent dispute arose between Pilate and the Jerusalem authorities when Pilate demanded that the Temple treasure bore the cost of an aqueduct which improved the city's water supplies and provided water to the Temple for ceremonial washing. The Temple leaders protested that the treasury money was dedicated to God and not to be used for secular purposes. When crowds gathered in protest, they were violently dispersed by Pilate's soldiers.[50] Pilate was eventually relieved of his governorship after a Samaritan delegation had protested to Rome that Pilate had violently suppressed a large crowd of Samaritan pilgrims who had gathered at Gerizim to witness one of their prophets unearth the sacred vessels of the Mosaic tabernacle which they believed had been buried there after the Israelite invasion of Canaan. Pilate's motive in taking such drastic action was the appeasement of the Jews who were enraged at the Samaritan prophet's claim to be an end-time prophet or *Taheb* whom Moses had prophesied would

46. Witherington III, *New Testament History*, p. 152.

47. Bruce, *New Testament History*, p. 32.

48. Ibid., p. 34.

49. Ibid., p. 35.

50. Ibid., pp.36-37.

come (Deuteronomy 18:15). Rome accepted the Samaritan petition and the Emperor, Gaius, appointed Marullus as Pilate's replacement.[51]

Pilate, however, had sufficient sense to see that Christ was an innocent man (Matt. 27:24; Mark 15:14; Luke 23:14-16; John 18: 38, 19:12). Of all the rulers who dealt with Christ in His last hours, it was this polytheistic, cynical Roman who came closest to seeing Christ for who He was. Yet it was Pilate's fear that the crowds would riot (Matt. 27:24) and that he himself would be accused of treason if he did not execute Christ (John 19:12) that led to his decision to crucify Christ. Christ was judicially murdered because He chose to be in accordance with His Father's will, because the ruling elite of Israel and their mob wanted Him dead, but also because the Roman governor wished to secure his position and power rather than release an innocent man.

The Gospel narratives of the attempted murder, persecution, torture, and finally execution of Christ is a story of God's willingness for the sake of humans to suffer unimaginably. But it is more than this. It is also a warning to those rulers whose behavior resembles that of Herod, the Sanhedrin, and Pilate that their ways of governing are wholly contrary to the will of God. God cannot govern as a dictator or support those who do for He is perfectly good. He cannot ill-treat His human creations or validate human regimes that do when He has made humans in His own image (Gen. 1: 26, 27). The fate of oppressive rulers is God's judgement of them (Judg. 13:1-16). On this count, God is not a dictator and Christians ought not to be either.

Song of Solomon

Hitchens' view of God is of a distant, tyrannical figure whose commandments are impossible to obey and who punishes eternally. If God is benevolent, Hitchens argues, He is intolerably paternalistic, ensuring that people get what is good for them whether they like it or not. God is therefore the enemy of human autonomy and self-respect and it is an excellent thing that He does not exist. Hitchens' images of God, however, are a travesty for all the reasons thus far given, but also because of the *Song of Solomon* which is a romantic and erotic poem nestled at the heart of the Old Testament. The *Song of Solomon* also demonstrates how wrong Hitchens is to identify sexual repression and disgust with natural bodily functions, particularly those of the female body, at the heart of Christian morality.

To understand the tone and imagery of this book, here are a number of ways in which the man and woman describe each other. The woman, or

51. Ibid., pp. 37-38.

the Shulamite as she is referred to, describes her beloved as having legs that are 'pillars of marble set on bases of fine gold' (5:15). The man celebrates the woman's breasts by describing them as 'two fawns, twins of a gazelle, which feed among the lilies' (4:5). The woman's desire is palpable, almost overwhelming, and is a celebration not a rejection of female desire:

> 'Like an apple tree among the trees of the wood, so is my beloved among the sons. I sat down in his shade with great delight, and his fruit was sweet to my taste' (2:3).

Male desire too is celebrated, not feared or trammeled, for the man declares:

> 'You have ravished me heart, my sister, my spouse; you have ravished my heart with one look of your eyes, with one link of your necklace' (3:9).

How is such poetry to be interpreted? According to Brueggemann, there is very little historical-critical data available for this text, and so the way to interpret it is through the methods of literary criticism.[52] The book is according to this hermeneutic deeply passionate love poetry.[53] The book is certainly love poetry, but not unrestrained, for though it is erotic, it stops short of being pornographic. Phyllis Trible interprets it as the redemption of *Eros* which in Gen. 2-3 is a narrative of disobedience and disharmony, whereas the *Song* presents love as harmonious.[54] The relationship between the Shulamite and her Beloved appears to be that of wife and husband. As seen in 3:9 quoted above, the Beloved addresses her as his spouse which he repeats in 4:10 and 5:1. If this is the case, the text exhorts married couples not to allow their sexual passion to die because of the pressures and responsibilities of conjugal life or over-familiarity with each other's body.

But there is a second reading of the book which arose early within Jewish and Christian criticism and which supplements the view that it is a celebration of human romance and sex: This love poetry allegorically represents the love between God and Israel and Christ and the Church.[55] Such an allegorical reading is indeed daring, for it describes God as lustful which does not normally feature in traditional theological descriptions of God.[56] (Lustful is not the best word as it has lurid connotations. The word

---

52. Brueggemann, *An Introduction to the Old Testament*, p. 324.

53. Ibid.

54. Phyllis Trible, *God and the Rhetoric of Sexuality*, p. 162.

55. Brueggemann, *An Introduction to the Old Testament*, p.325.

56. Ibid.

passion is preferable.) Contemporary critics have welcomed the allegorical reading. Paul Ricoeur and Andre Lacocque, for instance, support a variety of understandings of how the Song is metaphorical.[57] God through the lens of the book becomes a husband or lover who woos Israel and the Church. Such an interpretation receives support from Hos. 1-3 and Jer. 2-3 where God's love is metaphorically compared to that of a husband. Though there is no physical consummation of the love between God and His people, which is a monstrosity found in the sexual crimes of Zeus, for example, the intensity and focus of courtship is a vehicle of approximation for those who wish to find metaphorical representations of this love. What is important to emphasize again and again to Hitchens who argues that the Bible condones rape is that the Shulamite in the *Song* wholly consents with all her heart to the attentions of her Lover. So committed is she to him that she says that by night on her bed she seeks the one she loves (3:1). When she finds him, she holds on to him and does not let him go (v. 4). She pursues him as much as he pursues her and so there is symmetry of desire to this text.

Hitchens never mentions the *Song of Solomon* in his anti-theist pyrotechnics. His God is the heartless autocrat who inculcates a horror of sex and the human body and who rules with a titanium rod, turning human hearts to deserts and battlefields. If God is benevolent, He is the infantilizing 'Daddy' ever present to ensure we take our medicine. But the *Song* reveals how God cannot be the totalitarian. It invites us to His garden where we are loved and where we can love in return perpetually, and which is an exchange that is offered to all humanity. Whether God exists or not, the *Song of Solomon* reveals that at the heart of Judeo-Christian conceptions of God there is the image of Him as a Lover and a Husband and that Hitchens slanders God when he compares Him to a celestial Stalin or an eternal Mary Poppins.

Conclusion

The conclusion of this chapter is that God is not a totalitarian, whether malevolent or benevolent, but the creator and respecter of human free-will. This has been demonstrated in seven ways. God is neither capricious nor the author of unachievable rules. He is a God who acts consistently in keeping with His unchanging nature. Though humanity in its natural fallen state cannot keep God's laws, God has provided an alternative means of righteousness by faith, the new birth for believers by which they are able to keep God's laws and the glorification of all believers by which their sanctification is complete. It is because God seeks to be loved that he has given his human

57. Ibid., p. 301.

creation free-will, for love can only be called love if it is freely chosen. The disadvantage of this is that humans can exercise their free-will by rejecting God. The greatest totalitarian in existence is neither God nor the Devil, but the law of sin. Christ's death and the law of the Spirit are the means of liberation from sin's prison. Those who reject God and choose to do so everlastingly are those who by their choice go into and remain in hell. Hell is therefore not evidence of God the totalitarian, but of human free-will and God's respect for it. Christ Himself suffered at the hands of authoritarians, which demonstrates that God is the enemy of such a government style. Hitchens' view that God is a totalitarian has therefore been demonstrated to be a description of a god of Hitchens and others' own making rather than the God of the Jews and the Christians. Finally, the *Song of Solomon* reveals that the Judeo-Christian tradition celebrates human bodies and sexuality and that the repressive, misogynistic doctrines of the Church have no biblical sanction. If the text is considered as an allegory of God's love for Israel and the Church, it calls into question the view that God is a dictator and replaces it with God as lover and husband and Israel and the Church as consenting brides.

5

Democracy, Dictatorship and a Very Strange Choice of Hero

Introduction

THIS CHAPTER WILL ADVANCE a number of refutations to Hitchens' charge that Christianity is theocratic and so an opponent of the secular separation of state and church, teaches servility to oppressive governments and finally, that atheist dictatorships are theocracies in disguise. We shall proceed by granting Hitchens' axiom that the secular separation of state from church is desirable, but not because Christianity is harmful to political peace and social stability, but because there is warrant for such a separation in Scripture and in the writings of the Christian, or Unitarian, philosopher, John Locke. Moreover, rather than being the antithesis of democracy, it can be plausibly argued that Christianity has fostered democracy, an argument that Hitchens fails to consider, so convinced is he that Christianity is political poison. As for Hitchens' assertion that Christianity teaches submissiveness to tyranny, this chapter will demonstrate that Christians have an historical track record of resistance it. Hitchens argues that possibly the worst dictatorship of all, Stalin's, was not an atheist dictatorship, but rather a theocratic one, but this chapter will provide the unused example of Nikolai Khrushchev's government as an example of a militant atheist dictatorship that was not theocratic, but which persecuted Soviet Christians horribly. Finally, this chapter will explore, as Christian apologetics has failed to do thus far, the paradox of the libertarian Hitchens' admiration for the totalitarian and mass murderer, Leon Trotsky, who provides alongside Khrushchev an example of a militant atheist who colluded with the violent repression of Russian Christianity.

What unifies this chapter is therefore its desire to turn Hitchens' analysis of religion and dictatorship on its head by arguing that Christianity has been an ally of political and religious freedom and that atheism in its militant form has treated Christians in a bloodthirsty way. It seeks to demonstrate that Hitchens' political case against Christianity has been, like his spiritual case against God, built on insufficient evidence that ignores, whether deliberately or not, the abundant counter-data that ruin his simplistic dogma.

Christian Secularism

In his analysis of Locke's Letter, Mark Goldie paints a profoundly disturbing picture of religious divisions between Protestants and between Catholics and Protestants during the sixteenth and seventeenth centuries.[1] It is important to acknowledge this dark and disgraceful time in the history of the European Church as a means of avoiding the sententious hypocrisy of the New Atheists who cannot bring themselves to acknowledge the persecution and violence of militant atheists. But though these acts of violence are the deeds of Christendom, they cannot be called Christian if the core ethics of Christianity are taken to be the moral precepts of Christ. The prescription to love one's enemies, bless those who curse one and do them good (Matt. 5:44) certainly denunciates persecution and retaliation in the face of persecution as unChristian.

The oppression of Christians by Christians, if one can call the oppressors Christian, demonstrates the problem of Christianity becoming an official state religion. Though the Christian subjects of the Roman Empire no doubt were euphoric at the news that Constantine had converted and that they were safe from persecution, there are dangers in Christianity, or any other religion, being identified with the state. The primary problem is what to do with those minorities who will not bow the knee to official church doctrine and practice. Once a church becomes identified with the state, anyone who does not conform is not only seen as a heretic, which was enough to warrant being burned alive, but could be seen as a traitor.

But persecution of religious minorities was not simply a matter of political allegiance, but also a religious one of dogma and unity. Those who did not have the 'correct beliefs' threatened the Church's solidarity and endangered the souls of their neighbors if they converted them. Dissenters too were regarded as immoral, leading secretly depraved lives. The Scriptural justification for the use of physical compulsion against heretics supposedly

---

1. Mark Goldie, 'Locke On Religious Toleration' at https://oll.libertyfund.org/pages/locke-on-religious-toleration-by-mark-goldie (accessed 9 April 2017 at 16:08).

came according to St Augustine from Luke 14:23 where Christ's command to 'compel them to come in [*compelle intrare*]' was to be understood as referring to the Church. The Christian ruler was obliged to suppress heresy for he was God's minister of justice (Rom. 13:4).[2]

Scripture provides some evidence that the association of the state with Christianity is not the Christian way. In Matt. 22:15-21, it is recorded that the Pharisees sent their disciples accompanied by Herodians to attempt to incriminate Christ. The question they posed to him publicly was: 'Is it lawful to pay taxes to Caesar or not?' (v.17). Their question was a false but politically lethal dilemma. If Christ replied with a yes, He would have angered his listeners who resented the annual Roman tax.[3] If he responded with a no, He would have committed treason in the eyes of Rome. Christ's response is a masterstroke of logic. Rather than be trapped within the confines of the yes/no structure of the question, He asked for a visual aid, a coin, and split the two parts of their question. When presented with the coin, Christ asked whose image and inscription was on it. His interlocutors replied that it was Caesar's. Christ's response momentarily ended their questions: '"Render therefore to Caesar the things that are Caesar's and to God the things that are God's"' (vv.18-21). In this short interaction, Christ teaches a separation of duty towards the state and God. Roman currency belonged not to God, but to the Roman state, and if the state wished to have its money, then it was welcome to have it back in taxes. On the other hand, duties owed to God are to be rendered to God.

This principle can be extended to other things. If the state requires all to drive on the right-hand side of the road, it is good to obey this law for the sake of order and safety. If God commands our obedience, it is good to obey Him, for He is worthy of it. Though government by God through godly leaders is the preferred method of the Old Testament (2 Sam. 8) and is anticipated by the New at the end of the age (Rev. 21), human government is God's instrument for the historical age (Rom. 13:1-7), and within the relationship between the two kingdoms, that of the state and that of God, there is accommodation in that the state and God's demands are separate and can be met separately without the neglect of one for the other. When there is conflict between the state's demand and those of God, as we shall see later in this chapter, Christians owe their obedience to God and Christian disobedience is perfectly legitimate by the lights of Scripture.

2. Mark Goldie, 'Locke On Religious Toleration'.

3. Dale C. Allison, Jr., 'Matthew', ed. John Barton and John Muddiman, *The Oxford Bible Commentary*, p. 873.

John Locke's A Letter on Toleration

The idea of a separation of church and state can be found in *A Letter on Toleration* by John Locke, the devout philosopher of the seventeenth and early eighteenth century. Although Locke's view of a secular state was limited in the sense that he did not think that toleration ought to be extended to Catholics and atheists whom he regarded as a threat to political stability, nevertheless, his ideas were a philosophical move towards the contemporary secularism that Hitchens applauds.

Locke condemns Christian persecution as inhumane[4] and argues that the conversion of non-Christians such as Jews and Muslims was to happen not by force, but through the peaceful power of the Gospel.[5] Locke, however, is aware of the continuing reality of persecution and to solve this problem he advocates the same solution that Hitchens advocates: The separation of civil government from religion in order to prevent political and civil power being used to persecute those deemed heretics and to convert them forcibly.

Why does Locke think that the political leader cannot legislate in spiritual matters? He provides three reasons from the nature of civil magistracy before examining the nature of the Church. According to Locke, the commonwealth is the arena in which human beings gain, retain and improve their civil interests which he defines as such things as health and possessions.[6] It is the duty of the magistrate to ensure that each person has their ownership rights protected and to punish those who deprives others of their rights.[7] People's spiritual well-being is not the civil magistrate's responsibility, for religious faith is one of personal choice and conviction rather than the consequence of conforming outwardly to the will of another.[8] As the civil magistrate's power is external force, he cannot be responsible for individual salvation, for individual salvation is a private, personal decision.[9] Finally, the civil magistrates might be corrupt and therefore cannot lead their subjects on the path to salvation.[10] Locke concludes this section of his argument with the statement that civil government refers to earthly rather than spiritual interests.[11]

---

4. John Locke, *A Letter on Toleration*, trans. William Popple, p. 6.

5. Ibid.

6. Ibid., p. 7.

7. Ibid. p. 8.

8. Locke, *A Letter on Toleration*, p. 8.

9 Ibid., p. 9.

10. Ibid., p. 10.

11. Ibid., p. 10.

Just as the civil magistrate cannot impinge upon the functioning of the Church, neither can the Church take away a person's civil rights. Locke approves of the power of excommunication for anyone who continually transgresses civil and ecclesiastical law.[12] But excommunication does not also mean that the offender's civil goods are confiscated because these are under the magistrate's protection.[13] Neither can a person's civil rights be denied him because he is of another church as these civil rights too are under the civil magistrate's protection.[14]

The business of the Church is the salvation of the souls of all who have voluntarily joined them. According to Locke, the purpose of religious societies is to worship God and enable their members to attain eternal life. Ecclesiastical laws are therefore solely concerned with these two ends and have no authority over terrestrial goods.[15] Locke's political philosophy therefore makes a clear demarcation between the 'this-worldly' power of the civil magistrate and the eternal perspective of the Church which though it has its internal rules, has no say in civil matters.

Locke's position is that toleration must be extended to non-Christians. Since the commonwealth is not identified with any religion, there can be no discrimination against people on religious grounds. Native Americans, subject to a Christian King, were not to be persecuted.[16] Neither were Muslims, Jews, pagans and dissenting Christians.[17]

The weakness in Locke's argument concerns Roman Catholics and atheists. Locke denies toleration and civil protection to Catholics, not because of the differences between their religion and Protestantism, but because they owed allegiance to a foreign authority-the Pope.[18] This line of argument, however, is no different to Hitchens' intolerance for those Americans who enjoy the protection and privileges of American citizenship and yet because of their radical Islam and allegiance to foreign mullahs, kill their fellow Americans. Locke's intolerance of atheists is the consequence of his belief that they readily break rules because they do not fear divine punishment.[19] This is not the view of those Christian apologists who have debated Hitchens and it is certainly not my view. Readily do informed Christians

12. Ibid., p. 14.
13. Ibid.
14. Ibid., pp. 14-15.
15. Ibid., p.13.
16. Ibid., p. 32.
17. Ibid.
18. Ibid., p. 42.
19. Ibid., p. 43.

acknowledge that atheists can be, and for the most part are, people with moral values. The problem that atheists have is asserting objective moral values with warrant, though that is an intellectual problem which has no necessary bearing on the ability of atheists to live up to their society's moral code in ways no more and no less than their religious fellow citizens.

Though envisaging no civil rights for Catholics or atheists, Locke's position was a radical one for the late seventeenth century. What is most significant is that he was a Christian philosopher who sought to employ Scriptural text to justify his position as much as reason. Locke therefore stands as a testimony to the fact that a secular philosophical reading is possible on Christianity. Hitchens' blanket accusation that Christianity equals theocracy fails on the awkward fact of Locke and other Christians who have advocated a separation of church and state. As further evidence that Christianity is not synonymous with theocracy, we shall turn to the causal relationship that Maritain identifies between Christianity and democracy.

Christianity and Democracy

On 29 December 1949 at the annual meeting of the American Political Science Association and then on 19 February 1950 at Gettysburg College, the French philosopher, Jacques Maritain, gave an address called 'Christianity and Democracy'.[20] It was his fundamental proposition that Christianity works in two ways on history: from above in the form of the Church's teachings and from below through the influence of Christianity on secular culture. It was the stimulus of secular consciousness from below that is the subject of Maritain's paper.[21]

According to Maritain, it is Christian values that have transformed the secular consciousness away from barbarism and into becoming democratic. The Gospel has taught secularism the inherent value of each human being who though a member of the State also stands above and apart from it as a spiritual being. Secularists are now conscious of human rights.[22] It is under the Gospel's inspiration that secular consciousness has learned that though society is inevitably functionally unequal, humans are inherently equal which is necessary for democracy to be established and function.[23] Christianity teaches that all authority emanates from God ultimately. This means

---

20. Jacques Maritain, 'Christianity and Democracy' at https://www.3.nd.edu/Departments/Maritain/jm604a.htm (accessed 28 December 2016 at 00:30).

21. Ibid.

22. Ibid.

23. Ibid.

that no one can govern any other without his or her consent.[24] According to the Gospel, human government is accountable to God and the abuse of power and authority is damned by Him.[25] Secular consciousness has gained from the Gospel the view that humans are able to exercise freedom and this must find expression in political freedom.[26] Finally, the Gospel has taught the principle of love without which society cannot exist.[27]

The only political system Hitchens conceives Christianity can create is theocracy. Maritain argues the opposite: that democracy has been inspired and is sustained by Christianity. It is the faith in the values of democracy and in their triumph that sustains the democratic impulse and faith is that which Christ brought into the world.[28] It therefore follows that as Christian values are the bedrock of democratic thinking, Hitchens is enjoying the benefits of Christianity's influence on American civilization when he exercises his right to freedom of speech to censure religious belief.

Christian Disobedience

Paul's instructs everyone to be subject to the governing bodies for all such authorities are appointed by God (Rom. 13: 1,2). Yet the question arises as to what the Christian ought to do when the state commands him or her to do something that violates the commandments of God. In this case, the Bible is very clear from the examples it gives: that the command of God is superior to the command of the state and the state is to be disobeyed in ways that do not lead the believer into sin, such as terrorism and revolutionary violence. Three examples will suffice to prove this. Shadrach, Meshach, and Abednego (whose original Jewish names were Hananiah, Mishael and Azariah) refused to worship the gold statue that Nebuchadnezzar had erected. They were punished by being thrown into a furnace but were rescued by God and promoted by an astonished Nebuchadnezzar (Dan. 3:1-30). Christ defied the useless religious traditions of Israel's theocracy to demonstrate obedience to the higher laws of love. The strict observation of the Sabbath was a fundamental feature of the Pharisees' teaching and yet Christ defended his disciples for performing a form of work on the Sabbath-picking ears of corn in a grain field and eating them-by arguing that satisfying one's hunger was more important (Luke 6:1-5). Christ reinforced the point by healing

24. Ibid.
25. Ibid.
26. Ibid.
27. Ibid.
28. Ibid.

a man with a withered arm on the Sabbath, an act that was prohibited on
the Sabbath as it too was deemed to be a form of work (vv.7-11). Christ's
greatest defiance of human-made rules was to state his divinity which in the
eyes of the Sanhedrin was blasphemy punishable only by execution (Matt.
26: 64-66; Mark 14: 61-64; Luke 22: 66-71). Peter and John were arrested
for preaching in Jerusalem that Christ had risen from the dead and were
commanded by the rulers of Israel not to continue, but they refused and
continued (Acts 4:1-33).

Hitchens might dismiss these stories as mythological. It is not appropriate at this stage to enter a discussion of why the Bible ought to be
trusted as chapter three has already referred the reader to the work of Amy
Orr-Ewing in defending biblical trustworthiness. What is important to note
is that biblical stories mandate Christian disobedience when the state demands what is contrary to God's goodness and the well-being of people.

It is important in the debate with Hitchens to emphasize that there
is a tradition of Christian disobedience outside of the biblical narratives,
though warranted by those narratives. We have already discussed how the
Christian/Unitarian philosopher, John Locke, was instrumental in the development of liberal secular society through his advocacy of the separation
of state and church and the end of religious intolerance among Protestant
sects. It is important to note also that Locke advocated disobedience to the
temporal authorities when they abused their power. This is something that
Hitchens does acknowledge for he is impressed enough with Locke to include an analysis of his ideas in *Thomas Paine's Rights of Man*. Hitchens
begins his analysis by contrasting Locke favorably with Hobbes on the issue
of sovereignty within the political order. Whereas Hobbes saw the sovereign
authority as the one who would uphold and mediate the social contract that
bound people into an agreement of mutual interest without being held itself
to account by that contract, Locke argued that the sovereign is bound by
the contract also. According to Locke, government is to administer justice
impartially, create laws for the people's good and not raise taxes without
the consent of those being taxed.[29] The irony, of course, is that Locke, who
sought to circumscribe the power of the state and who taught civil disobedience in certain cases, was a Christian, or a Unitarian. On the other hand,
Hobbes, who upheld the state's sovereignty was, as Hitchens states, an agnostic.[30] It is therefore the religious philosopher who stands for political
liberty, whereas the irreligious philosopher argues for a powerful state.

29. Hitchens, *Tom Paine*, pp. 105-6.

30. Ibid., p. 205.

Hitchens not surprisingly omits to acknowledge Locke's Christian or unorthodox Christian faith and nowhere else in his writings does he acknowledge Locke's faith. Hitchens certainly cannot be unaware of Locke's religious views, but excludes them from his analysis probably because such a fact is inconvenient for someone who has the temerity to claim that all religion poisons everything.

Hitchens praises Locke by identifying how his ideas influenced and inspired the American Constitution. Most importantly, Hitchens notes that Locke was a supporter of the 1688 Revolution in England when the despised Catholic James II was deposed by the English aristocracy and replaced by the Protestant William of Orange. This revolution set a precedent in Locke's eyes for future rebellions if they became necessary.[31] The dethroning of James II certainly seems to have been the precedent for the dethroning of George II by the English-American colonists and their French allies who themselves were to topple Louis XVI in the French Revolution. Hitchens is therefore faced with the conclusion that a Christian thinker was at the root of the Constitution which he admires the most, but of course, he cannot bring himself to say this. Instead he diverts his readers' attention away from this on to the Founding Fathers of the USA whom he declares were religious sceptics and at most deists.[32]

Hitchens, however, if he cared to examine the historical record properly, would have recognized the role that a New England pastor, Jonathan Mayhew, played in stirring up the American Revolution. Jonathan Mayhew was not the only pulpit patriot to do so, and the American clergy by no means all shared his views, but he will be our focus for there is insufficient space to do justice to other revolutionary pastors. It is important to state that Mayhew was not an orthodox Christian, but probably a Unitarian,[33] but this is an irrelevant detail because Hitchens indicts all faiths and religions as poisonous and yet the religious Mayhew was instrumental to a revolution that Hitchens admires immensely. Whether the American Revolution was a morally good thing is not important within the present context. That Hitchens thinks it was is what is significant, for men of religious faith were integral in causing what in his opinion was the greatest revolution that led America's secular separation of state from church.

---

31 Ibid., p.108.

32. Christopher Hitchens, 'Yes, the Founding Fathers were Skeptics About Religion, *The Weekly Standard*, 11 December 2006.

33. 'Jonathan Mayhew' at https://www.totallyhistory.com/jonathan-mayhew (accessed 4 March 2017 at 14:54).

Mayhew is credited with formulating the Revolution's slogan: 'No taxation without representation'.[34] Mayhew delivered a sermon in Boston in 1750 grandly entitled 'A Discourse concerning Unlimited Submission and Non-Resistance to the Higher Powers: With some Reflections on the Resistance made to King Charles I. And on the Anniversary of his Death: In which the Mysterious Doctrine of that Prince's Saintship and Martyrdom is Unriddled'.[35] This famous sermon encouraged revolution and was the document that the Founding Fathers consulted when drafting the Declaration of Independence.[36] Whereas Hitchens would have people believe that authoritarian political structures are created and justified by religions such as Christianity, Mayhew's call to resist tyranny and absolutism on the part of Christian subjects and citizens was developed through an analysis of Scripture. His condemnation of monarchical mis-rule was a case of Christian hermeneutics determining politics. It is therefore because of Mayhew's code of biblical values that he denounced George II's government. Of course, it is not necessary to be a Christian to be an opponent of authoritarianism, but neither is such a role the preserve of the atheist, anti-theist, and secularist, and it is no less true that being a Christian or a Unitarian can lead a person, such as Mayhew, to serve the cause of liberty by using arguments from sacred text.

The East German Churches' Resistance

Hitchens likes to portray Christians as theocrats responsible for such things as inquisitions and witch hunts, or as servile colluders with totalitarian regimes. In his haste to smear Christians, Hitchens is either unaware or ignores counter-evidence such as the decisive contribution that the Protestant church played in pulling down the East German Communist regime through peaceful protest.

Though many East German Christians were involved in defying the regime, one pastor stands out: Christian Fuhrer, a pastor of a church in Leipzig. In 1982, Fuhrer initiated 'peace prayers' every Monday at the

---

34. Ibid.

35. Mayhew, Jonathan A.M., D.D. and Royster, Paul , Editor & Depositor, "A Discourse concerning Unlimited Submission and Non-Resistance to the Higher Powers: With some Reflections on the Resistance made to King Charles I. And on the Anniversary of his Death: In which the Mysterious Doctrine of that Prince's Saintship and Martyrdom is Unriddled (1750). An Online Electronic Text Edition." (1750). *Electronic Texts in American Studies.* Paper 44 at https://www.digitalcommons.unl.edu/etas/44 (accessed 5 March 2017 at 08:50).

36. Ibid.

Church of St Nicholas which became the focal point for those protesting at the oppression of Erich Honecker's atheist, Communist government.

The Monday prayer meetings culminated in a confrontation between the resistance movement and Honecker's government on 9 October 1989. When Honecker's supporters chose to occupy 500 seats in the church during the prayer meeting on that day, 70,000 people protested peacefully in the streets at Fuhrer's urging. The protestors, carrying candles and flowers, marched through Leipzig chanting, 'Wir sind das Volk!' ('We are the People'). The following week 120,000 people arrived to protest. The week after that, 320,000 came. The demonstrations shook the regime's confidence. A month later, on 9 November, the Berlin Wall was knocked down. East German communism was dead.[37]

The reasons for the fall of Communism in East Germany obviously extend much further than a popular prayer meeting and street demonstrations. But Fuhrer and his fellow protestors are a salutary lesson to Hitchens for whom religion is nothing but poison. In the peace prayer movement, we see Christians and their allies taking a stand against political oppression, but avoiding violence and therefore being more effective. Rather than acting like poison, East German Christians were salt and light to their nation, and in taking such brave and disciplined action, they helped to extract the poison from their nation-the atheist dogma of Leninist-Marxism. Locke and Mayhew would have been proud of them. Perhaps even Hitchens, the devotee of courage, might grudgingly applaud.

Khrushchev's Militant Atheism

The Soviet totalitarian, Stalin, fostered a personality cult. He achieved demigod status in the eyes of his people, both those who believed he was one and those who outwardly held this belief for their safety's sake. Stalin died in 1953 and was succeeded by Nikolai Khrushchev. At a closed session of selected party delegates in 1955, Khrushchev made a long speech denouncing Stalin's political crimes. He charged Stalin's cult of personality as betraying the ideals of the Revolution. The delegates listened in rapt silence, unused to criticism of the Great Leader and once the speech was done, dispersed quietly as no discussion was permitted. Khrushchev's speech did not mention Stalin's repressions before 1934, thus implying that such mass brutality as the forced collectivization of the peasants had been legitimate, and it made no mention either of Khrushchev's culpability in political murder.

37. David Henry, "Leipzig pastor whose 'peace prayers' rallied resistance to communism in the run-up to German reunification", *The Independent*, 8 July 2014.

It also failed to acknowledge that the Great Purge of 1936-8 had mostly affected the masses. The speech instead was concerned with the repression of leading members of the Party and public figures. Perhaps Khrushchev considered the extent of Stalinism's political murders too great for those more accustomed to propaganda than the stark truth. Instead of the cult of personality, Khrushchev intended for the Soviet Union to be governed collectively through regular meetings of the Central Committee and criticism of policy and of self.[38] The leader was no longer a quasi-deity, but *primus inter pares*. The process of de-Stalinization deepened at the Twenty-Second Party Congress in 1961 when public denunciations of Stalin were made. Fittingly for this iconoclastic environment, Stalin's embalmed body was removed from the Mausoleum where it resided next to Lenin. Instead of terror and a personality cult, Khrushchev adopted a popular approach in which he travelled the length and breadth of the Soviet Union talking to peasants and workers as a means of mobilizing them for the task of building communism.[39] The Soviet Union remained a dictatorship, but took the form of an oligarchy with Khrushchev as the head. It was also a militantly atheist dictatorship as shall be seen, something that Hitchens and Dawkins are unprepared to admit has ever existed.

Though Khrushchev's premiership saw a relaxation of the terror that was at the heart of Stalinism, it saw a return of the persecution of Christians which Stalin had suspended to win the Church's support in the Great Fatherland War. As Hosking concludes, Khrushchev wished to revive Communist and atheist militancy.[40] The change in policy towards the Orthodox Church came in 1961 when a synod of bishops under pressure from the Soviet state abolished the parish priests' role as the administrator of the parish and restricted their role to the spiritual. During the next three to four years, over half of Orthodox Church parishes were dispersed and 10,000 churches closed. It was suspected that local Communist activists had infiltrated the parish councils and authorized many of these closures.[41] Most monasteries were closed also. The Pochaev monastery survived because of international protest, but only after the KGB had harassed pilgrims, beaten up some of the monks and consigned others to psychiatric wards for having the delusion of religious belief.[42]

Soviet persecution of Christians of all stripes from the 1920s to the 1980s resulted in many turning their back on their faith. It is estimated that

---

38. Geoffrey Hosking, *A History of the Soviet Union*, pp. 335-337.

39. Ibid., p. 347.

40. Ibid., p.439.

41. Ibid., p. 440.

42. Ibid., p. 441.

80% of adults in 1920 were devout. In the 1980s, the figure was estimated to be between a quarter and a third of adults. Those who retained their faith appeared to be stronger in it. As Christianity did not die out in the Soviet Union, the state selected certain churches for official recognition and limited support on condition that those churches were loyal to the state. Nevertheless, whether it was Stalin's internal atheism/external theocracy or Lenin and Khrushchev's out-and-out militantly atheist dictatorship that was persecuting Christians, it was atheists who were doing the persecuting, and thus Hitchens and Dawkins who are zealous in calling for the Church hierarchy to apologize for historic collusions with Fascism ought to be prepared to apologize to Christians for the murder and imprisonment of their sisters and brothers by Soviet atheists. Of course, Hitchens and Dawkins might protest that Soviet atheists are not their kind of atheists, but if they do, it is legitimate for Christians to say that Fascist sympathizers in the Catholic Church are not their kind of Christian either.

Trotsky: A Strange Case of Hero Worship

Like Hitchens, the famous Bolshevik Leon Trotsky was an atheist.[43] Like Hitchens' rejection of his forebears' Christianity, Trotsky rejected the Judaism to which his parents had only lightly held.[44] Whereas Hitchens has made a name for himself as a journalist, literary critic and anti-theist, Trotsky is best known for being Lenin's second-hand man in the Russian Communist Party that took power in October 1917. In the light of the totalitarian methods that Trotsky used to protect the Revolution and his continuing justifications of its atrocities, one finds the democratic Hitchens' admiration for him a paradox. One also finds in Trotsky further evidence of murderous atheism which Hitchens and Dawkins refuse to admit exists.

When the Bolshevik Party unilaterally took power on the night of 25th-26th October, Lenin was careful to ensure that the government was dominated by the Bolsheviks and their allies; There was to be no socialist coalition government. Rather than proclaim the Congress of Soviets or the Petrograd Soviet as the new government, Lenin identified the Bolsheviks' Military Revolutionary Committee as the sovereign organ.[45] The heart of Bolshevik support was the urban proletariat of Petrograd and many soldiers and sailors, but Bolshevik control spread to the provinces either because the soviets (local committees of workers and peasants) had a Bolshevik majority

43. Robert Conquest, *Trotsky: A Biography*, p. 201.
44. Ibid., p. 17.
45. Hosking, *A History of the Soviet Union*, p.50.

or where the Bolsheviks were in the minority, Red Guards and sympathetic soldiers seized control on their behalf.[46] The executive committee of the All-Russian Congress of Soviets condemned the Bolshevik action as a coup and was replaced by Lenin's Council of People's Commissars (Sovnarkom).[47] By the end of December 1917, the Bolsheviks had extended their control to most of Russia, but there was one problem looming: the summoning of the Constituent Assembly. This was the long promised 'Parliament' whose deputies would determine Russia's government and constitution. Lenin sensed that the Constituent Assembly would not support the Bolshevik revolution, but he did not have the boldness to forbid the elections which his own party had demanded before the Revolution.[48]

The elections took place in November and though the Bolsheviks polled 9.8 million votes and won 168 seats, they came second to the Socialist Revolutionaries who were popular with the peasantry and who gained 15.8 million votes and 380 seats, making them the single largest party. The Bolsheviks permitted the Assembly to meet but interfered with its composition by banning the Liberal Kadet Party which had won seventeen seats in the Assembly. When the Assembly eventually met on 5 January 1918, it did so in the intimidating presence of the Red Guards. When the Bolshevik resolution to recognize their new government was rejected by the Assembly, the Red Guards forced the chairman to adjourn the session and locked the building so that no further meetings could take place. A workers' demonstration in favor of the Assembly was forcibly dispersed by the Red Guards who killed some of the demonstrators in the process.[49]

Hitchens holds democracy in the highest esteem, and yet his exemplar, Trotsky, was one of the leaders of a party that seized power without the mandate of a majority of the people and abolished two democratically elected governing bodies. After the closure of the Constituent Assembly, Trotsky proclaimed triumphantly that Communism had trampelled democracy.[50] When the Left Socialist Revolutionaries resigned from government in March 1918 in protest at the Treaty of Brest-Litovsk, Russia came under the Bolsheviks' single party rule. At that moment the Bolsheviks renamed themselves the Communist Party after the Paris Commune of 1870.[51]

---

46. Ibid., p. 53.
47. Ibid., p. 51.
48. Ibid., p. 54.
49. Ibid., p. 54-55.
50. Russell Tarr, 'Lenin in Power', History Review, Issue 55, September 2006.
51. Hosking, A History of the Soviet Union, p. 62.

To suppress enemies of the Party, the Bolsheviks extended and intensi-
fied their military dictatorship through the creation of the *Cheka*, or to give
its full name, the Extraordinary Commission for the Struggle with Coun-
terrevolution and Sabotage.[52] The Cheka abused viciously human rights
normally preserved in democracies. Hitchens found life in Castro's Cuba
intolerable because of the lack of personal freedom,[53] has denounced the
North Korean dictatorship for its mind-spinning excesses,[54] and has been
arrested by the Czechoslovakian police for attending a dissident meeting,[55]
and yet considers Trotsky his hero who either ordered or approved extraordinary levels of political violence to protect an unelected minority regime.
(It is an interesting question to ask how long Hitchens would have personally survived under Lenin and Trotsky's regime.) Unaccountable to any
soviet or party organ except Sovnarkom which gave it full rein to take the
class war to anti-Communists,[56] the Cheka eventually became responsible
not only for arresting suspects, but putting them on trial, deciding sentences
and executing them if the sentence was death.[57] With the Civil War underway and White monarchist and Czech troops in control of Kazan by August
1918,[58] Communist-held territories entered a violent period of emergency
justice which culminated in the 'Red Terror' which was proclaimed on 5
September. According to the decree, enemies of the Revolution were to be
incarcerated. This was a preventative measure and ensured that class enemies were kept away from the ordinary people.[59] Consequently, by 1922,
there were some 190 camps containing 85000 people. All those involved
in counter-revolutionary activity were to be shot.[60] What in time made the
situation particularly unjust was that proof that a middle or upper-class
person had committed anti-Communist 'crimes' became unnecessary. A
person's social origin alone was enough to convict him or her of treason. As
Latsis, the chairman of the Cheka on the eastern front told his operatives in
November 1918, their task was to exterminate the bourgeoisie, and it was a

52. Ibid., p. 68.

53. Hitchens, *Hitch 22*, pp. 112-113.

54. Christopher Hitchens, 'A Nation of Racist Dwarfs', *Slate*, 1 February 2010.

55. Hitchens, *Hitch 22*, pp. 337-338.

56. Hosking, *A History of the Soviet Union*, p. 68-69.

57. Ibid., p. 69.

58. Ibid., p. 65.

59. Ibid., pp. 69-70.

60. Ibid., p. 71.

person's social class that determined his or her fate rather than evidence.[61] One might coin a term for this: 'classicide'.

Historians do not know for sure how many people the Cheka killed. Robert Conquest has estimated that in total, around 500,000 perished between 1917 and 1923.[62] Though one might attempt to mitigate this grisly statistic by stating that the executions occurred during a civil war when the Communist regime was fighting to stay alive and when the Whites were also committing atrocities, the Communists recognized openly and proudly that terror was an essential part of the revolutionary process. Rather than a sickening necessity, if violence on such a scale was even necessary, brutality and illegal arrests became under the Communists a commonplace method of dealing with all real and suspected class enemies and were evidence of the Communists' revolutionary purity and devotion.[63]

Trotsky defended the Red Terror in his book, *Terror and Communism: A Reply to Kautsky*, published in 1920 during the height of the violence.[64] The German Social Democrat, Karl Kautsky, had argued that a revolution that went down the path of political violence was a revolution that had turned away from its true path and that the Red Terror was a product of the Bolsheviks' bloodthirstiness rather than a military necessity. Trotsky argued, however, that the Red Terror was necessary for the survival of the Bolshevik Government and that such extreme measures have been commonly used historically by revolutionary regimes to survive counter-revolution.[65]

To prove his point, Trotsky compares the Russian Communists' crisis with those of the French Revolution's Jacobins. Foreign troops had entered France with the aim of crushing the Revolution, there were civil wars raging among pro and anti-Revolution French, and in Paris, the center of the Revolution, there were internal enemies seeking to help monarchist forces. The new Soviet Government faced no less a crisis: White armies threatened from the east, south and the west, foreign troops had entered Russia to restore the Tsar, and enemies of the state were engaging in acts of sabotage behind the lines.[66] The bourgeoisie remained a potent threat within Bolshevik territories. So great was their resistance to the Communists, that 'severe measures

---

61. Ibid., p. 70.

62. Ibid., p. 71.

63. Ibid., p. 72.

64. The book is available online at https://www.marxists.org/archive/trotsky/1920/terrcomm/cho4.htm (accessed 24 December 2016 at 08:55).

65. Ibid.

66. Ibid.

of State terror' were required. Imprisonment was not enough according to Trotsky: What were required were executions.[67]

Trotsky mitigates the Red Terror by arguing that because it was so intimidating, only a few people needed actually to be destroyed.[68] This is either extraordinary ignorance, or a shameful denial of reality. Why if such a tactic was so successful is Robert Conquest able to estimate the deaths of half-a-million people? Is it really the case that a few individuals were killed in order to subordinate the majority when Trotsky earlier in his book declares that the revolutionary class will destroy its enemies?[69] Such declarations sound very much like descriptions of mass violence rather than the exemplary execution of a few.

Trotsky was also instrumental in the brutal repression of former allies who had turned against the Communist dictatorship, the most spectacular being the Kronstadt Naval Base uprising in March 1921. The Kronstadt sailors had a long revolutionary tradition. They had formed the first soviet in the 1905 Revolution and had played an essential role in bringing the Bolsheviks to power[70] on the assumption that the Bolsheviks did indeed mean what they said by their slogan, 'All power to the Soviets'. Disillusioned by the Communist Party's centralized control of the soviets which they believed ought to be self-governing, a delegation of sailors met with Petrograd workers on 1 March and asked for new soviet elections by secret ballot. The Communist response was to denounce the Kronstadt sailors as counter-revolutionaries[71] and on 10 March 50,000 of Trotsky's Red Army elite troops captured the Naval Base[72] but only after many casualties had been inflicted on both sides.[73]

In his article, 'Hue and Cry Over Kronstadt'[74] which appeared seventeen years after the rebellion, Trotsky continued to justify the suppression of Kronstadt because it was a counter-revolutionary act. In Trotsky's analysis, the Kronstadt sailors no longer consisted of pure Communists, but had been infiltrated by bourgeois and anarchist elements. Logically speaking, a regime will defend itself from its internal as well as its external enemies and that is Trotsky's logic. But if this much is granted to the Communist regime, it surely is surprising that Hitchens remains faithful to Trotsky who approved of the

67. Ibid.

68. Ibid.

69. Trotsky, *Terrorism and Communism*.

70. Hosking, *A History of the Soviet Union*, p. 90.

71. Ibid., pp. 90-91.

72. Figes, *Revolutionary Russia*, p. 167.

73. Ibid., p. 167.

74. Leon Trotsky, 'Hue and Cry Over Kronstadt', *The New International*, Vol. 4 No. 4, April 1938, pp. 103-106.

summary execution of 2,500 Kronstadt prisoners and of the slow starvation of hundreds of others in the labor camp at Soloviki.[75] Such injustice and capricious cruelty far outweighed the Kronstadt sailors' so-called crimes and speak more of the desire for revenge and the glorification of violence on the part of Trotsky and his Bolshevik colleagues than securing internal stability.

Conclusion

This chapter has covered a wide area of theology and history in refuting Hitchens' anti-theist political philosophy and interpretation of religious history. It has demonstrated how within Christianity a case can be made from Scripture and through the philosophy of Locke for a separation of state and church. It has explored the virtues of Maritain's argument that Christian values are the moral bedrock of democracy. Hitchens likens Christians to slaves to God and His priest-rulers, and yet Christianity provides excellent examples of the theology and praxis of disobedience. Christians played an instrumental role in inciting Hitchens' favorite revolution, the American one, and pursued heroic resistance against the East German Communist state. In both cases, Christians would not bow to taxation without representation or to the Leninist-Marxist state in East Berlin, but rather appealed to the higher authority of Christ. Hitchens attempts to deflect the argument that 20th century atheist dictators have been mass murderers of religious people by arguing that these regimes were theocratic. This is a plainly silly argument for as Peter Hitchens has pointed out, Stalin and Mao Tse Tung and others, though receiving their people's worship, nevertheless remained atheists and had believers murdered because they refused to abandon their worship of God. Moreover, the atheist dictator Khrushchev never sought to be glorified as a god and yet persecuted the Russian churches savagely. Hitchens' admiration for Trotsky is paradoxical when one considers Trotsky's totalitarian beliefs and behavior in Communist Russia. It is therefore possible to turn Hitchens' thinking on its head. Christianity, rather than the progenitor of theocracies, is, and ought to be if it is not, on the side of individual and political freedom, democracy, and the accountability of rulers to their people and to God. Atheist secularism on the other hand has demonstrated through the French, Russian and Chinese Revolutions how easy it is for it to fall into the trap of deifying political parties, states, and their leaders.

---

75. Figes, *Revolutionary Russia*, p. 167.

6

Four Responses to Hitchens'
Moral Philosophy and Anti-theodicy

Introduction

THE PURPOSE OF THIS chapter is to respond to Hitchens' moral philosophy and anti-theodicy with new lines of criticism. First, Hitchens regards certain moral values as good whatever people think of them and that these moral values have a natural origin within human evolution rather than in divine provenance. He also regards human beings as having intrinsic worth. On the contrary, this chapter will argue that Hitchens' view that the origins of that behavior we call good lies within the evolutionary process can only lead so far as moral pragmatism and relativism. To provide an objective basis for his moral code in which values are good in themselves, a moral principle that stands outside of humanity and nature would have to be invoked, and this worryingly for anti-theists takes us dangerously in the direction of a non-human intelligence and moral sensitivity. One of Hitchens' favorite philosophers was John Mackie who considered from an atheist perspective how objective morality might exist and presents two ways: through the apprehension of the Form of the Good according to Plato and the existence externally of something within moral situations that demands a moral response *a la* Samuel Clark. Though these are possible solutions, this chapter will argue that the Christian God provides the supreme ground for objective morality. It will show also that the humanist value of the intrinsic value of humans to which Hitchens subscribes is best guaranteed by the eternal value assigned to humans by God rather than the fluctuating value and no value often assigned to humans by other humans. This is not a moral argument for the existence of God, but it counters Hitchens' anti-theism in that it provides a reason for the desirability of God's existence. Second, it will argue that if there is no absolute reason to accept Hitchens' objective sounding discourse as an alternative to religious morality, there is no reason to reject those non-religious moral alternatives that Hitchens also rejects. We shall demonstrate this with reference to Nietzsche's moral philosophy which Hitchens censured as undemocratic. Third, this chapter will respond in diverse ways to Hitchens' Second Problem of Evil by providing reasons why evils and horrendous evils[1] co-exist with God. Finally, it will demonstrate inconsistencies in Hitchens' position regarding natural evil, or the problem of pain through an analysis of his attitude to his terminal illness and provide a possible reason as to why God might permit natural evil.

The Contradictions between Hitchens' Objective Ethics and His Metaethics

In chapter four we saw how Hitchens' assumption that humans are free to choose morally makes no sense within Hitchens' materialist universe where everything, including humans, is nothing more than matter in motion determined by those forces described by science's laws. In a materialist universe, a person might be responsible for a moral action in the sense that s/he is the one who has performed that action, but s/he cannot be held to be responsible in a praiseworthy or guilty way. For Hitchens' moral philosophy and anti-theodicy to be possible in the first place, Hitchens must assert the paradox of free-will and moral culpability within a deterministic universe.

Some biologists have expressed a skepticism regarding the extent to which natural selection can explain human behavior, which would include moral behavior. Can evolutionary force really explain human moral behavior? Dennis Noble, for example, has pointed out that the genome and the brain are information systems used by the organism rather than the determinants of the organism's behaviour.[2] He goes on to liken the human genome to an immense organ. The organ does not perform music of its own accord but requires an organist to do it; it does not compose music of its own accord but requires a composer for that.[3] Noble is insinuating that some grand intelligence is required to make the process work which, of course, naturalists such as Dawkins deny is necessary. The biologists Jerry Fodor and Massimo Piatelli-Palmarini, neither of whom identify as having

---

1. Marilyn McCord Adams, 'Horrendous Evils and the Goodness of God', in ed., McCord Adams and Merrihew Adams, *The Problem of Evil*, p. 210.

2. Dennis Noble, *The Music of Life*, p. 130.

3. Ibid., p. 32.

a religious belief, have expressed their disquiet over the way in which natural selection has spread from evolutionary biology to other disciplines as an explanatory mechanism when the evidence for the rationality of such an application to disciplines as psychology and philosophy, remains flimsy.[4] In their view, therefore, the nature of morality is not necessarily explained by natural selection as Hitchens would have us believe. Whether or not natural selection can bear the weight of such an explanation, it is nevertheless the case that if we run Hitchens' argument that morality is the product of evolutionary forces, we shall see that his argument becomes problematic.

The problem Hitchens has is that the argument to the evolutionary origins of morally good behavior cannot avoid invoking a justifying transcendent principle outside of the material world that evolutionary forces and their products, human beings, inhabit. Human evolution has favored cooperation, paternal investment, and altruism which we call good things, but it also has favored what we call evil things. Michael Price names xenophobia as a probable adaptation and violence as a psychological adaptation.[5] If such bad psychological adaptations exist within humans, it is because they confer some reproductive and survival value. They are no less important than cooperation, parental investment, and altruism in securing the propagation of our genes. To praise one set of psychological adaptations over another set therefore seems to be contrary to the amoral nature of natural selection in which those behaviors, whatever they may be, that lead to survival and reproduction are retained as part of the disposition of a species. To do so requires a person to stand outside of the evolutionary process and make that judgement. The question therefore is on what does that person stand? This is at first seemingly not a problem for Hitchens, but the problem for him becomes apparent when one begins the process of finding that alternative ground on which to stand. Is there anything else in the anti-theist world on which objective values can be founded by which certain psychological adaptations are judged good and certain judged bad? Such a question might after all be redundant in a purely material world such as the one Hitchens believes he inhabits. If everything is molecules, it is impossible to see how molecules can be called morally good or morally bad. But if we ignore this objection for the time being, assume that it is possible for values to exist in a purely material world and earnestly seek the ground of unchanging values, we see that we have limited options on the anti-theist point of view, none

4. Jerry Fodor and Massimo Piatelli-Palmarini, 'Survival of the Fittest Theory', *New Scientist*, 6 February 2010, pp. 28-31.

5. Michael E. Price, 'How Evolutionary Science Can Make Us Morally Better' at https:// www.psychologytoday.com/blog/darwin-eternity/201501/how-evolution-science-can-make-us-morally-better (accessed 19 November 2016 at 10:47).

of which satisfy. Where in the materialists' world is there an unchanging moral value to hand? The materialists' world is what it is and no 'ought' can be derived from it. If what we think ought to happen and not to happen is a matter of human nature or culture, which it has to be if the godless universe is an 'is' and not an 'ought', or does not contain 'oughts', it is hard to see how the different moral convictions of individuals and cultures over such issues as capital punishment and abortion can provide a stable ground on which to base our values. If it is argued that most humans and human cultures agree on certain moral principles and that that majority constitutes a moral ground, that is a working principle but no moral argument at all, for the unchanging rightness and wrongness of certain values and behaviors do not depend upon how many people recognize that rightness and wrongness. Once everyone in Christian Europe did indeed think that the immolation of those convicted of witchcraft was an act of mercy, but the enormous majority do not think that now. If there is no objective morality in the world, or inside humans, then if we wish to posit an objective morality, it can only be done on the basis of something beyond this world, but that of course is not the conclusion the anti-theists wish to draw.

Another way in which arguing that morality is objective but tracing its origins to evolution leads to relativism can be seen in what Stephen Jay Gould has proposed regarding evolution: that if evolution were re-played, it might be possible to get different results in terms of the species that emerge.[6]

It is conceivable that human beings might have been different in some way. Perhaps human beings might have evolved to be more physically powerful, less dependent as infants and solitary like tigers. They are still human in the sense that they are capable of sophisticated thought processes, creativity, and speech acts, but instead of using these gifts to form and sustain groups, their cleverness, ingenuity, and verbosity are exclusively tools by which to form temporary, loose alliances, outwit other humans in the competition for resources and seduce mating partners. Such humans would therefore not prize as highly as they now do cooperation, altruism, and trustworthiness. Self-reliance, independence, and suspicion would be highly prized. Therefore, there would be a reversal of moral priorities based on a different evolutionary result. Now Gould's speculation about re-running evolution producing different results might be wrong and he himself does not say whether he thinks that the same or different results would transpire, but his thought experiment places an interesting question mark over Hitchens' desire to trace the origins of the values he likes back to natural selection which might have thrown up a different set of values as the core values of humanity.

6. S. J. Gould, *Wonderful Life*, pp. 48-50.

The Plausibility and Necessity of Objective Morality

Though Hitchens speaks in terms of universal moral axioms, he fails to provide the universal, objective grounds for his moral philosophy. What alternative way of finding that ground is there for what Hitchens knew intuitively, but did not demonstrate philosophically? To demonstrate how objective morality is plausible and necessary, this chapter's next section will take John Mackie's moral philosophy as its starting point.

Mackie argues that there are no such things as objective categorical imperatives based on a kind of Argument from Queerness. The argument runs as follows: moral values are so weird it is very unlikely that they exist.[7] If they did exist, they would be unlike anything else in the material world.[8]

Mackie considers what instantiated moral properties would have to be like and concludes that they would have to have one of two properties. (1) The Good would have to have a special attraction in the way that Plato thought it had. If some good thing were somehow a participant in the Form of the Good, it would motivate a person to seek that good thing. (2) Alternatively, Samuel Clarke argues a situation would have a demand for a certain action built into it in some way. What is weird about these examples for Mackie is that in Plato's example, the weirdness lies in the recognition of the properties of the Good which reside in the good thing which *causally* induce motivation. In Clarke's example, the bizarreness resides in properties that *demand* action (and thus motivation). In other words, what is queer is the claim of morality to transcend all institutions."[9]

Christ as Superior to the Form of the Good

Mackie finds objective morality too bizarre to be real, but he does not stop to consider whether the very queerness of objective morality which resembles nothing else in the universe is because the source of that morality is indeed unlike anything in the universe, namely God who is immaterial. As we shall now see, God, whether He exists or not, would be a superior extra-world source for instantiated objective morality than Plato's Forms.

In Plato's theory, instantiated objective categorical imperatives would be mimicking shadows and momentary portrayals of the Form of the Good. Contrary to the Form, Christianity presents its belief in a Divine Person. In

---

7. Joyce, Richard, "Moral Anti-Realism", The Stanford Encyclopedia of Philosophy (Fall 2015 Edition), ed. Edward N. Zalta, at https://www.plato.stanford.edu/archives/fall2015/entries/moral-anti-realism/ (accessed 21 April 2016 at 09:11).

8. Mackie, *Inventing Right and Wrong*, p. 37.

9. Ibid., p. 59.

the matter of perfect goodness, Christians do not look to a Form of the Good, but to the nature of a Divine Person. On Plato's theory, instantiated objective morality is but a shadowy portrayal of the Form of the Good known only in its fullness by philosophers. The perfect goodness in the form of the Divine Person is known through the behavior of that Person known by all who met Him in His incarnation and laid bare for us in the Gospels. His goodness is known by those He has redeemed (John 10:14) who will at the Consummation know Him 'face to face' (1 Cor. 13:12). The unredeemed will know His goodness at the time of His judgement of them (Rev. 20:11-13). The knowledge of the Good is restricted to a privileged few on Platonism, but on Christianity it is known by the redeemed and will be known by all.

If the Form of the Good exists, the good that humans do are but pale representations or shadowy representations of the Form of the Good. On Christianity, the good that people do frequently is imperfect, impure versions of the good that God would do. X may give money to a charity assisting mendicants and homeless people, but he may do this for a variety of motives, both good and selfish. He might feel compassion for the people he is assisting, but he may also wish to be known for his compassion to garner votes in local elections. He might be performing his altruistic works to assuage a conscience troubled by his surreptitious criminal activities. But unlike the good caused by the Forms, Christianity regards the good done by people as being truly some good rather than being an appearance of the Form of the Good. On Christianity, people can be genuinely good if their actions accord with what is objectively good. There are several reasons for this. First, for humans to be fully the moral beings that God has made them, they must be able to perform moral actions rather than create appearances of the good. When X does that which is good, that which is good within what s/he has done is a fully morally good thing and is aligned with what God considers as the good thing to do in that situation. Second, God is affected by human moral behavior to reward it, forbearing with it and to punish it. If human moral behavior were only the appearance of the Form of the Good, it is difficult to see how God could have such powerful reactions to human moral behavior. Third, it is possible that the Judeo-Christian belief that humans are created in the image of God refers to humans as genuinely moral agents responsible for substantive good. (The image of God is marred in a human being when s/he does what is evil.) Fourth, the incarnation of God as a man called Jesus Christ who was morally perfect and who did the works of the Father reveals that human moral action has genuine substance that matters rather than the appearance of a Form.

God as the Best Guarantor of Intrinsic Human Worth

What then of Mackie's second way in which in a materialist universe instantiated moral values would appear too weird, namely Clarke's notion that in a situation there exists a moral demand somehow?

Let us take what might be called the moral situation which is a situation in which a human being feels obliged to come to a moral decision. Suppose X witnesses Z hitting Y with a stick for the fun of it. Y does not want Z to do this to him, but is unable to stop Z. X feels obliged to do something to help Y. What is it in that situation that makes X feel like this? Where is there the demand as Clarke thinks there ought to be if we are to speak of instantiated moral values, but which Mackie thinks are too bizarre? At the most fundamental level, there are movements of matter. What raises the movements of matter to a moral situation is the presence of two human beings, one of whom is being beaten and does not wish to be and one who condemns this beating. For both conclusions, there has to be more than consciousness: There has to be moral consciousness. Y may be conscious that his beating is morally wrong; but even if he cannot formulate the idea that his beating is morally wrong because he is too young and merely cries out in pain, X is present and condemns the beating. If there was no one to witness the beating for fun, it is the case that when we hear about such beatings, we are appalled. There is the human being who is acting in the sense that Z is beating Y for fun; there is Y who does not wish to be beaten and condemns what is being done to him; and there is X who condemns the beating. It could, however, be conceived that what is happening is an entirely natural thing and nothing is being instantiated. There is the movement of matter and there is human nature which has evolved a conscience and a sense of pity for the maltreated. A serious problem arises if what is happening to Y is within, for instance, the context of Nazism. If Y is Jewish and Z a member of the SS, X might approve of Y's beating, or be beaten himself if his sympathies were known. If Y feels the moral demand to help Y, T might feel the moral demand to help Z because she believes that Y is a member of a race that seeks global domination. The moral demands felt in this situation might conflict and so on this basis there is a relativism which is not the instantiation of a moral absolute. Secular humanists like Hitchens might argue that there are human rights which are forever morally correct regardless of what ideologies the human race concocts. Therefore, even if within a society of Nazis, it is regarded that it is always right to beat up Jews, it is really the case that in all situations it is wrong to beat Jews. But this brings us back to the question: What is it in any moral situation that demands absolutely that certain actions are deemed right and others wrong? If it is the human being in the situation who is being maltreated who is in him/ herself the demand for the morally correct action such as not to be beaten for fun and for the benevolent intervention on the part of others, then for that demand always to be morally true, that human being has to possess an everlasting and absolute value which can be recognized by other humans and which is intrinsic to their being human.

The problem is that for humans to have absolute value, it requires more than the recognition of other humans who as we have seen with our example of the Nazis often fail to recognize this value and often assign lesser value or no value at all to certain humans. The human race has been prolifically ingenious in creating political and economic systems that deny the absolute value of humans. Slavery is an excellent example of this moral degradation. So too is human sacrifice. Even in the West where human rights are frequently referred to, employees are known as human resources and no longer as personnel. If a society were run by the likes of Nicolas Walter whose secular humanism is a philosophical and ethical position that places an emphasis upon the value of human beings and their capacity to use reason and creativity to solve their problems,[10] human value would be protected, but unfortunately, many societies are not led by Nicolas Walter types, but by dictators who see their people as resources. Moreover, as a finite being, Walter cannot legislate everlastingly the value of humans. What is required is a source of human value that is independent of humanity and which is itself absolute and is unchanging in the absolute value it places on humans. Such a source is the Christian God who creates humans for His sheer pleasure in their being humans and for their sheer pleasure in being themselves and no other, and who values human beings everlastingly and as highly as He does Himself, seen in the giving of the Son for their redemption (John 3:16). There can be no greater value placed on humans than this, and it is Christianity that assigns this value. In a created universe, the Christian God is the guarantor of human worth. Therefore, in a moral situation the human being is an instantiation of the value God places on all human be- ings and it is the human being who by his or her presence demands a moral response which is in keeping with an everlastingly and totally valued being.

A Summary So Far

Hitchens posits a moral discourse that is objective and yet his evolution- ary metaethics lead him into moral relativism. Mackie regards instantiated

10. See Nicolas Walter, *Humanism-What's in the Word*, for a detailed discussion of the word humanism.

objective morality as too bizarre to be real but suggests two ways in which instantiated objective morality might be conceived: Plato's Form of the Good and some quality inherent in a moral situation that demands moral action. We have demonstrated that God is a superior source of objective morality than the Form of the Good, and it is the intrinsic worth of humanity as guaranteed by God that explains the sense of there being moral demands within the moral situation. If there is no objective morality within Hitchens' universe, it is impossible to see how we would justify picking his democratic convictions over those of Friedrich Nietzsche's contempt for the herd. It is to this problem that we now turn.

The Unanswerable Challenge of Nietzsche

Hitchens was interested in the works of the German philosopher Nietzsche, for on the testimony of Carol Blue, when Hitchens was admitted to hospital in Houston with pneumonia and unable to speak because he was intubated, he wrote down the names of writers whose books he wanted Blue to bring him from their guesthouse. One of those names was Nietzsche.[11] It is worthy of note therefore that despite this interest and even though both Nietzsche and Hitchens are famous (even infamous) anti-theists and anti-religionists, Hitchens does not deliberate in any developed way on Nietzsche's moral philosophy. At most there is a brief discussion of Nietzsche in Hitchens' *Morality*.[12] There is too a gnomic dismissal of Mencken as being too much an admirer of Nietzsche in *God is Not Great*.[13] Hitchens nevertheless knew Nietzschean scholarship well enough to avoid conflating Nietzschean philosophy with Social Darwinism and Nazism.[14] Apart from this, there is nothing. Nietzsche does not even merit a mention in Hitchens' cornucopia of atheist and antitheist writings, *the Portable Atheist*. Hitchens distances himself from Nietzsche because though both men despised what they understood to be Christian morality and did not see the 'death of God' as necessarily leading to nihilism, Hitchens says he found Nietzsche's anti-democratic views unsettling,[15] which is surely an understatement.

This section of the chapter will contend that Nietzsche is of enormous importance to Hitchens because Nietzsche's moral philosophy poses an

11. Carol Blue, 'The Last Word: Christopher Hitchens' widow on his life, his work, and his death', *Slate*, 27 August 2012.

12. Hitchens, *Morality*, pp. 60-64.

13. Hitchens, *God is Not Great*, p.250.

14. Hitchens, *Mortality*, pp. 61-62.

15. Ibid., p. 61.

unanswerable question to Hitchens: With the demise of religious morality, which morality ought to replace it, Nietzsche's revaluation of values or
Hitchens' liberal secular democracy? The question is made unanswerable
for Hitchens cannot provide an objective ground for his values.

To understand why this question is for Hitchens unanswerable, it is
important first to identify the methodology that will be used with regards
to Nietzschean primary texts and scholarship and second, to understand
why Nietzsche thinks that there had to be a revaluation of values whereas
Hitchens does not. Once the matters have been settled, we shall proceed to
the decisive discussion: the normative values that both thinkers proposed
and why there is no basis on Hitchens' own terms to prefer his moral code
to that of Nietzsche's.

To deploy Nietzsche against Hitchens is problematic because it raises
the question of which Nietzsche will be deployed. In Ashley Woodward's
text, *Interpreting Nietzsche*, the wide-ranging conclusions of thirteen prominent philosophers as to what Nietzsche's philosophy is are presented to us.
My method consequently is to identify and examine within Nietzsche's writings relevant moral expositions to the argument with Hitchens whilst being
guided by prominent scholars of Nietzsche where there is consensus among
those scholars as to what Nietzsche's moral philosophy is.

Nietzsche's ethics of beyond good and evil and Hitchens' moral con-
servatism begin with the rejection of belief in any god and religious morality.
In particular, they reject Christian values.[16] Both view religious morality and
priestly authority as a cause of sickness in human beings. Nietzsche identifies
this sickness' form as neuroticism.[17] Hitchens calls religion a poison capable of
destroying all enjoyment of life. Apart from this moment of congruence between the two, there is much divergence in their conclusions. As we have seen in
his critique of the New Testament in chapter two, Hitchens opposes Christianity
because it oppresses the weak. One of the best examples of this in Hitchens'
work is, as has been seen in chapter two, the psychological, physical, and sexual
abuse of children by the Church. This rightly appalls Hitchens. On the other
hand, Nietzsche interprets Christianity as a dogma that is founded on moral
values that favor the weak over the strong and seek to bind the instincts for
conquest of the strong through the enervating effect of the conscience.[18]

16. Friedrich Nietzsche, *The Genealogy of Morals* (New York: Dover Publications,
2003), p. 15.

17. Ibid.

18. Friedrich Nietzsche, *Twilight of the Idols with the Antichrist and Ecce Homo*,
trans. Antony M. Ludovici, p. 97.

For Nietzsche, the death of belief is a crisis for though belief in God diminishes value of humanity,[19] the death of God means a complete loss of all human significance.[20] The death of God meant also the collapse of Christian morality for he could not conceive of Christian morality surviving the death of its God. This was a crisis for it threatened Europe with what he called nihilism.[21] Though commentators such as Michael Gillespie have made a strong case that Nietzsche misunderstood nihilism, commentators from Heidegger to Danto have argued that nihilism is a central theme of Nietzsche's philosophy. To illustrate this, Nietzsche wrote his famous parable 'The Madman' that tells the story of a man who though it is a bright morning rushes into the market place with a lantern and to the derision of those there, cries over and over that he is seeking God before concluding that God has been murdered. The Madman's conclusion is that without God, humanity's values are lost and that the cold night of nihilism is therefore closing in.[22] The Madman, Walter Kaufmann declares, is Nietzsche himself: A prophetic voice who had realized the death of God before anyone else and who was already suffering the misery of that godless existence.[23] To escape nihilism or the devaluation of values was Nietzsche's great philosophical problem.[24] To solve nihilism, Nietzsche appears to have two undesirable choices: either to assert God's existence and deny this world of its ultimate significance, or deny the existence of God and deny everything of any value and meaning.[25]

For Hitchens there is no crisis but rather liberation. As Hitchens can see no good at all coming from God's existence and belief in His existence, it is best that God either as a being or an idea does not exist. As established in chapter two, Hitchens believes that religious moral codes are baleful, and so it is hard to see what sort of moral crisis might emerge if such ethical codes were consigned to history's ash can. In chapter two of this dissertation also, it was demonstrated that Hitchens believed that human decency was encoded by the evolutionary process and rather than abide by the preachments of a priestly caste, humans ought to follow the promptings of their conscience. As the knowledge and desire to do what is good is naturally present in the great majority of people, the loss of unnatural religious values does not create a nihilistic space but creates a secular space in which

19. Walter Kaufmann *Nietzsche: Philosopher, Psychologist, Antichrist*, p. 101.

20. Ibid.

21. Ibid., p. 101.

22. Friedrich Nietzsche *The Gay Science*, trans. Walter Kaufmann, pp.181-2.

23. Kaufmann, *Nietzsche: Philosopher, Psychologist, Antichrist*, p. 98.

24. Ibid., p. 101.

25. Ibid.

the exercise of natural goodness can take place. Hitchens, therefore, does not mind the retention of certain values of which he approves, but which are Christian values, for these values pre-date Christianity, are natural to human beings and therefore can survive Christianity's demise. The moral crisis therefore lies not within the loss of Christianity and its values, but within the continued influence of Christian moralities that cause so much ignorance and suffering and the theocracies that enforce them.

Nietzsche's answer on the other hand is to argue that as existence without God lacks any inherent meaning and objective values, the logical response is neither to assert that God exists and hope for otherworldly redemption nor collapse into nihilism because God does not exist, but to create a new set of values.[26] Whether such a logical response is made depends upon the value-creating agent and his capacity to avoid paralysis in the face of the great task of creating values despite an inherently valueless existence. Such a value-creating response in the face of the terrifying nature of reality as meaningless suffering and the devaluation of the highest values that have hitherto defended against meaninglessness is possible as it was managed, according to Nietzsche, by the ancient Greeks living during the time of Homer and the pre-Platonic philosophers. The highest form of the Greek capacity to see reality for what it is-a destroyer of individuals-comes in the form of Attic theatre. Though witnessing the wanton annihilation of heroes that drove them into a Dionysian delirium, the ancient Greeks emerged with an affirmation of the will and the drive to create new values evident in their construction of gods, philosophies, and personalities. This Nietzsche contrasts with the life-denying and life-escaping pessimism of Schopenhauer and the false consolations of religions' paradises.[27]

In seeking a revaluation of values, Nietzsche anticipates two directions, one of which is anathema to him, the other a glorious future of which he believed he was the prophet. The first is the well-trodden road of the herd-man which dominated, according to Nietzsche, the Europe of his day, and it is likely that this is how Nietzsche would have interpreted Hitchens' moral philosophy.[28] The herd morality is one which exalts those values that make an individual useful to the herd. These virtues consist of such things as kindness and sympathy.[29] In Nietzsche's formulation, one sees reflected back Hitchens' metaethics and normative ethics. Morality has been preserved

26. Wilkerson, 'Friedrich Nietzsche (1844-1900)', at https://www.iep.utm.edu/nietzsche/ (accessed 22 October 2018 at 13:05).

27. Ibid. See also Friedrich Nietzsche, *Ecce Homo*, trans. Anthony M. Ludovici, pp. 70-71.

28. Ibid.,

29. Friedrich Nietzsche, *Beyond Good and Evil*, trans. Marion Faber, p. 86.

by natural selection, for those humans capable of cooperating sufficiently with others have the greatest chance of survival and therefore the greatest chance of passing on their moral sense to their offspring. Though Hitchens personally was not always moderate or modest, his advocacy of rights and responsibilities is a form of public spirit, benevolence, and concern. His aversion to those who talk loudly in restaurants into their mobile phones is a protest at their lack of consideration. Underlying all is the belief that people have equal rights, equal responsibilities (depending though upon their moral maturity), equal responsibilities and the capacity for sympathy, the ability to feel for others.

Nietzsche disdains egalitarianism in favor of a simple hierarchy in which two categories of human exist: the slaves destined to make themselves useful by serving[30] and those destined to govern because of their intelligence and strength.[31] The vast majority, or the herd-men and their morality, are condemned by Nietzsche for they are degenerates who oppose great individuals who might upset their quotidian lives;[32] yet it is these great types who are needed more than the herd, for it is they who will have the capacity, like the Homeric Greeks, to face once again the horror of meaningless existence and create values.[33]

Here too one finds the division between Hitchens and Nietzsche that Hitchens recognized in his radio interview. It is in the common masses as an alternative to real leaders that one finds the origin of democracy,[34] the system that Hitchens prized, and Nietzsche despised. Whereas for Hitchens, the only solution left after the failed socialist revolutions of the Soviet Union, China and Cuba[35] and the failure of the EU to create a viable democratic constitution[36] is the fruit of the American Revolution and its democracy founded on the Bill of Rights,[37] for Nietzsche, whose target of censure was European democracy (though American democracy would not have impressed him either), democracy was the child of Christianity.[38] What unites demagogues is

30. Ibid., p. 55.

31. Ibid., p. 54.

32. Wilkerson, 'Friedrich Nietzsche (1844-1900).'

33. Ibid.

34. Nietzsche, *Beyond Good and Evil*, p. 86.

35. Ibid.

36. Christopher Hitchens, 'An Anglosphere Future', *City Journal*, 2007.

37. Hitchens, *Why Orwell Matters*, p. 105.

38. Nietzsche, *Beyond Good and Evil*, p. 90.

their fierce opposition to exceptional human beings.[39] Democracy, Nietzsche thunders, renders humans average and therefore useless.[40]

Where then is Nietzsche taking us that Hitchens will not and cannot? He is taking us to meet through his prose and poetry the future's exceptional men who will reevaluate values in the cold shadows of God's death. The past provided over-comers of nihilism such as the pre-Platonic Greeks and Napoleon.[41] He also uses the term Ubermensch which has been translated as the Supermen and the Overmen. What values will they subscribe to? Nietzsche seems more prepared to say what they will not value rather than what they will, as if to pry into the counsels of these great men undermines their greatness. The noble ones will reject the commonplace and embrace a strict hierarchy with themselves as the top.[42]

They will also feel no compassion for others or to themselves even.[43] Rather, they will stimulate suffering as the means to greatness.[44] Even cruelty Nietzsche considers as the foundation of great human cultures and knowledge, and so the free spirits will be cruel and therefore the harbingers and teachers of greater knowledge than Europe had hitherto known.

Moreover, they will be stimulated by the feeling of power. In contrast to Hitchens' values which seek the other person's good, in the second aphorism of *The Anti-Christ*, Nietzsche declares that the value of human actions is not to be measured by the goodness they do others. He writes that what is good is that which augments power and what enervates is bad.[45]

The greatest power of all, according to Nietzsche, is the capacity to command oneself and surpass oneself.[46] Therefore, the commanders of humanity will be commanders of themselves first whereas the weaker types will choose the easier path, which is to obey. The desire to command nevertheless is in the hearts of all people for according to Zarathustra who has examined the human heart, wherever he found humans, he found the desire to have and express power.[47] Those with the greatest vitality, the Overmen, will have this excess of life and this capacity to over-reach even themselves.

39. Ibid., p. 90.

40. Ibid.

41. Ibid., p. 86.

42. Robert C. Holub, 'Introduction' to *Beyond Good and Evil*, p. xix.

43. Ibid.

44. Ibid., p. 117.

45. Nietzsche, *Twilight of the Idols with The Anti-Christ and Ecce Homo*, p. 95.

46. Nietzsche, *Thus Spake Zarathustra* at https:www.nietzsche.thefreelibrary.com/ Thus-Spake-Zarathustra/36-1 (accessed 15 April 2017 at 13:27)

47. Ibid.

Two men, starting from the same point of anti-theism and anti-religion-ism, have ended up drawing opposite conclusions as to what moral values ought to replace those of Christianity. Nietzsche, a philosopher in exile from humanity and hardly read in his lifetime, concludes that with the loss of Christianity came the loss of its moral values, and so creators of value, the strong men of culture who will not be paralyzed in the face of creating value without any grounds on which to base them, will get to work, ignoring the rights and institutions of the masses as enshrined in democracy and socialism, to produce an ethics of suffering, cruelty, hierarchy and the abundant expression of the will to power, with the greatest value that of self-mastery. Hitchens, on the other hand, one of the most famous anti-theists of his generation, seeks to convince his audiences that they can know and do what is good and what is bad without the aid of religion because conscience and cooperation have been embedded by natural selection. Human beings are therefore sufficiently good naturally and therefore there is no chance of the moral collapse Nietzsche anticipated with the eclipse of God and religion. What threatens civilization is egregious religious values that sanction genocide, oppose scientific advance, and declare that a nuclear holocaust is not a problem because the good have the afterlife to look forward. It is in everyone's interests that religion ceases to have the influence that it does. In Hitchens' eyes, it is equality, democracy, and personal freedom of all that are the highest values.

The problem that faces Hitchens is the challenge of convincing us that his moral way is morally better than that of Nietzsche. Where is there the principle on which to decide? From a materialist perspective, which Hitchens claims to adhere to, there are no moral values that exist within the physical world; There is only matter. That was the starting point to Mackie's view that transcendent morality would be queer within the world. To describe what there is, as science does in a superlative way, is not tantamount to saying how things ought to be. As we know full well, the universe might have been a different place, and so conglomerations of matter are fascinating contingencies. In fact, the universe might not have been at all and value-valuing creatures such as humans nowhere to be seen.

So, from where does Hitchens' sense of moral rightness come? If the ethical standard does not lie within the material world and certainly does not emanate from a transcendent realm in Hitchens' view, it can only come from within humanity. But as we have seen this is an impossible argument. Both the good and the bad sit alongside each other within human nature, both having been retained by natural selection, and to distinguish them as a good and bad requires a principle that stands outside of humanity and the natural world. If Hitchens praises the altruism of his species, Nietzsche celebrates the pitilessness of the elite, something that on the basis of evolutionary psychology is no less selected. We therefore have no resource from Hitchens' perspective with which to reject objectively Nietzsche's philosophy. We might reject it because we do not like it, or that the majority opposes it, but Hitchens has never allowed other people's feelings or majority views to force him to abandon his moral position.

If Hitchens saw fit to reject criticism aimed at him by the majority and the consensus, Nietzsche is no less deserving of the same right to reject Hitchens and the liberal consensus' condemnation of his anti-democratic philosophy.

The Problems of Evil

Hitchens presents two kinds of problem of evil. These do not seek in the traditional sense to disprove the existence deductively nor to maintain probably that God does not exist. The first problem is the problem of the evil of God's existence. Hitchens' anti-theism proposes that if God did exist, that would be an evil, for God is a tyrant. It is therefore a good thing that there is no evidence that God exists. Chapter four has refuted the proposition that God is a tyrant, so this first problem of evil ought not to detain us. The second problem grants for the sake of argument the existence of God to show the impossibility of believing as Christians traditionally do that God is simultaneously all-powerful, all-knowing, and all-good. Hitchens' argument runs as follows: God has allowed humanity to suffer for thousands of years, only then finally to intervene to help humanity two thousand years ago through the advent of Christ. Hitchens cannot see what justified reasons there could be for God being tardy with His salvation. Surely if God is a God of love, complete knowledge, and infinite power, He would have done something about humanity's suffering long before the advent of Christ?[48]

In his catalogue of sufferings, Hitchens includes both moral evil and natural evil, or the problem of pain. The sorts of evil and suffering Hitchens has in mind when he impugns divine non-intervention are the most serious of kinds and which appear to have no rhyme or reason for their existence. He refers to humans as victims of predation, warfare, disease and the dangers of childbirth.[49] He seeks to present the greatest challenge to Christian belief in an all-good God by presenting the worst of suffering and is using examples of what Marilyn McCord Adams calls 'horrendous evil'.[50] Adams

---

48. 'Christopher Hitchens: "Heaven watches with folded arms"', You Tube, 25 February 2013 at https://youtube.com/watch?v=gQgHds6eIJo (accessed 23 July 2016 at 14:27).

49. Ibid.

50. Marilyn McCord Adams, 'Horrendous Evils and the Goodness of God', ed. McCord Adams and Merrihew Adam, *The Problem of Evil*, p. 211.

defines horrendous evils as those that seem to render a person's life worth-less.[51] Her examples of horrendous evil contain among many things such evils as cannibalism and genocide.[52] Hitchens, one would imagine, would not thus far disagree.

Hitchens' argument might also be classified as a 'noseeum' argument: First, he can see no good reason for divine non-intervention; second, he can see no good reason for the evil and suffering permitted by God's non-intervention, therefore there probably are no good reasons for God's non-intervention. Therefore, if there are no good reasons for non-intervention and evil and suffering, God cannot be omnibenevolent, or God does not possess to the maximum the traditional theist qualities of omniscience and omnipotence to pursue the good even if He is omnibenevolent. The follow-ing grid depicts the sorts of god that on Hitchens' reckoning Christians have as options in the light of evil and suffering.

51. Ibid., p.211.
52. Ibid., pp. 211-212.

Omnibenevolent	Omniscient	Omnipotent	Consequence
Yes	Yes	No.	This god is in the painful position of being all good and knowing the totality of evil and suffering in the world, and yet has not managed to find a way of doing something about it until He sent His Son Christ two thousand years ago. Despite His intervention through Christ, there are still many evils and sufferings which reflect His less than omnipotence.
Yes	No	No	This kind of god is all good, but his less than perfect knowledge and power is of the degree that has prevented him from intervening earlier than Christ's advent.
No	Yes	Yes	This is a most dangerous deity to deal with. This god has the capacity and knowledge to intervene much earlier than He has, but his mixed moral nature has meant that he has been torn between intervention and disinterest. Two thousand years ago, he decided to intervene.
No	No	Yes	A dangerous deity also but his capacity for intervention against evil and suffering has been retarded by his mixed moral nature and his less than perfect knowledge of when and how to intervene.

Omnibenevolent	Omniscient	Omnipotent	Consequence
No	Yes	No	A less than completely good god of all knowledge would have a perfect knowledge of the good and evil he could do, but the evil side of his nature and his less than perfect power could retard his capacity to intervene.
Yes	No	Yes	This god would have the perfect will to do good and prevent and solve evil and suffering, but his lack of complete knowledge limits his understanding of how to do this, and so his intervention has been tardy.
No	No	No	The lowest god of all the above types whose less than perfect nature is limited in its capacity to intervene by his less than perfect knowledge and power.

The above gods are less than the maximal Being of Christian theism and therefore no objects of worship. Even the closest of these gods to the maximal being of theism-the god that is all powerful and omniscient, yet not omnipotent, and the god that is all good and all-powerful, yet not all seeing-are not options for traditional theists. Yet on Hitchens' reckoning, there must be a weakening of one or more of the traditional attributes of God that is sufficient to explain God's tardiness in intervening, to accommodate God with the evil of His non-intervention over evil and suffering. Thus, to preserve their God, Christians must accept that He is a god, not God.

Hitchens' second problem of evil is premised on the assumption that God is obliged to help humanity, but it has been argued that God has no such obligation. If that is the case, this argument might be a means of meeting Hitchens' second problem of evil. Marilyn McCord Adams, for example, writes that God is not obliged to anyone.[53] Her reason for this opinion is that first, entities are obliged only to those entities who are responsible for

---

53. Marilyn McCord Adams 'Ignorance, Instrumentality, Compensation and the Problem of Evil,' *Sophia* 52, 2013, p. 16, emphasis in the original.

their existence. and second, God is humanity's patron and therefore is not obliged to humanity.[54]

In defense of her view, she claims two things: (1) that it is reasonable that God loves Himself above all as He alone possesses metaphysical goodness; and (2) that God owns the universe and can do what He likes with anyone and anything in it.[55]

Adams' notion of God as a patron or ruler in relation to His human clients and subjects through an honor code is unlikely to convince an antitheist like Hitchens who regards God as a totalitarian. To depict God as a feudal monarch who owns the universe and can do with whatever he chooses only reinforces in the minds of those who make the criticism that God is a dictator who is better off not existing.

The atheist Stephen Maitzen makes some strong criticisms of Adams' position.[56] He argues that it is foreign to our moral outlook to say that we have obligations only to those on whom we depend when the reverse seems true. On the contrary, we are obliged to help those who are dependent on us. [57]

Maitzen has no time either for Adams' 'honor code' for two reasons: (1) it regards injuries done to the client-subject as injuries done to the patron; (2) the restoration of the patron's reputation, which has suffered at the hands of the wrongs done to his client-subject, is deemed more important than justice for the client-subject.[58] Replacing a divine justice code with an honor code is thus in Maitzen's opinion a retrograde step.[59]

---

54. Ibid., p. 17.

55. Adams, "*Caveat Emptor!* Moral Theory and Problems of Evil" (presentation, Center for Philosophy of Religion, University of Notre Dame, 15 November 2013) at https://www.youtube.com/watch?v=K4rsQmM1cx4 (accessed 26 July 2016 at 11:26 am).

56. Stephen Maitzen, 'Perfection, Evil and Morality', ed. James P. Sterba, *Ethics and the Problem of Evil*, p. 6.

57. Ibid. One might add to Maitzen's argument that approval is accorded those who feel moral obligation to those who are dependent on them, but whom are not known personally by those feeling the obligation. When P sends money to a charity that feeds starving orphans in a poor country, he does so from moral obligation towards those who are strangers to him, and that is something that is regarded well. Additionally, it is part of our moral outlook to regard highly that sense of moral obligation to those on whom we do not depend and who do not depend on us. Q lives next door to S, and though Q and S are neighbours, not dependents on each other, Q's decision not to play loud music at night so as not to disturb S is a moral obligation felt towards another independent of her. Though such a sense of moral obligation may still have a self-helping element in it (Q knows that if she ever needs S's help, she ought to avoid playing loud music at night) her decision at the time not to play loud music is a selfless moral obligation felt from human decency.

58. Maitzen, 'Perfection, Evil and Morality', p. 6.

59. Ibid., p. 7.

Maitzen is right to attack the honor code and Christians ought to also. It is clear from Scripture that God regards the wrongs done as not only wrongs against Himself, but also against the humans He loves. When God makes a call to Israel to repent through the prophet Jeremiah, He depicts Himself as a husband wronged by Israel, His adulterous wife (Jer. 3:1-15). In this case, the offence is against Him; but He also warns Israel of its coming judgment for failing to plead the cause of the fatherless, or orphans (5:28) and for oppressing the stranger and the widows (7:6). In this case, the offence is against both vulnerable people and God, and not God alone.

It is possible to assert that God has no obligations to humanity, but it is important when dealing with anti-theists such as Hitchens to find another dimension of God's nature to demonstrate that He is committed to human flourishing that is stronger than obligation. God may not be obliged to help humanity, but He intervenes on behalf of humanity because He cannot act contrarily to His nature, which is one of unconditional love. It is possible to see why this is by looking at the meaning of two words obligation and *agapoo*.

Obligation refers to the gratitude and duties we owe to others.[60] With reference to (1), God has no obligation to anyone for as a necessary and self-sufficient Being He is in need neither of kindness nor help, though He can take pleasure in the kindness and help that humans render each other and in His own kindness and help he offers humanity. With reference to (2), God is neither duty-bound nor constrained by promises. Duties and promises, or contracts, only exist within the context of worlds in which there are times when people do not perform what is morally good. Duty, promise making, and contract signing are safeguards against this. Thus, if C says she is duty-bound, or has promised, to perform action D, she is saying she recognizes constraint on her actions when she knows that there is the possibility of refusing to recognize such constraints; whereas if C lived in a world where everyone only ever did the right thing and there was no possibility that this had been or could be otherwise, then C would not have to talk in terms of duty or make promises because she would do the right thing anyway. As God does the right thing only and always, and there is no possibility of His doing anything other than the right thing, He is under no obligation to do the right thing.

If God is not obliged to intervene, He freely *chooses* to intervene *in accordance with His very nature* which is that of unconditional love or *agapoo*. God's love is not born out of an affection for humans,[61] for it was 'while we were still sinners' and were enemies of God that 'Christ died for us' (Rom. 5:8).

---

60. Betty Kirkpatrick, *Webster's Word Power English Dictionary*, p. 223.

61. Vine, *et al.*, *Vine's Complete Expository Dictionary*, p. 382.

The human objects of God's love therefore contain no winsome excellence. God's *agapoo* is not 'a falling in love with', but the freely chosen decision to love despite the unloveliness of sinful humans who because of their sin, do not deserve and do not welcome God's intervention, but merit judgement. Such love also goes by the name of grace and its greatest and most complete manifestation is Christ's propitiatory sacrifice (Rom. 3:25).

Adams has described God as a patron-ruler, and it is true that God is depicted as a Master by the Scriptures (2 Tim. 2:21), yet His relationship to humanity is not one of cold command. For unredeemed humanity, His love is unconditional (John 3:16); for those redeemed, His love is that of friendship (John 15:15). The obedience of God's children, in turn, is the freely chosen act of love (15:14) rather than an act born of fear or self-interest.

If by Christian belief God has no obligation to intervene, but freely chooses in accordance with His nature to intervene, Hitchens' second problem of evil still demands a response: (1) why does God appear to have been for most of human history indifferent to human suffering, and (2) why is His intervention seemingly too little, for evil and suffering pervade His creation?

Responding to Hitchens' problem of evil, I shall adopt six strategies. First, I shall explore whether there is a contradiction between the anti-theist Hitchens who fears divine intervention and the Hitchens who censures Christians for believing in a God who has failed to intervene against evil. Second, I shall demonstrate that based on their faith in the biblical testimony, Christians ought not to conclude, as Hitchens does, that God has never helped humanity before Christ's advent. Third, I shall argue that rather than being indifferent to suffering, God is profoundly affected by it and suffers alongside His human creation. Fourth, I shall argue that atheism has two problems of evil of its own: the problem of evil's limits and the problem of justice. Fifth, I shall argue that alongside the intellectual and pastoral dimensions of the problem of moral evil and pain, there is what I shall call the problem of sin which reveals that all human beings as agents of moral evil are part of the problem of moral evil. The consequences of calling for the elimination of suffering would be the cancellation of human free-will, or the elimination of human beings. Finally, I shall present two reasons why God might permit moral evil. The first reason is that God allows human beings to experience moral evil in order to bring them to a point where they freely and gladly wish no longer to have the freedom to do moral evil, but only what is morally good, as a means of entering the new Jerusalem where human beings will no longer possess the moral freedom to do evil. The second argument is that through the experience or the perpetration of horrendous evil, God's love in its most gracious form is known experientially rather than only propositionally. Both reasons cannot bear the explanatory weight of horrendous evils, but they can play their part in moving towards an explanation, even if in this life and before the full revelation of God's Kingdom and will, no such full explanation is knowable. Moreover, they are glimpses of a deeper, fuller, eternal explanation for evil.

Hitchens dreads the existence of the God of theism because of His irresistible will. Yet, he appears angry when describing what he sees to be the ramification of Christian belief: that God has stood to one side for most of human history, indifferent to the terrors and pain of human existence. Hitchens, of course, is not angry with God, for in his opinion God does not exist. He is angry with those who believe in God either for not seeing the consequence of their belief, or if seeing it, continue to worship an unworthy God. But if Hitchens is angry with Christians for believing in an indifferent God, his anger is premised on the view that God ought to do something about human evil and suffering if He existed. The problem Hitchens has is defining how God ought to intervene without posing a threat to human free-will for some of the horrors Hitchens identifies are the result of human decisions. Hitchens fails to define how divine intervention might operate whilst simultaneously keeping human free-will intact and it is a flaw in his anti-theodicy.

According to the Bible, God's intervention in history did not begin with the advent of Christ. He has intervened since the creation. The promise of a Savior for all humanity was made to Adam and Eve, the first two human beings (Gen. 3:15). The nation from which the Savior would come, Israel, began with the calling of Abram (Gen. 12:1-3). The knowledge of this coming Savior was entrusted to the Israelites who were to make it known to all people (Isa. 49:6). The Temple in Jerusalem was intended to be 'a house of prayer for all nations' (56:7). The Old Testament is an account of the outworking of God's promise of a Savior and of His dealings with Israel to ensure that that prophecy came to pass. The birth, life, death, and resurrection of Christ are the fulfilment of those prophecies. The Jewish people occupy center place in the Old Testament, but God has dealings with other nations too of which there are many examples. Two prominent examples of God blessing Gentile nations are told in the stories of Joseph and Daniel. Through Joseph, God saved Egypt and the surrounding nations from starvation (Gen. 41:1-36). Daniel also interpreted the dreams of Nebuchadnezzar, the Babylonian potentate and imparted wise advice to him (Dan. 2). Hitchens may scoff at the idea that the Old Testament is historical rather than mythological, but the Christian worldview teaches that God has not stood with folded arms for all those thousands of years leading to Christ's coming.

Hitchens' Second Problem of Evil presents God as indifferent to suffering which in his eyes is inexcusable. Classical theism presents God as unchanging[62] and who therefore cannot suffer, for to suffer is to experience passively something that will affect and change the sufferer. The inability to suffer is not the same as indifference to suffering, for to be unable to suffer does not therefore mean that God is not concerned from a moral point of view to alleviate it. It nevertheless would appear a deep injustice on God's part to create a world that contains enormous amounts of moral evil and pain, and yet He Himself is indifferent to it, or is incapable of being affected by it. If God has made a world in which there is suffering, He ought at least to be decent enough to share in that suffering, if not to feel the suffering more than any other.

The God of the Bible fortunately is neither the cold god of Hitchens' imagination nor the pristine, unaffected God of classical theism. He is a God of unimaginable depths of suffering who suffers with humanity. The best example of God suffering is the tribulations of Christ. But in case anyone objects that Christ suffered as a man, but not as God, two examples, one from the Old Testament and one from the New Testament, will suffice to demonstrate this, though the Bible affords many more examples. In the sixth chapter of Genesis, God is 'sorry that He had made man on the earth' and that 'He was grieved in His heart (v. 6) because 'the wickedness of man was great in the earth' (v.5). God therefore has knowledge of moral evil which affects Him. In the New Testament, when Christ laments over Jerusalem, His lament was that of God through the voice of a man. Christ describes Jerusalem as 'the one who kills the prophets and stones those who are sent to her!' (Matt. 23:37). Christ's description is of the historical behavior of Jerusalem pre-dating His birth as a man. His declaration of wanting to gather Jerusalem's children together 'as a hen gathers her chicks under her wings' (v. 37) refers therefore to God's past desire to protect and nourish His people. That Christ describes the people of Jerusalem as 'not willing' (v. 37) surely was a source of frustration for God, which is a form of suffering. As Jürgen Moltmann concludes, the God of Christianity is a God of suffering and so Christians can offer genuine comfort to the victims of suffering.[63]

Hitchens' anti-theism commits him to concede an endlessly greater quantitative problem of evil and pain than that which the Christian position suffers. God's intervention through Christ's advent and death concludes with the promise that at the end of time 'a new heaven and a new earth' (Rev. 21:1) will be made and a paradisiacal existence will be provided for God's people within the New Jerusalem (21:9-22:5). Specifically, God promises that:

---

62. Brian Davies, *Philosophy of Religion*, p. 579.

63. Ibid., p. 580.

'God will wipe away every tear from their eyes, there shall be
no more death, nor sorrow, nor crying. There shall be no more
pain, for the former things will have passed away' (v. 4).

This condition of perfect happiness will be everlasting for God's people
who will 'reign forever and ever' (22:5). The misery experienced in individual lives is of short, temporary duration, whereas the perfect satisfaction
of living with and knowing God forever is a continual and ever-increasing
compensation for that suffering. If God has a good reason for evil and pain,
it is a small price to pay if regarded within the context of everlasting con-
tentment, though during great suffering, it can be impossible to keep this
everlasting perspective in view. On atheism, however, humanity is doomed
for the rest of its existence to evil and pain. Eventually the evolved descen-
dants of human beings will face in terror the universe's heat death.

A serious manifestation of moral evil is injustice and atheists face a
problem which is more serious and troubling than that which Christians
face. For Christians, the problem is one of comprehension: If God is perfectly
just, why is His justice delayed? Surely it is a quality of good justice that not
only is it fair, but that it is prompt also, thus deterring further criminality. As
with Hitchens' second problem of evil, there is a problem in understanding
what seems to be a delay in God's justice. But there is no doubt for Christians
that perfect justice will be eventually dealt out. Christians believe that there
will be a final judgement of all humans who have ever lived (20:11-15). This
judgement is perfect for 'each one' will be judged 'according to his works' by
God (v. 13). No one is above God's judgement, and no one will escape this
judgement. Christians can also advance the view that God Himself knows
what it is like to experience injustice, not only from the ill-treatment of His
followers by regimes and religions hostile to Christianity, but also through
the experience of Christ who suffered persecution at the hands of Herod the
Great, Israel's theocracy and the Roman executioners.

For the atheist, the problem of justice is even greater in that s/he has
no guarantee that justice will ever be done in many cases. Evil doers such as
dead despots who have enjoyed their lives and have avoided any judgement
while they were alive will never face judgement for when they die, they
cease to exist. The new authority that replaces the despot might denounce
the despot, (as Khrushchev did after Stalin died in March 1953), have his
or her accomplices arrested and compensate living victims, but nothing can
be done meaningfully to the despot directly and if his victims are dead too,
they will never receive their just due either. The problem of injustice cannot
be used to conclude that atheism is untrue in the way that the logical and
evidential problems of evil are used to attempt to show that theism is untrue

or probably untrue. Nevertheless, it is a horrifying fact that in an atheist universe there are instances of injustice that will never be redressed.

To respond fully to the problem of moral evil, Christianity recognizes three dimensions to the problem. John Lennox describes two dimensions as the intellectual problem in which evil and pain are objectively considered by the philosopher and the pastoral or experiential problem of how to cope with evil and pain when it is experienced.[64] Moral evil and pain can therefore be thought about, suffered, prevented, relieved, or reduced. I should like to add a third dimension: the problem of sin which concerns as much the moral evil perpetrated by humans as the moral evil each one suffers.

As seen in chapter four, sin is any thought, word or deed that falls short of the perfect moral standard of God. One is aware of other people's sins only too well, and this is how the problem of moral evil seems traditionally to be expressed: X suffers at the hands of Y; X is the victim and Y is the perpetrator. But what of the moral evil for which X is culpable? What of the moral evil of everyone? What of the moral evil of those who complain about the belief in God when there is so much moral evil? What about the moral evil for which *I* am guilty? The problem of sin is a problem for every person for as Paul writes: 'there is no difference: for all have sinned and fall short of the glory of God' (Rom. 3:22-23). But the problem is a deeply personal one for I am one of the 'all who have sinned'. There is no exception. The problem of sin therefore not only asks the question why does God allow moral evil, but why does God allow *my* moral evil? I may not be guilty of genocide or persecution, but the problem of sin is a problem of all sins: It is the problem of big, medium and small sins, or what might appear to be big, medium and small sins, for if we take the example of an apparently small sin, it may well be the touch paper for a much greater explosion of moral evil. Those who question the goodness of God for tolerating moral evil ought to be glad that He does, for by calling for the elimination of the causes of moral evil they are also calling for the elimination of themselves.

The problem of sin therefore personalizes the problem of moral evil by disconcertingly turning the problem back on ourselves. This is indeed a worrying situation, but it is important to state to Hitchens that this is a dimension of the problem of evil which God has solved. It is for this reason that Christians speak of the Good News that God has solved the problem of sin. Paul was acutely aware of sin's power to imprison humans in evil ways of living. He writes of the law of sin in the members of his body which sought to bring him into captivity (Rom. 7:23). To escape the besetting internal

64. 'The Hard Question: God and the Problem of Evil (with John Lennox)', You-Tube, 25th March 2015 at https://www.youtube.com/watch?v=Ssb47DEmn9U (accessed 26 July 2016 at 11:28).

power of sin, human beings need something or someone external to them to rescue them. Most happily, there is such a Being and He is Christ.

Chapter four has already established that God has defeated through Christ the tyranny of sin, but it is necessary to repeat this point within the context of the problem of evil, for it is God's solution to the problem of sin which is ultimately the end of the problem of evil. Humans, if they choose, can be 'justified freely by His grace through the redemption that is Christ, whom God set forth as propitiation by His blood, through faith . . .' (3:23). Now forgiven, repentant sinners begin the life of living by the power of the Holy Spirit which makes them 'free from the law of sin and death' (8:2). Though not morally perfect, the repentant now have the power and the desire to resist temptation. It is a common part of many churches' services that they have times when people testify to how the power of besetting sins such as alcoholism and violence has been broken. The solution to the problem of evil begins with the solution to individual humans' sin, for if God is to solve the problem of evil He must deal with the problem of sin. Those who do not wish to be forgiven their sins cannot be released from the power of sin, and so are contributing to the problem of evil which they use to dismiss the idea of God's existence or justify their anti-theism.

The underlying assumption of the above discussion is that human beings are endowed with moral free-will. If human beings could not but do what they do, for their behavior is the consequence of a chain of antecedent conditions or causes, there is no room to hold them personally culpable, even though they themselves are the cause of the action rightly attributed to them. It is a Christian axiom that humans are morally free to do what is good and what is evil. It has been argued by Mackie that God could have created a world in which humans have free will and yet without exception, freely chose the good thing to do.[65] Mackie's justification for this view is if there is no logical impossibility about a person freely choosing what is good to do on one occasion or a series of occasions, therefore there is nothing illogical about freely choosing to do good on all occasions. That God has not created human beings who freely choose always to do right is inconsistent with His being omnipotent and all-good.[66] Hitchens does not make these points personally, but possibly was probably aware of it and agreed as he had some knowledge of Mackie's philosophy.

---

65. John Mackie, 'Evil and Omnipotence' in ed. McCord Adams and Merrihew Adams, *The Problem of Evil*, p. 33.

66. Ibid., p. 33.

An objection to Mackie's argument is that making wrong decisions is logically necessary for moral free-will.[67] If people genuinely have moral free choice, eventually someone will do something wrong, and it would look very suspicious to an observer of humanity if s/he were assured that everyone had the freedom to choose morally and yet everyone only ever did what is right. Mackie meets this objection by stating that it renders human freewill as indeterminate, for if God has made humans good, but capable of acting contrary to their nature, their choices become random rather than decided by their nature. This enables God to escape the responsibility for human moral evil, for if He made them one way, and did not determine their wrong actions, their wrong actions are not determined by how He has created them. But as Mackie asks, if freedom is randomness, how can it be a matter of the will? How can it be the greatest good if free choices are random actions that have nothing to with the character of the moral agent?[68]

What appears to be the serious consequence of Mackie's reasoning is that if human beings have free-will and have chosen to do what is wrong (as well as right), their choice of doing the wrong thing is made possible by their possession of an evil nature. Like God who chooses in accord with his perfect nature of love to love unlovable humanity, humans have chosen in accord with their evil natures to do what is wrong. If God is the creator of humanity, He must be ultimately responsible for evil, for the evil portions of human nature are His creation. As God is omniscient, He would have known fully that when He created humanity with its evil nature, those humans would act in accord with that evil nature. God therefore created what is evil knowing full well what He was doing and the moral consequences of His creation of humanity.

In chapter four's discussion of the free-will, or libertarian defense of hell, we explored the idea that humans possess free-will in a sovereign way. In other words, one way of understanding how humans are made in God's image is from the nature of human freedom. I argued that in the matter of whether to love or reject God, humans exercise choice in the way God does. Like God, who acts only in accordance with His nature, but whose nature is not a prior cause of His actions, for they are spontaneous decisions, so humans choose whether to love or reject God in accordance with their nature, but not because of their nature. Therefore, both P and Q choose to love God, but they love God in different ways because of the different nature of their potential to give love. P may spend many hours in prayer because he is a contemplative type, whereas Q might choose to devote much of her time

67. Ibid., p.33.
68. Ibid., pp. 33-34.

to helping the poor because she demonstrates her love for God through acts of service. If on the other hand R rejects God, he does so in accord with his nature. Imagine that R is a bad tempered but talented writer. His rejection of God might therefore take the form of an angry tirade in book form.

The principle of sovereign free-will is true of all moral decisions. The freedom to accept God's love or reject it is a moral decision, for to reject the love of God is a sin for it is the dual rejection of God's salvation (therefore the person remains in his or her sin) and the power to live by the Spirit (which is life above sin). If there is freedom to choose in this, the greatest of matters, then there is probably freedom to choose in lesser moral decisions. But clearly for the Christian there is freedom in moral decisions for the Bible holds people as responsible for their sins and there cannot be moral responsibility unless there is freedom of decision.

Now if we argue that humans are free to choose morally, whether for good or bad, not because their good or bad natures are a cause of their decisions, but in a way that accords with their good or bad natures, we have not yet met Mackie's objection that God is ultimately responsible for evil. Mackie might rejoin that humans nevertheless possess evil natures and though on the view that humans are free in a sovereign sense, these evil characteristics are not the cause of human evil. Humans when they choose to do evil do so in a way that accords with the evil characteristics of their natures and these evil characteristics are the creation of God.

One way of meeting Mackie's objection is to argue that God did not create the evil characteristics of human beings, but only the potential to be evil. If a person has the potential to do evil, he or she cannot be called evil. Imagine Dr N who has all her life worked with unceasing care for her patients. Not once in her exemplary life has she ever used her hands to hurt someone. Her hands have only ever administered medical care that has saved many lives, cured many others, and made the last moments of some more comfortable when medical science could do no more. It would be hard to describe Dr N as an evil person, and yet the very hands she uses to administer drugs and palliatives could conceivably, though the likelihood is low inductively, pick up a pistol and shoot someone in a fit of jealous rage. But she has never done this. That she has the potential to do evil does not stop her from being described as a good person. Therefore, when God created humanity, He created good beings, who although with the potential to do evil, can only be described as good. Humans became evil at the moment they choose to realize their potential in some way to be evil.

The problem nevertheless of why God would create a world where evil was a possibility remains. Though God is not morally responsible for human evil, He is indirectly its cause, for He created people with the potential to do evil, and if He is omniscient and eternal, knowing full well that humans would exercise their ability to realize their evil potential. Perhaps the price of moral free-will is too high? Perhaps the evil that results from moral freedom outweighs the goodness of moral freedom itself. And if that is the price of human free-will, then perhaps God ought not to have created in the first place a world where free-will exists? Hitchens' begins the sixteenth chapter of *God is Not Great* by referring to Dostoyevsky's *The Brothers' Karamazov* in which the character Ivan asks Alyosha such a question: Would the world be worth creating if it meant the suffering of a small child?[69]

This question is used by Hitchens to preface a chapter on the abuse of children by the religions rather than to initiate a discussion of the problem of evil; however, the presence of the quotation in Hitchens' text raises the question of whether a world of free humans is worth the evil price.

Responding to Alyosha's question is at the heart of any theodicy dependent on the notion of human free-will. First, the price of evil is readily paid every day by the great majority of people who choose to continue to exist and who show signs of being happy that they exist in their state of free-will. Though evil and suffering are universal, and sometimes they are magnified to appalling levels, people continue to seek pleasure and purpose, are glad they are alive even in such a world as this and dread the end of their lives. Many people during great suffering or who have been through such a terrifying state choose to continue to live and seek an escape from their suffering or to be healed of its effects once the suffering has ended. These very same people also reproduce and bring others into this world of suffering. Hitchens himself was a father! Yet these same people question God's wisdom in making this world in the first place whilst enjoying their existence and giving existence to others.

Alyosha's question might also be posed to unbelievers, but in a modified way: The price of the evolution of humanity has been enormous levels of suffering caused by natural selection. Do you celebrate the existence of humanity despite such suffering? It seems to be the case that unbelievers do celebrate their existence. Was it not Richard Dawkins and his atheist bus campaign that enjoined us to enjoy our lives?

I wish to propose another reason for human free-will and the existence of moral evil. The eschatological vision of Christianity is of history culminating in 'a new heaven and a new earth' where there is no sin and suffering (Rev. 21:1). Where a person lives for eternity is his or her choice, for God will not force fellowship upon anyone. For humans to live in the new heaven and the new earth, they must be prepared to give up their potential

---

69. Quoted in Hitchens, *God is Not Great*, p. 217.

to act in accord with that dimension of their evil natures, for if they retain that potential and the ability to make it actual, they will ruin the perfection again as they did in the Garden of Eden. That beings can make evil choices within the context of perfection can be seen in the angelic revolt led by Lucifer who wished to usurp God (Isa. 14:12-15; 2 Peter 2:4). For human beings to live in such perfection, they must lose the potential and the will to do evil, but this cannot be taken away by force by God, for that would contradict His gift of free-will which is indispensable to the human capacity to love. Humans must therefore be brought to the point where they wish no longer to possess the potential to do evil and the capacity to actualize that potential. In other words, they reach that point where they reject their freedom to fulfil their potential to do what is wrong for they can no longer bear their wrongdoing. If a person hungers to be made perfectly morally good by God and *by nature* therefore incapable of doing what is morally wrong, s/he is giving up part of his/her their moral freedom, but if freely chosen, God is able to accept this giving up of the moral freedom He gave to him/her in the first place, thus rendering that person fit to live in the New Jerusalem where people only ever act in accord with their moral nature, which is perfectly good. Paul's exclamation of, 'O wretched man that I am! Who will deliver me from this body of death?' demonstrates how strong the desire to be free from even the possibility of sinning can be in the heart of the redeemed (Rom. 7:24). Fortunately for all God's children, Paul went on to write chapter 8 where he wrote of the Holy Spirit's power to enable the redeemed to live above the law of sin whilst they remain in this world. The writer of Hebrews writes of the ongoing process of sanctification by which the redeemed are metamorphosed into Christ-likeness (Heb. 2:11). Such a process might be accomplished instantly if God chose, but it is a process for it does not over-ride human free-will which will at times seek to resist this process by sinning. It is the process by which the redeemed who are appalled at their sin co-operate with God in removing that sinful nature and the ability to choose to do moral evil. In a way they are working with God to re-create themselves as is consistent with their new birth (John 3:1-21; Phil. 2:12). Moreover, the repeated personal experience of committing sin serves to reinforce the desire to be rid of it so that that desire becomes a conclusive and sustained decision.

Now it could be counter-argued that God might have created human beings ready for life in the New Jerusalem right from the start of their existence. Perhaps God might have given human beings a limited free-will in terms of being only able to choose between equally good courses of action. Why must God allow humans to go through the process of perpetrating moral evil and suffering from it themselves? The response lies in the dignity and status of humanity of which freedom is an essential part. Not only has God given human beings a genuine free-will in that they have the capacity to reject Him, but they also are given the choice as to what sort of moral beings they wish to be. With genuine free-will, there is a genuine possibility of choosing to actualize the evil in one's being and reject God wholly. One can make of oneself what one wishes to be. Those who are in the process of fashioning themselves into something godless and those who are in the process of sanctification will cause moral evil, but that is the necessary consequences of the greater good of human autonomy. Whilst this process is happening, humans are not left totally to the mercies of each other. God has instituted human government (Rom. 13:1) and God's justice is operational too (Gen. 15:16). But humans are explicitly told of the consequences of their evil self-modelling (Matt. 5:22).

It could be argued that God could remove the worst of moral evils and leave minor moral evils in existence. Surely humans could become sick of their sin through the experience of committing so-called small evils rather than horrendous evils? If a person is sick of smaller evils, they will certainly be sick of greater evils. In the light of this, I wish to suggest a reason for horrendous evil, but bearing in mind that the problem of such evil is far greater than any one reason or all the reasons suggested for it. But as stated earlier, we move closer toward that eternal understanding of which we have glimpses through our own philosophy. To make this response, I will treat the subject of horrendous evil from three perspectives: first, that of the victim, second, that of the perpetrator and finally that of the witness.

The victim of horrendous evil may ask a series of connected questions: Why did or does God permit this appalling suffering? Does God really love me? Can God still love me when this great evil that has befallen me has rendered me unlovable?

The second question is the consequence of the first, for it is difficult to conceive that someone who says he loves us would allow us to suffer horrendous evil. That God has not intervened, or prevented this great suffering, is surely evidence that He does not love us (or even that he does not exist or most likely does not exist). God's answer to the second question is that He does love us all. God is using human language to propose His love; we know His love propositionally, which is to know about His love but not to know His love. This situation reflects the division of knowledge into that by description and that by acquaintance. God's love is described as that which is love for us all, but it is our acquaintance with, even immersion in, the love of God which is sought by many of us (not all). There must be for many a continual experience of God's love which is one way of saying having a relationship with God. The questions remain as to what this love of God is, for if there is such a thing as God's love and at the same time there are horrendous evils that happen to those whom God loves, there has to be something about God's love that in some ways permits horrendous evil without being anything less than His love. It is the third question above that enables us to propose that there is such a thing as the love of God and horrendous evils.

Let us imagine that we have suffered or are suffering in such a way as to deny that our life has any positive value, that worse, our being has no positive value and that we are wholly unloved. Such a situation is one of the lowest we could come to, and probably the lowest. Imagine also that we have never known God's love, but we know that He is supposedly a God of love for that is how He has been described by those who claim to know Him. In that situation we might ask whether God loves us though no one else does. Someone might assure us that God loves us, but that would be of no use for it would be a proposition that appears to be untrue in the light of our suffering. If in that situation we came to know the love of God as someone loved by God rather than someone knowing about God's love for us, we would know that God loves us regardless of how low we sank. We would learn that nothing in us or in our situation stops God from loving us. Quantitatively, we would learn that God's unconditional, gracious love transcends human love which is often conditional upon the beloved reciprocating in certain ways. Each person is called by God to know His love (many do not respond to this call), but the question is whether God's love is available in every circumstance for every person. Is there a limit to God's love? Is there a type of situation in which His love ceases? By being allowed to go to the lowest point which we can bear, and each person has his/her own lowest point and limit of endurance, we no longer merely assent to the proposition that God loves all and at all times regardless of the nature of the person and his/her circumstance, but form the conviction, or trust, or what the Bible calls faith, in the nature of the all-loving God. The horrendous evil has been allowed by God to put His love to the test, and so has become the proof of His love rather than the proof of His evil, or His non-existence. Without our horrible circumstance, we may never have experienced the unconditional love of God in adversity and the security in God's love that accompanies the experience. We also may never have tasted one of the sweetest of God's loves made sweeter by its contrast with the bitterness of our situation. (A glass of ice cold mineral water scented with lemon slices is always sweet to the taste, but during a long walk on a hot day, it tastes even sweeter.) The situation may have engulfed us, but the love of God engulfs us in the situation and defeats it by proving our eternal value against the degradations of a finite, fallen world.

The perspective of the witness of horrendous evil who could have intervened but does not and the perpetrator is one of culpability and often a damning sense of guilt. What both have done is contrary to the will of the God whose command is clear: 'love your neighbor as yourself' (Lev. 19:18). Nevertheless, God takes the guilt of both classes of people and uses it for their own good. Just as the victim comes to know the reality of God's love rather than know God's love only propositionally through horrendous evil, the bystander and the perpetrator may know through their repentance the mercy and forgiveness of God which are greater goods than the horrendous evils they have ignored or perpetrated. A good example of this is the criminal who repented of his evil as he was dying next to Christ (Luke 23:40-43). This criminal must have committed appalling crimes to merit the worst form of execution the Romans possessed, but what immense relief he must have felt when he heard Christ say, "'Assuredly, I say to you, today you will be with Me in paradise'" (v. 43). What is more, victim, bystander and perpetrator are called to the highest moral manifestation: that of forgiveness. The victim is called to forgive the bystander and the perpetrator (Matt. 6:14-15), whereas the bystander and the perpetrator are called to forgive themselves (though face the justice of this world). Without anything to forgive, there is no superlative good such as forgiveness.

However, if there is no satisfying reason or collection of reasons known for horrendous evils, it is best to leave this issue at the point where Marilyn McCord Adams leads us. Adams' response to horrendous evil is to argue that generic or global reasons are sufficient to explain why God might permit non-horrendous evils, but to try to explain why God might permit horrendous evil is impossible. Adams' is certain that no package of non-transcendent goods can balance off or defeat horrendous evils, but God who is the Being a greater than which cannot be conceived is greater than any horrendous evil and created goods. Her response is not to explain why there is horrendous evil, but to describe the way in which God defeats horrendous evil. What overwhelms and nullifies the horrendous evil suffered by an individual is the love of God. An overwhelming is the first stage of God's response according to Adams; the second stage is defeat by which God integrates participation in horrendous evils into a person's relationship with Him. Adams suggests this is possible by identifying with Christ who Himself participated in horrendous evil through His trial and crucifixion.

Natural Evil or the Problem of Pain

Natural evil is that evil that is not caused by human agency, whether intentionally or unintentionally, but is caused by the world in which humans live.[70]

---

70. Sharon Dirckx, *Why? Looking at God, evil & personal suffering*, p. 130.

This evil is sometimes also called collectively the problem of pain for the word evil suggests moral agency, whereas a hurricane that destroys a city and kills many people cannot be held morally responsible. Having said this, with growing scientific knowledge, it is easier to see how human behavior causes or contributes to some of what has hitherto been called natural evil. According to the World Meteorological Organization, the world is five times more prone to natural disasters now than it was during the 1970s due to climate change, of which human activity is the cause.[71]

For Hitchens, pain is certainly a problem for all of humanity, but it does not exist as a theological problem. As God does not exist, there is no reason to find the reasons why He allows natural disasters and diseases. For Hitchens, this is just how the universe is and humanity must find ways of coping with these features as best it can. If people are hurt by purely natural phenomena, such as a hurricane, that is a consequence of living on the sort of planet that we happen to live.[72] He took the same attitude to being diagnosed with metastasized esophageal cancer.[73]

Of course, Hitchens is content to challenge Christians to explain how they can believe in an all-benevolent and omnipotent God in the face of natural evil, thereby ensuring that natural evil is a theological problem for them! As we saw in chapter two and earlier in this chapter, Hitchens presents his a-theodicy in the following graphic way and for the sake of this chapter's argument I shall repeat it here: In his list of evils that have permeated the earth whilst heaven watched with folded arms and did nothing, Hitchens refers to the fact that almost all species that have ever existed are now extinct and died out in callous circumstances over billions of years. In the case of *homo sapiens*, Hitchens estimates that our species has been around for 100,000 years. If Christ came to earth to attempt a rescue of humanity, it means that for 98,000 years, humans suffered alarming levels of infant mortality, a life expectancy of 20-30 years kept low by infections and diseases, and permanent fear of natural disasters such as earthquakes and lightning strikes.[74] The horror of natural evil to which God has left His creation to face is compounded by the fact that

71. Suzanne Goldberg, 'Eight ways climate change is making the world more dangerous', *The Guardian*, 14 July 2014.

72. '#141 Debate-Christopher Hitchens vs Timothy Jackson-How Religion Poisons Everything-2007', You Tube, 26 December 2015 at http://www.youtube.com/watch?v=WFXotOT7uY (accessed 26 July 2016 at 11:31).

73. Hitchens, *Mortality*, p.6. Hitchens' response is a typically atheist response. Dawkins talks of a world characterised by 'blind, pitiless indifference'. See Richard Dawkins, *River Out of Eden*, p. 133.

74. 'Christopher Hitchens: "Heaven watches with folded arms"', You Tube, 25 February 2013 at https://www.youtube.com/watch?v=gQgHds6eIJO (accessed 26 July 2016 at 11:35).

it has occurred for billions of years in the case of animals and thousands of years in the case of humans. A response to Hitchens' a-theodicy therefore requires a response to the problem of natural evil. The present discussion will include an examination of terminal illness, the natural evil that tapped Hitchens on the shoulder and escorted him away from the fun of life.[75] This response will not present a complete theodicy, but instead will, as in the case of moral evil discussed above, provide some lines of argument that could play a role in a complete theodicy.

Terminal diseases such as Hitchens' esophageal cancer might be termed as horrendous natural evils or as horrendous problems of pain in an analogous sense to horrendous moral evils. Certain natural evils such as mild headaches and stiff muscles do not overwhelm people; on the contrary, terminal diseases are horrendous natural evils for both the sufferer and his or her family and friends. They cause great pain and cause their victims to waste away. They cut people down in their prime and prematurely finish their lives. They take away spouses, parents, children, relatives, and friends. The treatment for cancer often feels as severe as the symptoms. Accompanying the physical symptoms are the emotions of fear, anxiety, loneliness, and frustration. If the patient has a belief in God, there is also the question as to the justice of his or her predicament and the question too of whether God is good after all. The patient may question too whether it was ever good for him/her to have been born in the first place if this is how his/her lives will finish. What s/he may have achieved in life from his/her new perspective now seems dissolved by the valley of suffering into which s/he has descended. His or her dignity seems undermined by the humiliation of their condition.

Terminal illness is a horrendous natural evil, but it is often not a purely natural evil as it can be caused or exacerbated by human agency. Many people who have chosen to smoke knowing the health risks have indeed ended up developing lung cancer. Hitchens himself recognized the role his smoking and drinking played in provoking his cancer when he warned others after his diagnosis to cut back on their drinking and smoking.[76] Hitchens castigates God for failing to intervene to prevent human suffering; on that basis, it is pertinent to ask Hitchens whether he would have welcomed God's cancellation of his enjoyment of cigarettes and his favorite alcoholic drink, Johnnie Walker Black,[77] in order to preclude his cancer? It appears not, for

75. Mick Brown, 'Godless in Tumourville: Christopher Hitchens interview', *The Daily Telegraph*, 25 March 2011.

76. Andrew Anthony, 'Christopher Hitchens: "You have to choose your future regrets"', *The Observer*, 14 November 2010.

77. 'Christopher Hitchens on life, death and lobster' at https://www.bbc.co.uk/

surely no anti-theist such as Hitchens would have tolerated such an intrusion into the exercise of his free will. Hitchens used alcohol because it made him a better writer.[78] He also said that it was worth taking the risk with drinking because writing was the most important thing to him.[79] Hitchens therefore risked the natural evil consequences of considerable alcoholic consumption for the sake of his art and accepted the price of that art when it was exacted.

Hitchens' position on natural evil therefore seems confused and contradictory. As a universal principle, he challenges Christians to explain why their God has chosen not to prevent the horrors with which humanity has to contend, and yet with specific reference to himself, he would wish to deny God the liberty to remove his enjoyment of liquor to prevent the natural evil of cancer. The question one might put to Hitchens is this: If God were to put an end to earthquakes and floods, why might He not put an end to cancer too, and if He ought to put an end to cancer, why might He not take away the enjoyment of copious amounts of alcohol which is a contributing cause to esophageal cancer? Hitchens' position appears to suggest that God ought to eliminate certain natural evils whilst permitting others. All can agree that the world would be a better place without cystic fibrosis, a condition that afflicts people genetically and therefore through no one's design or negligence, but what of the question of excessive drinking of alcohol? X might drink copiously to be an inspired writer and stoically endure the consequences when the oncologist confirms the prognosis, but Y to whom X is married might be appalled at having to watch X decline slowly and painfully and wish that X had never drank at all. Y might ask God to prevent X's copious drinking and extend that to all those in danger of provoking the same disease with too many whiskeys.[80]

There is some irony in that Hitchens' defense of his decision to drink abundantly to lubricate the engines of creation is reminiscent of the Christian philosopher Swinburne's theodicy regarding natural evils. Swinburne interprets natural evil as the means by which a greater good can be achieved. Natural evil teaches humans to be interested in the natural world

news/uk-16214466 (accessed 3June 2016 at 08:10).

78. Christopher Hitchens, 'A Short Note on the Grape and the Grain', Slate, 6 June 2010.

79. Brian Palmer, 'Does Alcohol Improve Your Writing? Putting Hitch's theory to the test', Slate, 16 December 2011.

80. Jack Daniel's Black Label Whiskey was Christopher Hitchens favourite drink. See debate with Timothy Jackson at '#141 Debate Christopher Hitchens vs Timothy Jackson How Religion Poisons Everything 2007, You Tube at https://youtube.com/watch?v=WFXot4OT7uY (accessed on 26 July 2016 at 11:39).

to prevent natural evil and it provides humans with the opportunity to demonstrate great moral qualities such as courage and compassion.[81] The price of the greater good is the lesser evil without which the greater good would not exist. The greater good emerges after the emergence of the lesser evil. Hitchens' argument is presented not as a universal principle of why there is natural evil in the world but relates to a specific case that pertains to him. Hitchens' greater good of exceptional writing does not arise after the occurrence of the lesser evil of esophageal cancer but occurs through taking the risk of incurring the natural evil of cancer for the sake of a greater good of his writing. The greater good of Hitchens' thinking is excellent writing which satisfied him first, but with which no doubt he intended to satisfy his audience. Nevertheless, within Hitchens' view, there is the idea, as there is in Swinburne's theodicy that the price of natural evil is worth paying for the sake of a greater good.

Hitchens' riposte might be to ask why has there to be a price of natural evil in the first place for human agency. For instance, why could God not have created the world such that a writer could enjoy his or her drinks and smokes as a means of enjoying the greater pleasure of writing fluently without incurring deadly tumors? Why not create a world in which humans are already interested in the natural order without their attention having to be gained through natural disasters and where humans can still manifest compassion and courage in dealing with lesser natural evils without having to be provoked into doing so by horrendous ones? What too of animals who are already deeply interested in and integrated into the natural order, and who are regarded by Christians as not having a moral nature and who therefore cannot learn to be morally better through the experience of pain? For Hitchens, God's guilt remains.

One response to this problem is what the Bible teaches about the relationship of humanity to the natural world. In their natural state, all humans are destined to die. Death serves the present state of the natural world very well, for with its finite resources ever increasing populations of any one or more species would be impossible to sustain. Death therefore enables and sustains life, but for each living being, that life is limited. Yet according to Christian theology, death was never originally an intended feature of creation. Death entered the created order through the rebellion of humanity against God. The Genesis account reveals that Adam was informed after he chose to eat the forbidden fruit that his life would be a struggle to survive until he returned to the ground (3:19). Relationship with the Creator

---

81. 'Swinburne: The Problem of Evil' at https://homepages.wmich.edu/~baldner/
swinburne.pdf (accessed 27 May 2016 at 08:20).

means that one shares some of His attributes for He is the source of those attributes in His creation. One of these attributes is everlasting life. Continued rebellion against God, which is the stance all humans take, means the loss of some of those attributes for the connection with the source is severed. Humans somehow have not lost a sense of right and wrong, and for good reason, for it is the prompt to seeking salvation from the wrong they have done, but they no longer live forever bodily without God's saving intervention. Hitchens' own rebellion against God meant that he too bore the consequence of physical death.

Another response is to understand the role that humanity was given regarding the natural world. The government of the created order was delegated by God to humanity (1:28), but by listening to the serpent in the Garden of Eden who was Satan (Revelation 12:9) and by continuing to listen to him, Adam first and then all of humanity have handed over the government of this world to satanic authority. Satan is called 'the ruler of this world' (John 12:31) and 'the prince of the power of the air' (Eph. 2:2). The created order, by a free act of the original humans and subsequently confirmed by the whole of humanity's rebellion, has remained in the hands of devilish government ever since. The problem with this line of argument is that the one who delegates authority has the right to overrule the misuse of that delegated authority. If a doctor is mandated by the British Medical Association to practice as a doctor and that doctor fails to follow clinical procedure and this leads to a patient's death, the BMA is within its rights to remove that doctor's license to practice. Surely then, God the delegator of authority ought to take back the world from Adam and Eve who have sinfully given away their authority to an evil being who has no right to it?

One response to this argument is to ask what if humanity's role in subduing and having dominion as it was commanded to do in Gen. 1:28 was something that only they could do and not even God could do because that is how God has created the world in such a way that this is the case? Undoubtedly, God is the creator of the natural order and sustainer (Col. 1:17), but what if there is a part in maintaining this order that humans uniquely can do, but who can refuse to do because of their sovereign free-will. It makes sense from the perspective of the eternal value of humans that they are irreplaceable within God's creation, and that if they refuse to perform their delegated role of maintaining order in the way that God has given them, which is the best way, there is no other being who can perform that role. As human authority is limited and God Himself continues to intervene in His creation (Exod. 14), the world does not fall into total chaos, but the freely chosen and continued submission of human authority to the Evil One and the sin distorted attempts of humans to continue to bring order, means that natural evil is an unfortunate phenomenon in the created order. Someone might object that this is an intolerable limitation on God's omnipotence, but if Christians are prepared to accept that God has limited his omnipotence by creating humans who are made in His image and therefore who are free and that humans are eternally valuable, there is nothing intolerable about proposing that part of the exercise of that sovereign free-will and part of that eternal value is the notion that humans are free to exercise a governmental role over the created order that only humans can exercise.

One further observation is useful. Just as the atheist can provide no end to the problem of moral evil if humans possess the propensity for moral evil, so the atheist cannot provide an end to the problem of natural evil as long as natural evil exists and exceeds the power of humanity to control it. If Christian theism is true, there is a limit to the duration of suffering which is provided for by Christ's Cross and Resurrection. Paul teaches that it is when God's children are revealed as sons of God, in other words, when His people are fully sanctified at the Consummation (Rom. 8: 19), then creation, like the sons of God, will be 'delivered from the bondage of corruption into the glorious liberty of the children of God' (8: 21). For a time, creation was 'subjected to futility' for the sake of human salvation, for until that moment when all predestined to salvation are fully sanctified, the natural world remains under the curse of the effects of human sin. But this subjection was done as Paul teaches 'in hope' (8:20) of that moment when the sons of God are revealed. Death too, the final enemy, will be thrown into the Lake of Fire (Rev. 20:14).

Conclusion

This chapter has been a long and complex one to write. It has covered some very complex and serious questions in much detail, so it is time to summarize once more what this chapter has asserted.

It is the case that Hitchens uses a moral discourse that is objective sounding, and yet his decision to identify the origins of morality not within the divine realm, but as an evolutionary phenomenon means that his morality remains sincere, yet relative and contingent. Mackie argues that the queerness of objective transcendental values makes them implausible. The objective morality of Christianity is more powerful than the Form of the Good that Mackie sees as being the basis of objective morality. Relationship with Christ is the essence of Christianity and knowing Christ and his goodness is available to all, whereas knowing the Form of the Good is only possible for philosophers. The beauty of the Form of the Good in the good deeds of people attracts others to do the same goodness, but a relationship with Christ is a greater motivator of the good. Humanists like Hitchens assign intrinsic worth to human beings, but human worth has fluctuated historically. The Christian God who has assigned total intrinsic worth to humans is the best guarantor of perpetual human worth in his consistent love.

If there is no objective morality within the anti-theist universe, there is no reason to choose Hitchens' democratic and egalitarian views over those of Nietzsche's elitism on the basis that Hitchens' morality is more good. Both men begin with anti-theism and anti-religionism and yet reach such contradictory ethical conclusions. Nietzsche never doubted the relativism of morality and prophesies the free spirits who will emerge to fashion values in defiance of the groundlessness of values. Hitchens retains many Christian values, but he believes an ethical life can be lived independently of religion.[82] As there is no objective ethical standard by which to choose between the two philosophies, the choice can be made based on what we like and do not like or based on the moral consensus around us. But Hitchens does not accept moral choices being made on either of these two grounds. His choice is made on what he takes to be self-evidently right and wrong, but if there are no such things, the objective choice of democracy over Nietzsche is illusory.

Hitchens' first problem of evil, which is God's totalitarian nature, was rebutted in chapter four, so it does not feature in this chapter. Hitchens' second problem of evil attempts to demonstrate to Christians that if He exists, He is evil in that He has been indifferent to human moral evil and suffering and has intervened tardily. To respond to this problem, this chapter has revealed that the argument that God is not obliged to help is no defense, for though He is not obliged, God is moved by His character to help nonetheless. If that is the case, the second problem of evil still stands. But it is not the case that God has not intervened before Christ's advent, and this chapter has provided biblical data for God's benevolent intervention throughout history. God is a God of love, and rather than being indifferent to moral evil suffers alongside His human creations and suffers because of them. Whereas atheism cannot guarantee that moral evil will ever cease, Christianity does with its hope in the Final Judgement and the Consummation of Time. For those who never received justice in this life, atheism can give no hope, but on Christianity, there is hope in the form of God the perfect Judge. The problem of moral evil is the problem of sin which demonstrates to people that the problem of moral evil is as much the problem of their evil as it is the problem of others. Christ has provided the solution to this by defeating the judicial consequences of sin and the power of sin to enslave.

Human free-will has been an important part of theodicy. Mackie has argued that God is responsible for moral evil because for free-will not to be

82. Hitchens, *God is Not Great*, p. 6.

random and indeterminate, humans have to choose in accordance with their natures. It could be argued therefore that God is responsible for moral evil because He gave human beings the capacity to choose to do wrong and therefore made them part evil. This chapter has argued that God has given humans free-will, but only the potential to do evil; the actualization of that evil is the responsibility of humans. It could be argued that the price of free-will is too high as the moral evil that has resulted is enormous. This chapter has suggested that the presence of sin in people's lives is a way of preparing people to wish to renounce their evil natures and their freedom to choose evil to be ready for life in heaven. Lucifer and his followers reveal that it is possible to live in God's presence and yet still sin, therefore for the redeemed to be able to live sinlessly in the presence of God, they are brought to the point through their being sick of sin that they freely choose to renounce their freedom to sin. The capacity of the redeemed to live forever perfectly in the presence of God is worth the price of moral evil. If anyone asks why give human beings the choice in the first place, this chapter has asserted that humans have the genuine choice of what sort of person they wish to be. This is part of the status of human beings. They either can work out their salvation with God or choose to fashion themselves into something evil. Whilst these choices are being made and reaffirmed over lifetimes, human and divine justice keep society for the most part tolerable. Being sick of sin can be achieved through non-horrendous evils, so why do horrendous evils exist? One reason is that through horrendous evils, victims come to know the true reality of God's love in the worst of circumstances; perpetrators and bystanders who could have intervened to help come to know the forgiveness of God in its fullest form.

In Hitchens' Second Problem of Evil, there is the problem of natural evil or suffering. Yet there is a contradiction between Hitchens' Problem of Evil and his own behavior. Hitchens has justified his health-destroying consumption of whiskey claiming it gave him inspiration as a writer, yet he demands that God remove all natural evils. Would he wish God to remove his capacity to drink which he enjoyed so much? More, there is an ironic parallel between the Christian philosopher Swinburne's view that natural evils produce moral goodness and Hitchens' view that destructive drinking gave rise to his work. But if it were possible for God to remove all natural evils, why should He not do so? The response to this is that humans have been gifted authority over the natural world by God and have tasks which only they can perform in the regulation of the natural world. But humans have chosen not to perform their responsibilities under the authority of God and so through their sin have gifted it in turn to the superlative evil being, Satan, now prince of this world. Unlike atheism, however, there is an end to natural evil when God redeems the natural world and sets it free from its bondage.

7

The Rationality of Christianity

Introduction

HITCHENS MAKES MUCH OF his view that Christianity is irrational and is immoral in the way that it propagates and enforces irrational beliefs. His worldview divides strictly into two on the matter: On the side of irrationality is all religion and on the side of rationality is atheism and secularism. What follows are diverse challenges to Hitchens' simplistic dualistic thinking. First, this chapter will demonstrate how rationality is prized within the Old Testament by providing biblical data of individuals famed for their intellectual and practical abilities and through a discussion of the importance of the book *Ecclesiastes* in demonstrating the quality of Old Testament philosophy. Second, it will present an interpretation of the Apostle Paul's view of the relationship between reason and faith which reveals a coherent and strongly compatibilist epistemology that makes room for both human and divine reason. It will also argue that Angus Menuge's theology which attempts to close the gap between natural theology and intimate knowledge of God, demonstrates the integral role of rationality within saving repentance. It will assert that Menuge's view provides us with a spectrum of rationalisms which lead a person to Christ and will consider in a way that Menuge does not the rational nature of the work of the Holy Spirit in conversion. Finally, the chapter will examine Christian praxis by demonstrating how the focus on truth is an indispensable part of Christian daily living.

God's Intelligent Servants of the Old Testament

Those who have been gifted with thinking abilities (and the term thinking abilities covers many forms of thinking from intellectual to common sense and practical reasoning) combined with a good moral character and emotional maturity are held in high honor within the Old Testament. Four individuals are eminent for their intelligence and good moral application of it: Adam the first human, Joseph the Viceroy of Egypt, Solomon the third King of Israel, and Daniel the principal adviser to Babylonian and Persian emperors.

Adam is best known for his foolish decision to eat of the Tree of the Knowledge of Good and Evil (Gen. 3:1-6). Adam, however, is described in Genesis as being given the task by God of tending and keeping the Garden of Eden (v. 2:15) and of giving names to 'all the cattle, to the birds of the air, and to every beast of the field' (2:20). At first glance these do not appear to be important details, but both reveal that an understanding of the natural world was important in God's opinion for Adam to have. By being given the work of managing a garden, Adam would have employed botanical knowledge. To name the animals and birds, Adam probably would have observed them first before deciding their names. He was therefore acting as a zoologist. How far Adam's knowledge went is impossible to tell, but there is evidence that God gave Adam intellectual autonomy in the naming of the creatures. God brought the animals and the birds to Adam to 'see what he would call them. And whatever Adam called each living creature, that was its name' (v. 15). God therefore accepted the names Adam gave them. Adam's investigation of the natural world preceded his sin (3:1-19) which means that the pursuit of scientific knowledge is not a transgressive unlocking of Pandora's Box, but is mandated by God. As for the sexist view that men make better scientists than women because they are by nature more rational, it must be emphasized that when Adam named the animals and birds, Eve was part of his being for the rib from which she was fashioned had not yet been removed from Adam (v. 21, 22). Eve therefore is shown to share in Adam's capacity to observe and classify the natural world and there is no reason to assume that after she had been drawn out from him she ceased to possess a scientific and rational capacity.

Joseph the Viceroy of Egypt provides our second example. The gift that first became apparent in Joseph was supernatural revelation rather than of reasoning. He anticipated his own greatness through a dream and was tactless enough to tell his brothers who hated what they regarded as his conceit and his father who rebuked what he saw as arrogance (Gen. 37: 1-11). Whilst in prison for the false accusation of sexual molestation, he interpreted correctly the dreams of two other prisoners (40:1-23). It is

Joseph's interpretation of Pharaoh's dreams warning of widespread famine that elevated him to the role of Viceroy (41:1-44). Joseph's belief in the precognitive nature of dreams is enough to disqualify him in the eyes of the New Atheists. The Bible, however, presents Joseph as also a man of reason. Once he had interpreted Pharaoh's dream, Joseph presented a plan to deal with the coming food crisis. He advised Pharaoh to:

> 'select a discerning and wise man, and set him over the land of Egypt. Let Pharaoh do this, and let him appoint officers over the land, to collect one-fifth of the produce of the land of Egypt in the seven plentiful years. And let them gather all the food of those good years that are coming and store up grain under the authority of Pharaoh, and let them keep food in the cities. Then that food shall be as a reserve for the seven years of famine which shall be in the land of Egypt, that the land may not perish during the famine' (41:33-36).

The Hebrew adjective which is interpreted as wise is *hakam*; the Hebrew noun for wisdom is *hokmah*.[1] In advising Pharaoh so well, Joseph demonstrated that he possessed *hokmah*, or sound decision-making.[2] Joseph had proved this through his diligent service as Potiphar's slave (39:1-6); his refusal to be sexually immoral (vv. 7-12); and his crediting God rather than himself with the interpretation of dreams (41:16).

If there is a biblical name most closely associated with wisdom, it is King Solomon. God appeared to him in a dream and asked him what he would like to be given. Solomon requested 'an understanding heart' to judge God's people and 'discern between good and evil. God was so pleased with Solomon's answer, He gave him 'a wise and understanding heart' greater than any other person before or after him (1 Kings 3:5-12). Solomon's mind was so wise and creative, he 'spoke three thousand proverbs' and composed 'one thousand and five' songs (4:32). Like Adam, Solomon had botanical and zoological understanding for he had great knowledge of trees, animals, birds, insects, and fish (4:33). It is clear from the text that Solomon's wisdom, creativity, and scientific knowledge were a blessing from God.

Daniel is our final example. According to the book named after him, Daniel was taken into exile by Nebuchadnezzar, the Babylonian emperor, when he conquered Judah and captured Jerusalem (Dan. 1:1-7). Along with others, Daniel was selected from among the young people of Israel because he was 'gifted in all wisdom, possessing knowledge and quick to understand' to be trained to serve in Babylon's government and speak Chaldean (v. 4).

---

1. Vine *et al.*, *Vine's Complete Expository Dictionary*, pp. 290-291.
2. Ibid., p. 291.

During his training God gave Daniel and three other Israelites called Hananiah, Mishael and Azariah 'knowledge and skill in all literature and wisdom'. Like Joseph, Daniel was also gifted by God to understand visions and dreams (v. 17). This no doubt also disqualifies Daniel as it does Joseph in the eyes of the New Atheists, but it is important to assert that regardless what one thinks of supernatural gifts, Daniel had genuine intellectual and practical ability and God is the source of this gift. Daniel enjoyed a very successful career serving Nebuchadnezzar as the ruler over the province of Babylon and chief administrator of the Babylonian wise men (2:48). He also enjoyed the confidence of the Persian Emperor, Darius, who promoted him to viceroy (6:3, 28).

Of course, we might, as Hitchens does, dismiss the above data as myth not history. But the problem Hitchens faces is that even if none of the above persons existed or did not exist in the way the Old Testament claims they did, we nevertheless have examples of Scripture holding rationality in its intellectual and practical forms in very high regard within narratives that are at the heart of the text. But such a concession is not necessary because there is good extra-biblical evidence that supports the Old Testament. The story of Adam and Eve might appear to be an obvious myth, but it is generally agreed that in the creation of myth and legends, original simple accounts of events which are close to the truth are adorned and embellished over time. The Hebrew creation story contrasts with other ancient societies' creation stories in that it is remarkably free of their embellishment and hyperbole. This suggests that Gen. 1-11 was the historical account that was turned into elaborate myths by Babylon and Sumeria.[3] There is not enough room to present all the extra-biblical evidence which demonstrates the plausibility of the narratives featuring Joseph, Daniel, and Solomon,[4] however, certain details are worth presenting here. According to Howard F. Vos, it was not unheard of for foreigners like Joseph to be highly promoted at the court of Pharaoh. A Semite called Yanhamu or Jauhamu was appointed as deputy to Amenhotep III with responsibility for the delta granaries, a responsibility like that of Joseph.[5] Though there is no known extra-biblical evidence for Daniel, the fact that Judah went into Babylonian captivity is not in dispute. Records located in Babylon's Hanging Gardens record that the exiled King of Judah Jehoiachin and his five sons were provided with a monthly ration, a place to live and were treated well which matches the account of 2 Kings 25: 27-30. As for Solomon, the conclusion among archaeologists has traditionally been that there is no corroborating

3. Norman L. Geisler, *Baker Encyclopedia of Christian Apologetics*, pp. 48, 49.

4. Josh McDowell presents the evidence in detail in his apologetics primer, *The New Evidence That Demands a Verdict: Evidence I & II*, pp. 108-115.

5. Howard F. Vos, *Genesis and Archaeology*, p. 106.

evidence for the biblical testimony,[6] though there is evidence of the existence of his father, David, whose dynasty is referred to in a Semitic inscription.[7] *National Geographic*, however, has reported that in the opinion of an Israeli archaeologist, Eilat Mazar, a tenth century B.C. defensive wall excavated on the edge of ancient Jerusalem is the same wall as the one recorded as being built by Solomon in 1 Kings 9:15. Israel Finkelstein of Tel Aviv University agrees that the wall is possibly King Solomon's.[8] The conclusion to draw is that Hitchens' dismissal of the Old Testament as myth and legend fails simply to consider the archaeological evidence.

Ancient Jewish Philosophy

The Old Testament book of Ecclesiastes is a monologue by someone who is referred to as the Preacher. Traditionally, the book's authorship has been ascribed to Solomon, which was decisive in ensuring the book's canonization which was achieved after much opposition and debate.[9] Scholars conventionally date the text to the late Persian or Hellenistic era.[10] However, as with the Epistle to the Hebrews, the anonymity of the Preacher and the author, if the two were separate people, is an incidental issue to the importance of the method and content of the book in demonstrating that Christianity and, of course, Judaism are rational world views.

The method of the Preacher is a rational one. He states that he devoted himself to study and to explore by wisdom life (1:12). He does not rely upon supernatural revelation but upon his own capacity to think. Summaries of the book's teachings agree that the book's composition was a rational one. Gerhard von Rad writes of the book's rational evaluation of life which concludes that life is meaningless.[11] James Crenshaw sees the Preacher's purpose as demonstrating or proving the claim that life is preposterous.[12] Daphne Merkin describes the book as philosophical.[13] Whatever one might

---

6. 'What evidence is there that the Temple of Solomon existed?' at https://www.bbc.co.uk/sn/tvradio/programmes/horizon/solomon_qa.shtml (accessed 1 April at 18:31).

7. Avaraham Biram, 'House of David', *Biblical Archaeology Review*, March/April 1994.

8. Mati Milstein, 'King Solomon's Wall Found-Proof of Bible Tale', *National Geographic News*, 27 February 2010.

9. Brueggemann, *An Introduction to the Old Testament*, p. 329.

10. Ibid.

11. Gerhard von Rad, *Wisdom in Israel*, pp. 227, 228.

12. James Crenshaw, *Urgent Advice and Probing Questions*, p. 509.

13. Daphne Merkin, 'Ecclesiastes' in ed. David Rosenberg, *Congregation: Contemporary Writers Read the Jewish Bible*, p. 397.

think of the book's conclusions, one cannot doubt that an analytical process has led the Preacher to them.

The conclusion that the Preacher reaches about life is that it is meaningless. He identifies specifically what he concludes is meaningless. Though the Preacher is a man seeking wisdom, he concludes that wisdom is meaningless, not because wisdom is not wise somehow after all, but because the same fate awaits the wise and the foolish: both will die in due course and be forgotten (2:12-16). Though the Preacher has owned many things which is described as amounting to that of a great potentate, when he surveyed all the wives, slaves, and property he had amassed, he concluded that it was 'meaningless, a chasing of the wind' as 'nothing was gained under the sun', presumably because such wealth is impermanent (vv. 1-11). Riches too are meaningless because 'whoever has money never has money enough' (5:10). Work or toil has no meaning because each 'must leave all he owns to someone who has not worked for it' (v. 21). Because of the oppression and injustice in the world, the Preacher concludes that better is it for the one 'who has not yet been' (4: 3). Death is the 'common destiny' of all whether they are good or evil (9:2). Death is evil for the dead are forgotten (v. 5). The advice of the Preacher in the light of life's meaninglessness is to live keeping in mind the certainty that God will judge everyone:

> 'fear God and keep His commandments, for this is the whole duty
> of man. For God will bring every deed into judgement, including
> every hidden thing, whether it is good or evil (12: 13, 14).

Hitchens has presented religion as irrational because it demands the acceptance of irrational propositions and suppresses independent thought, criticism, and dissent. The inclusion of Ecclesiastes in the canon demonstrates that there is space for dissent within Judaism and Christianity. The Preacher recognizes the legitimacy of the divine moral code and that ultimately God has control for He renders reward and punishment according to each one's deeds, but he also presents the view that God is inaccessible and indifferent to human fate. This is a bold challenge to the optimism of Old Testament faith.[14] The heterodoxy of Ecclesiastes therefore cannot be assimilated into Israel's confidence in their divine destiny[15] and glaringly challenges Christ's message of loving intimacy with God as Father and the indwelling of the Holy Spirit in His followers (John 14). Ecclesiastes is therefore marked by a courageous candor in that the Preacher is prepared to state exactly how life and God appeared to him within the context in

---

14. Brueggemann, *An Introduction to the Old Testament*, pp. 393-398.

15. Ibid., p. 331.

which he lived. If the writer was Solomon and it was written towards the end of his life when he had time to ruminate on human life, then the text suggests repentance for his descent into idolatry under the influence of his many foreign wives (1 Kings 11:1-13). If the text was written during the late Persian or Hellenistic periods, the destabilized socio-economic conditions that prevailed in Palestine at that might account for the text's gloominess.[16]

Christianity, faith, and reason

In his essay 'Faith and Reason',[17] James Swindall provides an overview of the historical analysis of the connection between faith and reason.[18]

a. The conflict model. Here there is a rivalry between faith and reason in explaining and justifying religious beliefs. Fundamentalists side with the power of faith to provide justification and scientific naturalists side with the power of reason.[19]

b. The incompatibilist model. Here faith and reason are two distinctly different methods with different aims and objects. There is no rivalry between the two for as Swindall succinctly summarizes: Rationality seeks scientific truth; religion searches for the truth about God. The model divides further in three ways. The transrationalists see faith as higher than reason with reason only able to construct an understanding of what is already known by faith. The irrationalists regard religious beliefs as irrational, therefore they cannot be subject to rational scrutiny. Fideists hold that faith ought not to be subject to rational assessment at all.[20]

c. The weak incompatibilist model. On this view, though faith and reason occupy separate domains, interaction is possible between them.[21] In other words, though separate ways of thinking, they can help illuminate the nature of things for one another.

16. Ibid., pp. 329, 330.

17. James Swindall, 'Faith and Reason' at https//www.iep.utm.edu/faith-re (accessed 26 March 2017 at 18:11).

18. Ibid.

19. Ibid.

20. Ibid.

21. Ibid.

d. The strong compatibilist model. Reason and faith are seen to inter-
relate and even have parity. The claims of faith can therefore be demonstrated using reason. [22]

Swindall understands Paul as providing a range of ways in which faith
and reason relate. He notes how Paul engages in rational discussion with the
Epicurean and Stoic philosophers in Athens (Acts 17:18) and in Romans 1: 20
he sees Paul asserting a natural theology in which anyone can from using his
or her reason to reflect on the nature of the natural order concludes that God
exists. Swindall sees in 1Corinthians 1:23 evidence of Paul's incompatibilism
for Paul claims that Christian revelation is foolishness to the Greeks.[23] Though
Swindall does not charge Paul with contradiction, it is important to take these
three instances and propose that there is coherence here in Paul's approach.

Before Paul spoke to the Athenian philosophers, he was already reasoning in the synagogue and market-place with the Jews and God-fearing Greeks
(Acts 17:17). Paul's message to the philosophers demonstrates a method of
evangelism. Paul finds the entry point into their polytheistic worldview
through their altar to an unknown God (17:23). Paul then takes the opportunity to testify to who that unknown God is: The God of the Old Testament
who raised Christ from the dead. According to Walter Klaiber, Paul follows
Stoic patterns of argument, presenting God as the Creator and quoting from
a stoic hymn to Zeus.[24] Traditionally, this sermon has been understood to be
the use of indigenous concepts for missionary evangelism.[25] This is true, but
Paul makes it clear that the God he is referring to is not the sort of god that
his audience might conceive the unknown god to be (v. 23). He is superior to
Greek gods because He is omnipresent and self-sufficient (vv. 25, 28). As He is
omnipresent, Paul testifies that people can reach out to Him (v. 27). By saying
this, Paul is assuring his Greek audience that his God is not a tribal deity, but a
universal Lord. He also describes God as not like gold, silver or stone, thereby
distinguishing between God and the Greek idols (v. 29). God according to
Paul will judge the world justly through a man appointed by God whom God
raised from the dead (v. 31).

The religiosity of Athens as described by Luke and Paul's acknowledgement of it (v. 22) is a consequence of natural theology's ability to form within a
culture the conclusion that gods, or God exist. This phenomenon is discussed
by Paul in Romans 1:19-23. The knowledge of God's 'invisible attributes' is
possible by observing the things He has made. Paul provides two examples

22. Ibid.

23. Ibid.

24. Walter Klaiber, *Call and Response*, pp. 83, 84.

25. Ibid., p. 84.

of these attributes: God's 'eternal power' and His divinity (v. 20). To create
a temporal universe, the Creator must be outside of time, hence eternal and
powerful. Even to create a universe, which is not self-creating, for something
cannot come from nothing, the Creator must be something other than the
universe He has made, namely that He is capable of original creation. On both
occasions-testifying to the Athenian philosophers and writing to the Roman
Christians-Paul is presenting a strong compatibilist case between the contem-
plation of natural phenomena and the *sensus divinitatus*.

What unites Paul's speech to the Athenians and his epistle to the Romans is his assertion that the knowledge of God is not itself sufficient for
his proper worship, for what denies this is the wickedness of human hearts
which substitutes idolatrous images for what it knows about God (vv. 21-
23). Though New Atheism does not accept the claims of natural theology
and denies the existence of all gods, thereby denying that there can be a
crime of idolatry as envisaged by Paul, it is important to assert that it is
the case that truth, which is best served through epistemic virtue, can be
suppressed because of evil motives. It is incumbent upon all to examine
whether their beliefs are the consequence of evidence or the consequence of
the denial of truths which they do not want to be truths. The New Atheists
like to argue that Christianity is wish-thinking, but if we are challenged to
examine our beliefs for evidence of self-delusion, it is equally legitimate to
challenge the New Atheists as to whether their atheism is a denial of what
they know is true, but do not wish to be so: That God exists and that the
natural order is testimony to that.

Swindall's final example of Paul's attitude towards rationality suggests that Paul was presenting faith in an incompatibilist way. He quotes
1 Corinthians 1:23 in which Paul declares the Corinthian Christians that
he and they preach 'Christ crucified' which is 'foolishness to the Gentiles'.
Paul therefore seems to place at the heart of Christianity a belief that is
irrational but which to be a Christian must be accepted by faith. But the
context of this verse disproves that Paul is not talking in a strictly incompatibilist sense if we accept the existence of the higher reason of God.
Paul's purpose in this passage is to teach that God's wisdom is far greater
than human wisdom (v. 20), and that what might seem foolish from a
human perspective is entirely wise and reasonable from God's. Therefore,
to preach that a crucified man is the means to salvation is a foolish message to those who are perishing (v. 18), no doubt because they can see no
necessary connection between the crucifixion and salvation, but to those
who are being saved, Christ crucified is the power and wisdom of God (v.
24). The crucifixion of Christ, though unreasonable from an unredeemed
perspective, is entirely wise from God and the redeemed ones' point of

view. Christianity is therefore grounded in a higher reason than human reason which is God's. The goal of the renewed mind (Romans 12:2) is to have 'the full riches of complete understanding' so that the mysteries of God are known in Christ in whom dwell 'all treasures of wisdom and knowledge' (Colossians 2:2-3). The Cross is one of those mysteries; so too is the Trinity, but there are many, many others. Christianity far from closing the mind seeks the restoration of it to full knowledge. This is probably what Paul means when he tells the Corinthians that he and they have 'the mind of Christ' (1 Cor. 2:16).

Paul's theology of reason is not therefore diverse as Swindall suggests, but coherent. Paul presents a strong compatibilist view in that he adopts a reasoned approach with the Athenian philosophers and argues that God's existence and attributes of eternal power and divinity can be inferred from the natural order. Paul is an advocate of epistemic virtue in that he castigates humanity for suppressing their knowledge of God because of their wickedness. Paul argues that the efficacy of the Cross which appears ridiculous to the sinful mind is a manifestation of God's wisdom which is immeasurably greater than human wisdom. Finally, Paul provides glimpses of what a fully redeemed mind is like, complete in the knowledge and understanding of the mysteries of Christ.

Angus Menuge and Ramified Personalized Natural Theology: A Third Way

The life of the Christian is one of daily repentance because of an awareness of the holiness of God and though the Christian is steadfastly sanctified, there is the continuing presence of old sinful desires. One problem within Christian philosophy is that it is possible to assent to the proposition that God exists based on natural theology without having a deep conviction that it is the case and a desire to live as Christ's disciple. Angus Menuge resolves this problem by positing a third intermediary way that closes the gap between the objective, distant knowledge of God through natural theology whereby the philosopher concludes there is a God because of logical and empirical argument and direct, intimate knowledge of God.[26]

Menuge clearly has made much room within his approach for Christian rationality, but he does not think it is enough if repentance and the salvation of people is the Christian's goal. What is required is that the Christian

---

26. Angus Menuge, 'Ramified Personalized Natural Theology: A Third Way', at https://www.epsociety.org/library/articles.asp?pid=195&mode=detail (accessed 1 April 2017 at 22:15), p. 1.

philosopher (and any Christian engaged in discussion with unbelievers) lives and relates to unbelievers in a way that draws them to Christ. There is a personal appeal to the unbeliever to enter into a Christo-centric life and acceptance that Christ is the only cure for the sickness of sin.'[27]

There is much to commend in Menuge's approach, particularly his determination to unite logical argument with the personal call to repent. What is important to note in his framework is that reason and faith work together within apologetic discourse. The reason of natural theology can take a person as far as accepting there is a God and ramified natural theology can take a person as far as accepting that there is a God who is the God of the Bible revealed in Christ, but there is the testimony of how the Christian relates to the unbeliever that makes the invitation to trust Christ.

We have therefore moved from assenting to propositions, which is the consequence of reasoned thought, to trusting in a Person, which is the move of faith. Faith is reasonable because trust is extended if the Person is trustworthy, in other words as long as there is evidence that He can be trusted, which He is content to supply. Faith therefore is a dynamic process wherein questions about the One in whom we trust are asked and the level of trust experienced by us fluctuates or even momentarily disappears according to the conclusions we draw about the One whom we are learning to trust.

The relationship between reason and faith can therefore be seen as a spectrum of rationality. We begin with natural theology which leads to a personalized appeal which in turn leads to faith's inductive confidence whereby God is trusted because He has proven trustworthy in the past. Moving a person from natural theology to a living relationship with Christ is the work of the Holy Spirit. It is important not to see the Spirit as some sort of irrational Force. Christ calls the Holy Spirit 'Counsellor' (John 16: 7) and the Spirit of Truth (v. 13). The work of the Spirit in conversion is to convict the word of its guilt because of sin (v. 8). This is not a process whereby a person is presented through revelation with some esoteric piece of information, but a true evaluation of what the person is and probably what the person knows already. The conviction of the Holy Spirit is therefore the enablement of a person to see what s/he really is, which is a sinner in need of a Savior. The work of the Spirit is therefore empirical: He presents the facts of a person's being to that person. It is also personal, which is not irrational, because He calls for a response called repentance and the challenge to trust God.

27. Ibid.

Meditating on the Truth

How is the Christian mind to work in everyday practice? It is the proposition of this section of the chapter that rather than wish-thinking which according to Hitchens is the hallmark of the Christian mind, it is regular reflection upon the truth which God requires of His people.

In Philippians 4:8 Paul urges the Philippian Christians to meditate on 'whatever things are true, whatever things are noble, whatever things are just, whatever things are pure, whatever things are lovely, whatever things are of good report' and upon 'virtue' and 'anything praiseworthy'.

To understand Paul's exhortation better, it is necessary to understand what he meant by truth, and by doing so, one will discover that Christians are required to operate to a high epistemic standard. The word Paul uses is the Greek word *aletheia* which can be translated in two ways: first as the objective truth which lies behind what appears to be true.[28] It can also be used subjectively to refer to the integrity of a person.[29] Paul is using the word *aletheia* in the objective sense for he writes of things not people that are true.

Christians, therefore, are not to accept what appears to be true, but to seek what really is the case. Christians are required to make enquiry into the true nature of reality both as people making sense of reality from an everyday, common sense view and from an academic view, such as that of science. Christians are thus mandated by Scripture to be skeptical over what appears to be the case until they have evidence as to what is really the case, which is precisely the habit of mind that ranks highly with Hitchens who as we have seen, speaks highly of skepticism as an epistemic virtue.[30]

One final observation needs to be made about this verse in Philippians. Paul exhorts his audience to meditate on the truth, but also upon many pleasant things such as things that are noble, pure, and just. Why would he do this? One possibility is that meditating on the truth means focusing not only on pleasant but also unpleasant truths and worse. To provide some mental balance to the apprehension of disquieting realities, Paul suggests keeping in mind those things that are genuinely uplifting. It is the emotional health of the mind that is as important to Paul as its truth-perceiving capabilities.

28. Vine *et al.*, *Vine's Complete Expository Dictionary*, p. 645.
29. Ibid.
30. Hitchens, *God is Not Great*, p. 255.

Conclusion

In this chapter, we have seen how Christianity can claim to be a rational worldview. Adam and Eve engaged in scientific activity and individuals in the Old Testament received God's approval because of their reason. Ecclesiastes provides an example of ancient Jewish philosophy which demonstrates the space there is within Judeo-Christianity for dissent. The Apostle Paul's epistemology has been shown to be coherent and strongly compatibilist and which acknowledges the importance of human and divine reason. It has also argued that Menuge's combination of reason and faith reveals the role of deduction and faith's induction within salvation. It has also shown how rational the Holy Spirit's actions are in conversion. Finally, this chapter has shown how the focus on truth is an indispensable part of Christian daily living.

8

Conclusion

My Findings

HITCHENS' ANTI-THEISM AND ANTI-RELIGIONISM consist of four propositions:

1. There is no good evidence that God exists.

2. It is a good thing that He does not exist, because if He did, He would be a dictator.

3. Religion is poisonous because it is superlatively immoral.

4. Religion is irrational because there is no evidence for its propositions.

For Hitchens, so-called evidence for God such as arguments for the fine tuning of the universe and the truth of Christ's resurrection lack any credible evidence. He therefore concludes that there is no good reason to believe that there is a God and that it is highly probable that God does not exist. Hitchens rejects the term agnostic because he sees it as a fudging of the question. It is not the case that we cannot know if there is a God whether because the evidence for and against seem evenly matched, or because God, if He did exist, could not be known because He is inaccessibly transcendent. What we do know is that there is no good evidence for God's existence and so we can proceed on the reasonable conclusion that there is no God. Or so Hitchens says.

At a deeper level, Hitchens' worldview rests on three axioms: His deep love of personal and political freedom, his profound conviction as to what is right and wrong, and his view that being rational is the best way, if not the only way, of understanding the truth of what is the case. Therefore, God the totalitarian and immoral, irrational religion are anathema to him.

Though Hitchens is a member of the New Atheist leadership, he disagrees at certain points with his fellow leading New Atheists. Hitchens does not think that religion will disappear and his reason for saying this is that the defect of religion has been selected for during human evolution. In this he betrays the influence of the Old Right which sees human nature as flawed and politics as the practical means of coping with this weakness. The struggle against religion is therefore ongoing for Hitchens and secularism will not necessarily win the struggle. Because of this, Hitchens' view is a form of secular Manicheanism. Hitchens approves of the use of military violence against extremist religion such as jihadism. He approves too of 'regime-change' to topple theocracies and replace it with democratic regimes and in this Hitchens demonstrates the influence of neo-conservatism on his thinking. To keep moderate religion tame, Hitchens advocates that religion is kept out of the political sphere and restrained by law within a secular democratic society. But Hitchens is guilty of a greater heresy: He does not wish to see religion disappear. One reason he gives is because he enjoys the debate with religion and sees it as the most important one because by debating with the religious, one can define more sharply the contours of reason and civilization. But there is another reason, though one that I infer because Hitchens never says this: To remove religion totally is a totalitarian act, and therefore contrary to Hitchens' libertarian instincts.

Hitchens' thinking, like that of his fellow New Atheists, is not postmodernist. He is a foundationalist who seeks evidence for his beliefs and challenges his opponents for theirs. He is not a moral relativist either, being convinced that certain moral values are true whether we like them or not. In this he is counter-cultural, though from conviction, not because of the need to appear contrarian. It is Hitchens' foundationalism that enables debate between himself and Christian apologists because both sides agree that there is such thing as the truth of the matter.

Hitchens thinks and writes like anyone else within a context. Within the context of the history of thought, Hitchens sits within an intellectual tradition stretching back through the Russian thinkers Goldman and Bakunin and all the way back to Lucretius. With such a weighty tradition at his back, it is forgivable that Hitchens has really nothing new to say, but because he has a way of packaging ideas in novel ways, such as the Hitchens' Challenge and the Hitchens' Razor, and has a ubiquitous, enduring presence in the Media and on the Internet, a robust, comprehensive refutation of his beliefs is required.

The Christian critical response to Hitchens has been by and large successful, though it is guilty of failing to distinguish how Hitchens differs from his fellow New Atheist leaders. Christian apologists such as John Lennox have welcomed Hitchens' anti-postmodernism as it makes debate possible. Christians have asked what is new about New Atheism and have concluded that it is the intensity of its angry tone that is unprecedented caused by the durability of religion and atheism's low status. Hitchens is angry with religion's privileges and its harmfulness, but not with religion's failure to disappear because he neither expects it to disappear nor does he want it to. Hitchens is a high status anti-theist who is respected by both anti-theists and religious believers; he is not likely to be angry about his lack of status. New Atheism appears to Christian apologists as evangelistic, but Hitchens seems less concerned about converting others and more interested in having the debate for its own sake and enjoying his celebrity status. According to Alister McGrath, the center of New Atheism is the online communities it has spawned, but Hitchens, unlike Dawkins, has never set up his own homepage, though websites about him have been established. Albert Mohler thinks that the worst thing about New Atheism is its derisive attitude to religious beliefs, but though Hitchens has ridiculed Christianity, he is also friendly with many Christians and has engaged in cordial debate with some of them.

Christian apologists have had much success in the refutation of Hitchens' assertions. Terry Eagleton has demonstrated that faith is not irrational, but trust in God based on the evidence of God's behavior. Mark Roberts has elucidated Hitchens' factual errors when writing about the New Testament. Alister McGrath and John Lennox have presented compelling argument in favor of biblical morality and David Bentley Hart has shown how the Christian revolution led to unmatched benevolence. Peter Hitchens has informed us that his brother had answered his own 'Challenge' with reference to Lech Walesa and Solidarity and has demonstrated how Stalinism might have had a theological carapace, but its heart was atheist. William Lane Craig has cogently argued for the *kalam* cosmological and teleological arguments in contrast to Hitchens' jejune criticisms of them. McGrath and Lennox have disproven Hitchens' view that religion and science are antagonistic. McGrath interestingly has explored the arguments of historians of science who see Christianity as the cradle of modern science. Lennox, McGrath, and Peter S. Williams have argued from Scripture that Christianity is rational. With regards to the shortcomings of materialism, Hitchens has been shown to have no answer. The Argument from Desire reveals how the Christian God's existence is desirable. Terry Eagleton's cultural criticism of New Atheism as regarding Western civilization as superior to parallel civilizations does not apply to Hitchens. Neither does the Christian feminist accusation that New Atheism is a privileged white male club apply to Hitchens. However, Christian feminists have argued *contra* Hitchens that Christianity ought not to be seen as a sexist worldview because of Scripture.

Atheist critics can be divided into four groups which overlap: Old Atheism, the New New Atheism, Atheist Feminism and 'Pure' Atheism. Both Old Atheists and New New Atheists dislike the angry, hateful tone of New Atheism's attitude towards religion and its way of representing all religion as irrational and immoral without differentiating between those religionists who are irrational and immoral and those who are not. New New Atheism is also prepared to admit that there are certain features of religion which ought to be preserved, albeit in a secular form. Atheist Feminists of both the Old and New New type have complained about the lack of women in the New Atheist leadership and have protested at sexist behavior they have experienced at atheist conventions and conferences. Pure Atheists, who take atheism to its logical conclusion, regard New Atheism as under the influence of Christianity through its belief in free-will and objective morality. Pure Atheists take atheism to its logical conclusion and deny the existence of free-will and objective values.

In searching for ways to develop existing arguments against Hitchens and find new ones, I chose to begin my case with the nature of God. I demonstrate He cannot be a totalitarian by examining two attributes of God which have not featured in the debate so far: That He is unchanging, and therefore not capricious, and He does not impose impossible laws. I have emphasized too within the debate that for free-will to exist within a determinist universe, it would have to come from outside the universe, and as God wishes to be loved, which means to be chosen freely by His human creation, God is the author and guarantor of free will. My thesis has added to the debate a discussion of how sin, not God, is the worst totalitarian in the world, and that God is our liberator from it. I have defended a libertarian view of hell and have concluded that those who go there are not consigned there by a despotic deity, but freely choose to go and remain there. I have also supplemented Christian criticism by turning attention to how Christ defied totalitarian regimes and suffered at their hands and how the Song of Solomon presents a radical and startling image of God as a loving husband of his people and of the beauty of the human body and eroticism.

My book presents the evidence that Christianity ought to be no friend of theocracy and fascism. I have emphasized that the separation of church and state can be grounded in biblical data. I have also used the evidence of John Locke to show how the notion of state and church separation is contained within one tradition of Christian political philosophy and the arguments of Maritain who sees Christianity as the cradle of modern democracy. Christianity too has a tradition of resistance to tyrants. I have already referred to Locke, but I add to the debate the theology of disobedience that the 18th century Boston Pastor Jonathan Mayhew taught which did much

to stir the American Revolution. A recent example of Christian resistance
to dictatorship is that of the East German Protestants who through their
mass, peaceful demonstrations contributed decisively to the fall of Communism in that country in 1989. Peter Hitchens has done much to demonstrate
that Stalin's regime was atheist rather than theocratic, so I have introduced
Nikolai Khrushchev, the Soviet premier, as an example of a militant atheist
leader who did not festoon his regime with theocratic trappings, and yet
persecuted Christians. Finally, I have engaged with Hitchens' strange hero-
worship of Trotsky and have shown how inconsistent this is with Hitchens'
democratic values.

In chapter six I consider the flaws in Hitchens' moral philosophy
and atheodicy. Hitchens speaks in terms of objective morality, and yet his
metaethical belief that human values are the product of evolution provides
only the ground for moral relativism. God is the best ground for objective
morality and for the belief that humans are intrinsically valuable. These are
the extensions of established arguments, but they needed to be applied to
Hitchens. As Hitchens can provide no objective ground for his morality,
there is no reason not to prefer Nietzsche's anti-democratic philosophy
to Hitchens' secular liberalism. As for the problem of the moral problem
of evil, chapter six suggests that Hitchens fails to define how God might
intervene to prevent suffering without compromising human free-will. On
Christianity there are limits to evil that atheism cannot provide, and that
justice will prevail for all cases of injustice on Christianity whereas on atheism, many cases of injustice will go unpunished. Again, these are established
arguments, but they need application to Hitchens' atheodicy. One reason
why God might permit horrendous evil among other reasons is to persuade
people to give up freely their freedom to sin or commit moral evil, thus
rendering them fit for His kingdom. Hitchens' natural atheodicy is shown
to be contradictory, for he was never prepared to give up the alcohol that
contributed to his esophageal cancer. Moreover, if there is natural evil, it is
because humans have ceded control of the world to the satanic powers, but
creation will be restored. Once again, Christianity provides a limit to evil,
in this case the natural kind. There is nothing new to that argument, but it
needs to be restated in riposte to Hitchens.

Chapter seven joins the debate over the rationality of Christianity. It
provides details about the rationality of a number of Old Testament figures.
Ecclesiastes is discussed as an example of ancient Jewish philosophy which
forms part of the Christian Bible. Ecclesiastes demonstrates what space exists within the Judeo-Christian tradition for questioning orthodoxy. Paul's
epistemology is shown to be coherent and strongly compatibilist in terms
of the relationship between faith and reason. Menuge's closure of the gap

between natural theology and Gethsemane epistemology shows how intrinsic reason is to the conversion of people to Christianity and to the relationship of people to God. The work of the Holy Spirit too in conversion is a rational one. Finally, Christianity is shown to teach a focus on truth as part of the Christian lifestyle.

Further Study

This text is certainly not the last word with Hitchens and the debate with him, and if not with him specifically, with anti-theism, will continue for the foreseeable future. Studies of further examples of Christian resistance to authoritarian regimes would be profitable in the argument with Hitchens' anti-religionism. Hitchens likes to charge the Catholic Church with collusion with Fascism, and yet an exposition of Catholic resistance to Polish communism through the Catholic Church and trade unions would be a powerful counter-example. A developed comparison of Nietzsche's anti-theism with Hitchens and New Atheism would be a doctorate-level study in its own right. The problem of evil is an enduring problem within theology and philosophy and it is certain that further arguments can be brought to bear on Hitchens' use of this problem in its moral and natural forms. Another profitable line of inquiry would be an in-depth study of the Christian influences on Hitchens' worldview of which Hitchens was aware.[1]

A Final Appeal

Though this book may stimulate further study, one thing this book cannot do is make an appeal to Hitchens himself as he is deceased. Though Hitchens, as far as we can tell, remained true to his anti-theism in his final hours, we can still appeal to the living, to those who have read and listened to Hitchens, over the questions that he took very seriously and enjoyed debating: that of the nature of God and Christianity.

---

1. Hitchens, *God is Not Great*, p. 11.

Bibliography

Adams, Marilyn McCord. "Caveat Emptor! Moral Theory and Problems of Evil" (presentation, Center for Philosophy of Religion, University of Notre Dame, 15 November 2013) at https://www.youtube.com/watch?v=K4rsQmM1cx4.

———'Horrendous Evils and the Goodness of God', ed. Marilyn McCord Adams and Robert Merrihew Adams, *The Problem of Evil* (Oxford: OUP, 1990).

———'Ignorance, Instrumentality, Compensation and the Problem of Evil', *Sophia* 52, 2013.

Aikman, David. *The Delusion of Disbelief* (Carol Stream, IL: Salt River, 2008).

Akhmatova, Anna. *The Complete Poems of Anna Akhmatova*, trans. Judith Hemschemeyer, Roberta Reeder, ed. (Boston: Zephyr and Canongate, 2000).

Allison, Jr., Dale C. 'Matthew', ed. John Barton and John Muddiman, *The Oxford Bible Commentary* (Oxford: OUP, 2007).

Akkoc, Raziye. 'Mapped: These are the world's most religious countries', at http://www.telegraph.co.uk/news/worldnews/11530382/Mapped-These-are-the-worlds-most-religious-countries.html.

https://www.amazon.co.uk/God-Not-Great-Religion-Everything/dp/1843545748.

Anthony, Andrew. 'Christopher Hitchens: You Have to Choose Your Regrets', *The Guardian*, 14 November 2010.

Aristotle, *Metaphysics* 1005 b19-20.

Aslan, Reza. 'Sam Harris and the "New Atheists" aren't new, aren't even atheists', *Salon*, 21 November 2014.

Augustine, *Confessions* (Oxford: Oxford Paperbacks, 1998).

Ayer, A. J. *The Central Questions of Philosophy* (London: Penguin, 1973).

Baggini, Julian. 'Nyateismen virker mot sin hensikt', *Fri Tanke* 2009/1, March 2009.

Baggini, Julian and Fosl, Peter S. *The Philosopher's Toolkit: A Compendium of Philosophical Concept and Methods* (Oxford: Blackwell: 2003).

Barbour, Ian G. *When Science Meets Religion: Enemies, Strangers, or Partners?* (New York: HarperCollins, 2000).

'Barbour's Typologies' at https//serc.carleton.edu/sp/library/sac/examples/barbour.html.

https://www.bbc.co.uk/religion/religions/isla/ataglance/glance.

Beattie, Tina. *The New Atheists: The Twilight of Reason and the War on Religion* (London: DLT, 2007).

Biram, Avaraham. 'House of David', *Biblical Archaeology Review*, March/April 1994.

Blackburn, Simon. *Oxford Dictionary of Philosophy* (Oxford: Oxford University Press, 2005).

'Blair and Hitchens keep the gloves on' at https://news.bbc.co.uk/today/hi/today/newsid_9234000/9234386.stm

Blue, Carol. 'The Last Word: Christopher Hitchens' widow on his life, his work, and his death', *Slate*, August 27th 2012.

Botton, Alain, de. *Religion for Atheists* (London: Penguin Group, 2012).

Brigham, Jamie T., Carroll, Sean M. and Thornton, Joseph W. "Evolution of Hormone Receptor Activity by Molecular Exploitation', *Science* 312:5770, April 7, 2006.

Brooke, John Hedley. *Science and Religion: Some Historical Perspectives* (Cambridge: CUP, 2014).

Bruce, F. F. *New Testament History* (New York: Doubleday 1980).

Brueggemann, Walter. *An Introduction to the Old Testament: The Canon and Christian Imagination* (Louisville: Westminster John Knox, 2003).

https://www.theguardian.com/commentisfree/andrewbrown/2009/apr/30/religion-atheism-dawkins-contempt.

Brown, Mick. 'Godless in Tumourville: Christopher Hitchens interview', *The Daily Telegraph*, 25 March 2011.

Butt, Riazat. 'Atheist bus campaign spreads the word of no God nationwide', *The Guardian*, 6 January 2009.

Carroll, Rory. 'Pope says sorry for sins of church', *The Guardian*, 13 March 2000.

'Children Targeted in the Genocide' at https://www.hrw.org/reports/2003/rwanda0403/rwanda0403-03.htm

Cook, David. *Blind Alley Beliefs* (Leicester: Inter-Varsity, 1996).

Conzelmann, H and A. Lindemann, A. *Interpreting the New Testament: An Introduction to the Principles and Methods of N. T. Exegesis* (Peabody: Hendrickson, 1988).

Conquest, Robert. *Trotsky: A Biography* (London: Macmillan, 2009).

Council for Secular Humanism, 'What is Secular Humanism?', at http://www.secularhumanism.org/index.php/3260.

Craig, William Lane. 'The Resurrection of Theism', *Truth Journal*, updated 8th August 1997 at www.leaderus.com/truth/3truth01.html.

Crenshaw, James. *Urgent Advice and Probing Questions; Collected Writings on Old Testament Wisdom* (Atlanta: Mercer University Press, 1995).

Daley, David. 'Camille Paglia takes on Jon Stewart, Trump, Sanders: "Liberals think of themselves as very open-minded, but that's simply not true!"', at https://www.salon.com/2015/07/29/camille_paglia_takes_on_jon_stewart_trump_sanders_liberals_think_of_themselves_as_very_open_minded_but_that%E2%80%99s_simply_not_true/

Davies, Brian. *An Introduction to the Philosophy of Religion* (Oxford: OUP, 1989).

Davies, Brian. *Philosophy of Religion: A Guide and Anthology* (Oxford: OUP, 2000).

Dawkins, Richard. 'Is Science a Religion?', *The Humanist*, Jan./Feb. 1997.

————*River out of Eden* (New York: Basic Books, 1995).

————*The God Delusion* (London: Bantam Press, 2006).

————*The God Delusion: 10th Anniversary Edition* (London: Black Swan, 2016).

Dawkins, Richard. *The Selfish Gene* (Oxford: Oxford Paperbacks, 1989).

Dennett, Daniel. *Breaking the Spell: Religion as a Natural Phenomenon* (New York: Viking, 2006).

———'The Bright Stuff', at https://www.the-brights.net/vision/essays/dennett_nyt_article.html.

De Silva, Bruce. 'Pundit Christopher Hitchens picks a fight in book, "God is Not Great"', *Rutland Herald* [Vermont], 25 April 2007.

Dirckx, Sharon. *Why? Looking at God, evil & personal suffering* (Nottingham: IVP, 2013).

Eagleton, Terry. 'Faith, Knowledge and Terror' in ed. John Hughes, *The Unknown God: Sermons Responding to the New Atheists* (Eugene, Oregon: Cascade Books, 2013).

———*Reason, Faith, and Revolution: Reflections on the God Debate* (New Haven: Yale University Press, 2009), p. 111.

Eaton, George. 'Preview: Richard Dawkins Interviews Christopher Hitchens' at https://www.newstatesman.com/blogs/the-staggers/2011/12/dawkins-hitchens-catholic.

Ehrman, Bart. *Misquoting Jesus: The Story Behind Who Changed the Bible and Why* (New York: HarperCollins, 2005).

Elwell, Walter A. and Yarbrough, Robert W. *Encountering the New Testament: A Historical and Theological Survey, Second Edition* (Grand Rapids, Michigan: Baker Academic, 2005).

Figes, Orlando. *Revolutionary Russia, 1891-1991* (London: Pelican, 2014).

Fitzpatrick, William. 'Morality and Evolutionary Biology' in ed. Edward N. Zalta, *The Stanford Encyclopedia of Philosophy* (Fall 2014 Edition), at https://plato.stanford.edu/archives/fall2014/entriesbiology/>

Fodor, Jerry and Piatelli-Palmarini, Massimo. 'Survival of the Fittest Theory', *New Scientist*, 6 February 2010.

Ford, David. *Theology: A Very Short Introduction* (Oxford: OUP, 2000).

Geisler, Norman L. *Baker Encyclopedia of Christian Apologetics* (Grand Rapids: Baker, 1998).

Gillespie, Michael Allen. *Nihilism Before Nietzsche* (Chicago: University of Chicago Press, 1995).

Gillespie, Michael Allen and Strong, Tracy B. ed. *Nietzsche's New Seas* (Chicago: University of Chicago Press, 1988).

Goldberg, Suzanne. 'Eight ways climate change is making the world more dangerous', *The Guardian*, 14th July 2014.

Goldie, Mark. 'Locke On Religious Toleration' at https://oll.libertyfund.org/pages/locke-on-religious-toleration-by-mark-goldie.

www.goodreads.com/quotes/47422-my-own-opinion-is-enough-for-me-and-i-claim.

Gould, Stephen Jay. *Wonderful Life: The Burgess Shale and the Nature of History* (New York: W. W. Norton, 1989).

Gray, John. *Black Mass: Apocalyptic Religion and the Death of Utopia* (London: Penguin, 2007).

———'The atheist delusion', *The Guardian*, 15 March 2008.

Groothuis, Douglas. *Christian Apologetics: A Comprehensive Case for Biblical Faith* (Downers Grove: IVP Academic and Apollon, 2011).

Grudem, Wayne. *Systematic Theology: An Introduction to Biblical Doctrine* (Leicester: InterVarsity Press and Zondervan, 1994).

Habermas, Gary. *The Historical Jesus* (Joplin, Mo: College Press, 1996).

Haldane, John. *Atheism and Theism* (Oxford: Blackwell, 2nd edition, 2003).

Hall, Chris. 'Forget Christopher Hitchens: Atheism in America is undergoing a radical change', *Salon*, 5 June 2014.

Harris, Peter, Hitchens, Peter and Turner, Ed. 'Unbelievable? Was Christopher Hitchens right about religion? at'https://www.premierchristianradio.com/Shows/Saturday/Unbelievable/Episodes/Unbelievable-Was-Christopher-Hitchens-right-about-religion-Peter-Hitchens-Ed-Turner-Peter-Harris-plus-Unbelievable-2016-announced.

Harrison, Peter. *The Bible, Protestantism and the Rise of Science* (Cambridge: Cambridge University Press, 1998).

Harris, Sam. *Letter to a Christian Nation* (New York: Kopf, 2006).

———*The End of Faith: Religion, Terror and the Future of Reason* (New York: W. W. Norton, 2004).

———*The End of Faith: Religion, Terror and the Future of Reason* (London: The Free Press, 2006).

Hart, David Bentley. *Atheist Delusions: The Christian Revolution and Its Fashionable Enemies* (Yale University Press, 2010).

———'Believe it or Not', at http://www.firstthings.com/article/2010/05/believe-it-or-not.

———'David Bentley Hart interview on New Atheism', You Tube, 19th April 2013, at https://www.youtube.com/watch?v=99onNksSYAo (accessed Saturday 26th September 2015).

Hawkins, Benjamin. 'Dembski, Hitchens debate God's existence', *Baptist Press*, November 23rd 2010).

'Hardcover Notification-New York Times', *The New York Times*, 3 December 2006.

Henry, David. "Leipzig pastor whose 'peace prayers' rallied resistance to communism in the run-up to German reunification', *The Independent*, 8 July 2014.

Hitchens, Christopher. 'A Nation of Racist Dwarfs', *Slate*, 1 February 2010.

———.'Assassins of the Mind', *Slate*, 5 January 2004.

———.'A Short Note on the Grape and the Grain', *Slate*, 6 June 2010.

———.'An Anglosphere Future', *City Journal*, 2007.

———.'An Atheist Responds', *Washington Post*, 14 July 2007.

———.'Axis of Evil' at https://fora.tv/2007/05/10/Christopher_Hitchens.

———.'Believe Me, It's Torture', *Vanity Fair*, 2 July 2008.

———.'Bush's Secularist Triumph: 'The left apologizes for religious fanatics. The president fights them', *Slate*, 9 November 2004.

———.'C4 Right to Reply - Christopher Hitchens vs Mother Theresa', You Tube, 7 May 2016 at https://www.youtube.com/watch?v=DWSU9Y2Fa8E.

———.'Christopher Hitchens: "Heaven watches with folded arms"', You Tube, 25 February 2013 at https://www.youtube.com/watch?v=gQgHds6eIJO.

———.'Christopher Hitchens vs John Lennox Is God great' [sic], You Tube, 8th May 2015 at https://www.youtube.com/watch?v=sHiGsL4bzmM.

———.'Christopher Hitchens-On BBC Radio 4 "Great Lives" Discussing Leon Trotsky [2006]', You Tube, 16 September 2012 at https://www.youtube.com/watch?v=98uw-qzFq88.

———.'Christopher Hitchens On God and North Korea', You Tube, 16 June 2009 at https://www.youtube.com/watch?v=f4oTRJl5vvI.

———.'Christopher Hitchens on Hannity & Colmes about Rev. Falwell's Death', You Tube, 17 May 2007 at https://www.youtube.com/watch?v=doKkOSMaTk4.

———.'Classic: Christopher Hitchens on The Death Of Jerry Falwell', You Tube, 16 January 2008 at https://www.youtube.com/watch?v=iq939cZv2Uc.

———.'Christopher Hitchens: "Heaven watches with folded arms"', You Tube, 25 February 2013 at https://youtube.com/watch?v=gQgHds6eIJo.

———.'Christopher Hitchens on life, death and lobster' at https://www.bbc.co.uk/news/uk-16214466.

———.'Christopher Hitchens responds to a Jihad sympathizer', You Tube, 20 August 2009 at https://www.m.youtube.com/watch?v=axHR8AOXXKC.

———.'Christopher Hitchens: Talks at Google', YouTube, 16 August 2007 at https//:www.youtube.com/watch/v=DoB-X9LJjs.

———.'Christopher Hitchens vs. Douglas Wilson Debate at Westminster', YouTube, 30th November 2011 at https://www.youtube.com/watch?v=g6UU9C-WmvM.

———.'#9 Debate-Christopher Hitchens vs Tim Rutten-God Is Not Great-2007', You Tube, at https://m.youtube.com/watch?v=wNW4DeM6ZVo.

———.'#141 Debate Christopher Hitchens vs Timothy Jackson How Religion Poisons Everything 2007, You Tube at https://youtube.com/watch?v=WFXot4OT7uY.

———.'Does God Exist? William Lane Craig vs. Christopher Hitchens-Full Debate [HD]', You Tube, 28 September 2014 at https://www. https://www.youtube.com/watch?v=otYm41hb48o.

———.'Faith-Based Fraud', Slate, 16 May 2007.

———.'Free Exercise of Religion? No, Thanks: The taming and domestication of religious faith is one of the unceasing chores of civilization', Slate, 6 September 2010.

———.God is Not Great: How Religion Poisons Everything (London: Atlantic, 2007).

———.Hitch 22: A Memoir (London: Atlantic Books, 2011).

———.https//:hitchensdebates.blogspot.co.uk/2010/08/hitchens-vs-kresta-ave-maria-radio.html.

———.Hitchens vs. Blair: Is Religion a Force for Good in the World? (London: Black Swan 2010).

———.'Holiday in Iraq', Vanity Fair, 12 March 2007.

———.'In Defense of Endless War', Slate, 19 September 2011.

———.Is Christianity Good for the World: A Debate (Moscow ID: Canon, 2009).

———.Collision: Is Christianity Good for the World, (LEVEL 4: 2008).

———.'John Paul II's Other Legacy', Slate, 1 April 2005.

———.Letters to a Young Contrarian (New York: Basic, 2001).

———.https://library.fora.tv/search?q=Christopher+Hitchens+

———.'Mommie Dearest: The pope beatifies Mother Teresa, a fanatic, a fundamentalist, and a fraud', Slate, 20th October 2003.

———.Mortality (London: Atlantic, 2013).

———.No One Left to Lie to: The Triangulations of William Jefferson Clinton (London: Atlantic, 2014).

———.'On God and North Korea', You Tube, 16th June 2009 at https://www.youtube.com/watch?v=f4oTRJl5vvI.

———.'Simply Evil', Slate, 5 September 2015.

———.'Stop the Masochistic Insanity', Slate, 23 May 2005.

———.'The Four Horsemen-Hitchens, Dawkins, Dennett, Harris', YouTube, 23 July 2012 at https://www.youtube.com/watch?v=n7IHU28aR2E.

———.The Missionary Position: Mother Theresa in Theory and Practice (London: Atlantic in 2013).

———.'The Moral Necessity of Atheism (2/8), YouTube, 8th September 2007 at https://www.youtube.com/watch?v=JiBvgAS7vKQ.

———.'The New Commandments', Slate, 4 March 2010 (with Jacque del Conte).

———.the Portable Atheist: Essential Readings for the Nonbeliever (Philadelphia: Da Capo, 2007).

———.The Trial of Henry Kissinger (London: Verso, 2002).\

———.'To Hell With the Archbishop of Canterbury: Rowan Williams' dangerous claptrap about "plural jurisdiction"', Slate, 18 February 2008.

———.Tom Paine's Rights of Man (New York: Grove, 2006).

———.'Trotsky with Hitchens and Service'. YouTube, 3 August 2009 at https://www.youtube.com/watch?v=cuzXR-5w4Qu.

———.'Why Women Aren't Funny', Vanity Fair, 1 January 2007.

———.'Yes, the Founding Fathers were Skeptics About Religion, The Weekly Standard, 11 December 2006.

Hitchens, Peter. The Rage Against God: How Atheism led me to Faith (Grand Rapids: Zondervan, 2010).

Hobson, Theo. 'Richard Dawkins has lost: meet the new new atheists', The Spectator, 13th April 2013.

Hosking, Geoffrey. A History of the Soviet Union (London: Fontana, 1985).

Josephus, The Jewish War, Book 1, Chapter 33, 5. 656, trans. William Whiston, The New Complete Works of Josephus (Grand Rapids: Kregel, 1999), p. 726.

'Jonathan Mayhew' at https://www.totallyhistory.com/jonathan-mayhew.

Joyce, Richard,. "Moral Anti-Realism", The Stanford Encyclopedia of Philosophy (Fall 2015 Edition), ed. Edward N. Zalta, at https://www.plato.stanford.edu/archives/fall2015/entries/moral-anti-realism/> .

Kahane, Guy. 'Should We Want God to Exist?' in Philosophy and Phenomenological Research, May 2011, Volume 82, Issue 3.

Kaufmann, Walter. Nietzsche: Philosopher, Psychologist, Antichrist (Princeton: Princeton University Press, 2013).

Kenny, Anthony. 'The Wisdom of Not Knowing', The Philosopher's Magazine, Issue 37, 1st quarter 2007).

Kirkpatrick, Betty. Webster's Word Power English Dictionary: With Easy to Follow Pronunciation Guide (Glasgow: Geddes & Grosset, 2001).

Klaiber, Walter. Call and Response: Biblical Foundations of a Theology of Evangelism (Nashville: Abingdon, 1997).

Lacocque, Andre and Ricoeur, Paul. Thinking Biblically: Exegetical and Hermeneutical Studies (Chicago: University of Chicago Press, 1998).

Lennox, John C. God's Undertaker: Has Science Buried God? (Oxford: Lion, 2009).

———Gunning for God: How the New Atheists Are Missing the Target (Oxford: Lion Hudson, 2011).

——— 'The Hard Question: God and the Problem of Evil (with John Lennox)', YouTube, 25th March 2015 at https://www.youtube.com/watch?v=Ssb47DEmn9U.

Lewis, C. S. Mere Christianity (London: Fount, 1997),

Lindsey, Hal. The Late Great Planet Earth (Grand Rapids: Zondervan, 1970).

Livingston, James C., Fiorenza, Francis Schussler with Coakley, Sarah and Evans Jr., James H. Modern Christian Though, Volume 2, Twentieth Century, 2nd ed. (Minneapolis: Fortress, 2006).

Locke, John. *A Letter on Toleration*, trans. William Popple (Pennsylvania: Pennsylvania State University, 1998).

Mackie, John. 'Evil and Omnipotence', ed. McCord Adams and Merrihew Adams, *The Problem of Evil* (Oxford: OUP, 1990).

———*Inventing Right and Wrong* (New York: Viking, 1977).

Maitzen, Stephen. 'Perfection, Evil and Morality', ed. James P. Sterba, *Ethics and the Problem of Evil* (Indiana: Indiana University Press, 2017).

Maritain, Jacques. 'Christianity and Democracy' at https://www.3.nd.edu/Departments/Maritain/jm604a.htm.

https://www.marxists.org/archive/trotsky/1920/terrcomm/cho4.htm.

Mayhew, Jonathan and Royster, Paul, ed. "A Discourse concerning Unlimited Submission and Non-Resistance to the Higher Powers: With some Reflections on the Resistance made to King Charles I. And on the Anniversary of his Death: In which the Mysterious Doctrine of that Prince's Saintship and Martyrdom is Unriddled (1750)', ed. Paul Royster, *Electronic Texts in American Studies, Paper 44* at https://www.digitalcommons.unl.edu/etas/44.

Mawson, T. J. *Belief in God: An Introduction to the Philosophy of Religion* (Oxford: Oxford University Press, 2005).

McGrath, Alister. *The Dawkins Delusion* (London: SPCK, 2007).

———*The Science of God* (London: T&T Clark, 2004).

———*Why God Won't Go Away: Engaging with the New Atheism* (London: SPCK, 2011).

McDowell, Josh. *The New Evidence That Demands a Verdict: Evidence I & II* (Nashville: Thomas Nelson, 1999).

Mohler, Albert. 'The New Atheism?' at https:// www.albertmohler.com/commentary_read.php?cdate=2006-11-21

Medawar, Peter B. *The Limits of Science* (Oxford: Oxford University Press, 1985).

Menuge, Angus. 'Ramified Personalized Natural Theology: A Third Way', at https://www.epsociety.org/library/articles.asp?pid=195&mode=detail.

Merkin, Daphne. 'Ecclesiastes' in ed. David Rosenberg, *Congregation: Contemporary Writers Read the Jewish Bible* (San Diego: Harcourt Brace Jovanovich, 1989).

Milstein, Mati. 'King Solomon's Wall Found-Proof of Bible Tale', *National Geographic News*, 27 February 2010.

'Jonathan Miller-On the ineffectiveness of 'New Atheism', You Tube, 4th March 2009 at https://www.youtube.com/watch?v=pZ9uWuEifrA (accessed 26th September 2015).

Moreland, J. P. and Craig, William Lane. *Philosophical Foundations for a Christian Worldview* (Downers Grove: IVP Academic, 2003).

Nietzsche, Friedrich. *Beyond Good and Evil*, trans. Marion Faber (Oxford: OUP, 1998).

———*Ecce Homo*, trans. Anthony M. Ludovici (New York: Dover Inc., 2004).

———*The Gay Science With a Prelude in Rhymes and an Appendix of Songs*, trans. Walter Kaufmann (New York: Vintage, 1974).

———*The Genealogy of Morals* (New York: Dover, 2003).

———*Thus Spake Zarathustra* at https:www.nietzsche.thefreelibrary.com/Thus-Spake-Zarathustra/36-1.

———*Twilight of the Idols with the Antichrist and Ecce Homo*, trans. Antony M. Ludovici (Ware: Wordsworth Editions, 2007).

Noble, Dennis. *The Music of Life: Biology Beyond the Genome* (Oxford: Oxford University, 2006).

Orr-Ewing, Amy. *Why Trust the Bible: Answers to 10 Tough Questions* (Nottingham: InterVarsity, 2005).

Orwell, George. *1984* (London: Penguin, 1989).

Palmer, Brian. 'Does Alcohol Improve Your Writing? Putting Hitch's theory to the test', *Slate*, 16 December 2011.

Parker, Ian. 'He Knew He Was Right: How a former socialist became the Iraq war's fiercest defender', *The New Yorker*, 16th October 2006.

Pinker, Steven. *The Blank Slate* (London: Allen Lane 2002).

Plantinga, Alvin. 'Is Belief in God Rational?' in ed. C. F. Delaney, *Rationality and Religious Belief* (Notre Dame: University of Notre Dame Press, 1979).

Plantinga, Alvin. *God and Other Minds* (New York: Cornell University Press, 1967).

Pritchard, Duncan. *What is this thing called knowledge?* (London: Pritchard, 2007).

Price, Michael E. 'How Evolutionary Science Can Make Us Morally Better' at https://www.psychologytoday.com/blog/darwin-eternity/201501/how-evolution-science-can-make-us-morally-better

Rachels, James. 'God and Human Attributes', *Religious Studies* (1971).

Rad, Gerhard von. *Wisdom in Israel* (Nashville; Abingdon, 1972).

Ragland, C. P. 'Hell' at http://www.iep.utm.edu/hell/.

Reicke, Bo. *The New Testament Era: The World of the Bible from 500 B.C. to A.D. 100*, trans. David E. Green (London: Adam & Charles Black, 1964).

'Religion – the "Root of all Evil?"' at https://humanism.org.uk/2006/01/05/news-194/?desktop=1 (accessed 20 February 2017 at 16:29).

Roberts, Mark D. *Can We Trust the Gospels: Investigating the Reliability of Matthew, Mark, Luke and John* (London: Crossway, 2007).

———'Is Hitchens a Reliable Source of "Facts"?', 7th June 200 at https://markdroberts.com/?p=94.

Rosenberg, Alex. *The Atheist's Guide to Reality: Enjoying Life Without Illusions* (New York: Norton 2011).

Rushdie, Salman. 'Christopher Hitchens, 1949-2011', *Slate*, 6 January 2012.

Russell, Bertrand. Why I am Not a Christian, at https://www.andrew.cmu.edu/user/jksadegh/A%20Good%20Atheist%20Secularist%20Skeptical%20Book%20Collection/Why%20I%20am%20Not%20a%20Christian%20-%20Bertrand%20Russell.pdf.

Schweitzer, Bernard. *Hating God: The Untold Story of Misotheism* (Oxford: OUP, 2010).

Shermer, Michael. *Why Darwin Matters: The Case Against Intelligent Design* (New York: Times Books, 2007).

Shores, Monica. 'Will "New Atheism" Make Room for Women?', *Ms Magazine*, 1 November 2010.

Sire, James W. *Naming the Elephant: Worldview as a Concept* (Downers Grove: InterVarsity, 2004).

Smith, Quentin. 'The Metaphilosophy of Naturalism', *Philo Vol. 4, Number 2*, 05 January 2002 at www.philoonline.org/library/smith_4_2.htm.

Solomon, Deborah. 'The Contrarian: Questions for Christopher Hitchens', *The New York Times*, June 2nd 2010.

Stern, David H. *Jewish New Testament Commentary* (Clarksville, Maryland: Jewish New Testament Publications, Inc., 1996).

Stone, Jon R. ed., *The Routledge Dictionary of Latin Quotations: The Illiterati's Guide to Latin Maxims, Mottoes, Proverbs and Sayings* (London: Routledge, 2005).

Swindall, James. 'Faith and Reason' at https//www.iep.utm.edu/faith-re.

'Richard Swinburne: The Problem of Evil' at https://homepages.wmich.edu/~baldner/swinburne.pdf.

Tarr, Russell. 'Lenin in Power', *History Review, Issue 55*, September 2006.

Taylor, James E. 'The New Atheists', *Internet Encyclopedia of Philosophy* at http://www.iep.utm.edu/n-atheis/.

Van Til, Cornelius. *The Defense of the Faith, 4th ed.* (1955; reprint, Phillipsburg, N.J.: P &R, 2008).

Trachtenberg, Jeffrey A. 'Hitchens Book Debunking The Deity Is Surprise Hit', *The Wall Street Journal*, 22nd June 2007.

Trible, Phyllis. *God and the Rhetoric of Sexuality* (Philadelphia: Fortress, 1978).

Trotsky, Leon. 'Hue and Cry Over Kronstadt', *The New International, Vol. 4 No. 4*, April 1938.

Vine, W. E., Unger, Merrill F. and White Jr., William, *Vine's Complete Expository Dictionary: Old and New Testament Words* (Nashville: Thomas Nelson, 1984).

Vos, Howard F. *Genesis and Archaeology* (Chicago: Moody, 1963).

Wahlquist, Calla. 'Richard Dawkins stroke forces delay of Australia and New Zealand tour', *The Guardian*, 12 February 2016.

Walter, Nicholas. *Humanism- What's in the Word* (London: Rationalist Press Association, 1997).

Ward, Keith. *Why There Almost Certainly is a God: Doubting Dawkins* (Oxford: Lion, 2008).

What evidence is there that the Temple of Solomon existed?' at https://www.bbc.co.uk/sn/tvradio/programmes/horizon/solomon_qa.shtml.

Wilby, Peter. 'Christopher Hitchens obituary', *The Guardian*, 16 December 2011.

Wilkerson, Dale. 'Friedrich Nietzsche (1844-1900)' at https://www.iep.utm.edu/nietzsche/

Williams, Peter S. *A Sceptic's Guide to Atheism: God is not Dead* (Milton Keynes: Paternosta, 2009).

————*C.S. Lewis vs the New Atheists* (Milton Keynes: Paternoster, 2013).

————'Understanding the Trinity', at https://www.bethinking.org/god/understanding-the-trinity.

Witherington III, Ben. *New Testament History: A Narrative Account* (Grand Rapids: Baker Academic, 2001).

Wolf, Gary. 'The Church of the Non-Believers', Wired, November 2006 at http://www.wired.com/wired/archivew/14.11/atheism_pr.html.

Wolterstorff, Nicholas. 'Reading Joshua', presented at the conference My Ways Are Not Your Ways at the University of Notre Dame, 10-12 September 2009.

Woodward, Ashley. ed. *Interpreting Nietzsche: Reception and Influence* (London: Continuum, 2011).

Index

9 781532 651984